WITHDRAWN BY THE
UNIVERSITY OF MICHIGAN

Political Participation
and American Democracy

**Recent Titles in
Contributions in Political Science**

Conflict Resolution and Public Policy
Miriam K. Mills, editor

Surveillance in the Stacks: The FBI's Library Awareness Program
Herbert N. Foerstel

Sheathing the Sword: The U.N. Secretary-General and the Prevention of International Conflict
Thomas E. Boudreau

Teaching Public Policy: Theory, Research, and Practice
Peter J. Bergerson, editor

The U.S. Constitution and Foreign Policy: Terminating the Taiwan Treaty
Victoria Marie Kraft

Power and Civil Society: Toward a Dynamic Theory of Real Socialism
Leszek Nowak

Public Policy and the Public Good
Ethan Fishman, editor

The U.S. Consul at Work
William D. Morgan and Charles Stuart Kennedy

Reluctant Ally: United States Foreign Policy Toward the Jews from Wilson to Roosevelt
Frank W. Brecher

Ethics for Public Managers
Harold F. Gortner

Power and Service: A Cross-National Analysis of Public Administration
Hardy Wickwar

Richard M. Nixon: Politician, President, Administrator
Leon Friedman and William F. Levantrosser, editors

Gubernatorial Leadership and State Policy
Eric B. Herzik and Brent W. Brown, editors

The West European Allies, the Third World, and U.S. Policy: Post–Cold War Challenges
Richard J. Payne

POLITICAL PARTICIPATION and AMERICAN DEMOCRACY

Edited by WILLIAM CROTTY

Prepared under the auspices of the Policy Studies Organization
STUART S. NAGEL, *Publications Coordinator*

Contributions in Political Science, Number 279

GREENWOOD PRESS
New York • Westport, Connecticut • London

JK
1764
.P6651
1991

Library of Congress Cataloging-in-Publication Data

Political participation and American democracy / edited by William
  Crotty.
      p.   cm. — (Contributions in political science, ISSN 0147–1066
  ; no. 279)
      "Prepared under the auspices of the Policy Studies Organization."
      Includes bibliographical references and index.
      ISBN 0-313-27652-8 (alk. paper)
      1. Political participation—United States. 2. Voting—United
  States. 3. Political participation. 4. Voting. I. Crotty,
  William J. II. Policy Studies Organization. III. Series.
  JK1764.P665 1991
  323'.042'0973—dc20   91-9175

British Library Cataloguing in Publication Data is available.

Copyright © 1991 by William Crotty

All rights reserved. No portion of this book may be
reproduced, by any process or technique, without the
express written consent of the publisher.

Library of Congress Catalog Card Number: 91-9175
ISBN: 0-313-27652-8
ISSN: 0147-1066

First published in 1991

Greenwood Press, 88 Post Road West, Westport, CT 06881
An imprint of Greenwood Publishing Group, Inc.

Printed in the United States of America

The paper used in this book complies with the
Permanent Paper Standard issued by the National
Information Standards Organization (Z39.48–1984).

10 9 8 7 6 5 4 3 2 1

Contents

Preface		vii
1.	Political Participation: Mapping the Terrain *William Crotty*	1
2.	Theories of Turnout: An Empirical Comparison of Alienationist and Rationalist Perspectives *Jack Dennis*	23
3.	Nonvoting in America: Attitudes in Context *John R. Petrocik* and *Daron Shaw*	67
4.	When Turnout Matters: Mobilization and Conversion as Determinants of Election Outcomes *Thomas E. Cavanagh*	89
5.	Legal-Institutional Factors and Voting Participation: The Impact of Women's Suffrage on Voter Turnout *Jerrold G. Rusk* and *John J. Stucker*	113
6.	Political Participation and Discrimination: A Comparative Analysis of Asians, Blacks, and Latinos *Carole Jean Uhlaner*	139
7.	Voting for Judges: Race and Roll-Off in Judicial Elections *Richard L. Engstrom* and *Victoria M. Caridas*	171

8. Participation and Political Knowledge
   Jane Junn   193

Bibliography   213

Index   225

About the Contributors   231

Preface

The present era could be said to be the most promising of times for democratic nations. The signs are everywhere: nations worldwide are joining a growing community of interest in democracy, instituting democratic forms of government and employing standards of democratic performance to judge their own and others' actions. The U.S.S.R., most dramatically, as well as other countries in Eastern Europe, Latin America, Asia, and Africa—many long noted for their authoritarian or, in some cases, totalitarian governments—are adopting, even if only grudgingly, universally accepted democratic norms of behavior.

All of this is to be welcomed. Yet the world's major democracies have problems of their own that international shifts in political climate should not mask. These problems range from social inequality and poor economic performance to decline in the quality of people's lives. The United States clearly is not immune to such trends and, to an extent, personifies the difficulties being encountered by advanced industrial nations. The country faces many challenges.

One area that is beginning to receive increasing attention is the quality of public life. In this context, no concern can be greater than the political involvement of citizens in self-government. The questions raised are fundamental to the operation and preservation of democratic governance. What is, or should be, the role of the citizen in a democracy's political life? What is, or should be, the impact of the individual on the conduct of the affairs of a representative government? How democratic can a society be in which one-half of its citizenry does not vote, which is participation at the most basic level? What kind of future can such a society anticipate? How is its political life likely to develop?

These broad questions underlie the concerns in the chapters that follow. The information in the individual studies should provide those interested with a better basis for entering into their own personal judgments. The chapters are intended to investigate issues of significance within a closely reasoned and empirically grounded analytic format. Taken as a whole, the studies in this volume should assist people in making more informed judgments on some of the most fundamental issues to confront a democratic society.

Political participation or, more accurately, the nonparticipation of significant numbers of its citizens in its political life, is one of the more severe and intractable problems the United States faces. The concern is not new. And, if anything, the situation may be worsening. Yet evaluations of the comprehensiveness and quality of participation receive a relatively modest amount of attention from social scientists. The social issues addressed are fundamental; the extent of the research available disappointing. In this regard, these studies can make a contribution. Is there a fundamental and systematic bias in participation patterns? Do social condition, class status, and social identity relate to the quality and likelihood of representation? Are there observable differences in ideological and policy commitments between voters and nonvoters? If so, are the differences significant enough to affect election outcomes and the policy mandates based on these? Is the active electorate representative of the entire public's concerns? If, demographically or in issue terms, significant numbers of the nonparticipants were included in the electorate, what effect could it have, if any, on the nation's political agenda? Would it affect the government's distribution of society's resources?

In another vein, do institutional structures within the society aid or inhibit the mobilization of voters? Do legal and electoral forms (for example, registration practices, ballot formats, or the type of electoral rules used to decide election outcomes) affect participation and representation? Or to pursue another perspective, do patterns of involvement vary among minority and politically underrepresented groups, such as women, blacks, Hispanics, and Asians? The list could go on.

These are some of the questions we can address. We cannot explore them all or always in the depth we might like. But we can begin to isolate the significant issues open to empirical examination, outline the factors of importance in influencing participation, and suggest some of the ramifications of present tendencies.

The opening chapter, "Political Participation: Mapping the Terrain," outlines the characteristics of the nonparticipants, using data from the 1988 presidential election, and issues raised by their noninvolvement. Many of the latter are treated from a variety of perspectives in the studies that follow. In chapter 2, "Theories of Turnout: An Empirical Comparison of Alienationist and Rationalist Perspectives," Jack Dennis tests two competing theories, one emphasizing alienation from the political system as the major cause of nonparticipation, the other a rational judgment as to the benefits and costs of involvement, and then gives one purely demographic explanation in terms of their ability to predict turnout. Each approach helps in explaining participation; no one approach succeeds to the extent its proponents would like.

In "Nonvoting in America: Attitudes in Context," John R. Petrocik and Daron Shaw analyze the attitudes and issue preferences of nonvoters compared to voters, employing data from both presidential and congressional elections. The authors also explore other factors that might affect involvement. They conclude that while the attitudinal and issue differences among participants and nonparticipants are modest, they have a powerful effect on turnout. They also argue that the increased voter participation would not necessarily favor one party or the other nor would it challenge the legitimacy of election outcomes, curiously perhaps a concern of many theorists.

Thomas E. Cavanagh, in "When Turnout Matters: Mobilization and Conversion as Determinants of Election Outcomes," points out the contradictions and limitations in our knowledge concerning participation and then goes on to employ a comparative perspective to specify the conditions under which the mobilization of disadvantaged groups within the electorate, especially African-Americans, can be effective. Highly competitive races, often at levels below the presidential, offer the environment in which such mobilization drives can achieve the greatest impact.

In "Legal-Institutional Factors and Voting Participation: The Impact of Women's Suffrage on Voter Turnout," Jerrold G. Rusk and John J. Stucker assess the effects of electoral laws on political participation and, most specifically, the impact of women's suffrage on turnout. They investigate varying approaches to measuring such consequences, including the development of their own explanatory model. Placed in historical perspective, they show that the inclusion of women in the electorate decreased turnout but increased mobilization rates, although the impact varied by region of the country (as, for example, showing little effect in elections in the western United States).

Carole Jean Uhlaner, in "Political Participation and Discrimination: A Comparative Analysis of Asians, Blacks, and Latinos," breaks new ground by assessing the effects that perception of prejudice can have on the participation of two of America's newest immigrant groups, Asians and Latinos, and of one of its oldest targets of discrimination, blacks. The study is set in California. Prejudice is believed to exist, especially by those most active in politics, and such beliefs may actually contribute to greater electoral mobilization. The strength of feelings of discrimination varies by ethnic group, generation in this country, and existing group participation rates.

Relatively little attention has been paid to turnout in lower level elections. Citizen interest in these is low. This is particularly true of elections for judicial offices. While the stakes can be high—justice is hardly blind—the large number of choices facing voters, the information required to vote intelligently, and the test of persistence needed to make such decisions all contribute to "roll-off" or a drop-off in votes as one moves down the ballot. Richard L. Engstrom and Victoria M. Caridas, in "Voting for Judges: Race and Roll-Off in Judicial Elections," analyze the dynamics of a decreasing involvement in low-stimulus elections with particular attention to the differences between blacks and whites. The authors find the racial gap in turnout accentuated in lower level contests, in effect resulting in a different electorate (and one increasingly more white) in, for example, judicial races compared with the presidential or gubernatorial vote. The consequences of a systematic bias in turnout in a broad range of low involvement elections can only be guessed.

Jane Junn, in "Participation and Political Knowledge," investigates the role an understanding of the political system plays in participation. Is political knowledge a prerequisite for political involvement? The relationship is tested with both panel data from the 1980 presidential election and cross-sectional data from the 1987 General Social Survey, which replicated Sidney Verba and Norman H. Nie's path-breaking study of two decades earlier (published as *Participation in America* in 1972). Education, exposure to political information, and political knowledge in general relate positively to the probability of increased participation. Political learning does relate to involvement and consequently has direct implications for the quality of political life.

More than likely, the quality of political involvement will be tied to the social forces active in a society and will serve as a barometer of political vitality. If so, it becomes even more important that an adequate understanding of the dynamics of participation be available and that the problem in all its complexity be addressed with the seriousness it deserves. It is hoped that the essays in this volume will make their contribution to such an understanding.

As editor, I wish to thank the Policy Studies Organization and its Secretary-Treasurer, Stuart S. Nagel, for the opportunity to address in this context an issue of importance to me. At Greenwood Press, Mildred Vasan, Maureen Melino, and Todd Adkins have been particularly helpful. M. L. Hauch, Lucille Mayer, Dale D. Vasiliauskas, Molly Crotty, and Patrick Crotty have all contributed at various stages in the development and production of the manuscript. To all, we are grateful.

Political Participation
and American Democracy

1 Political Participation: Mapping the Terrain
William Crotty

When it comes to political participation, some things are indisputable. Much of the research in this area is uncertain or even contradictory in its findings and arguments as to the importance and efficacy of the vote or of other forms of political participation. The studies of and debates over the value and necessity of widespread participation often proceed from incompatible sets of value preferences or assumptions as to what constitutes acceptable levels of democratic representation and operation (see Dennis in this volume). Still, from this diverse and at times confusing body of information, certain basic points stand out.

THREE PROPOSITIONS

First, the United States has the weakest levels of political participation, as measured by the vote, of any major industrial democracy. This point has been made repeatedly. The United States ranks well below other advanced democratic nations (except Switzerland, a nation noted for its constant electioneering and refusal, until recently, to allow women to vote) in cross-national turnout. While this chapter is less concerned with the barriers to the vote than with identifying the characteristics of the nonparticipants and the consequences of such actions, a general concurrence does exist that participatory levels reflect institutional characteristics of the society. If a society wants and facilitates high rates of turnout, it gets them. When it does not (South Africa, Switzerland prior to 1971, the American South prior to 1965, a number of Third World countries), turnout is anemic and limited by law, social custom and the tolerance of ruling officials. Comparing patterns of participation in 19 modern democracies, G. Bingham Powell, Jr. concluded that "voter turnout in the United States is severely inhibited by its institutional conflict. ... The U.S. was disadvantaged by voluntary registration, unevenly competitive electoral districts, and very weak linkages (perceptual and organizational) between parties and social groups" (Powell 1986, 25–26). Powell estimates that institutional and party system factors depress turnout by 13 percent and registration procedures by an additional 14 percent, major reasons the United States' average 54 percent turnout falls well below the 80 percent of other nations.

Robert W. Jackman, in a related analysis of turnout in 19 industrial democracies, while disagreeing with Powell over the role of a nation's political culture in affecting levels of political participation, emphasizes the function of political institutions—nationally competitive electoral districts, political parties and electoral laws—in shaping electorates. Jackman concludes: "Where institutions provide citizens with incentives to vote, more people actually participate; where institutions generate disincentives to vote, turnout suffers. Thus, the meaning of national differences in voting turnout is rather clear: turnout figures offer one gauge of participatory political democracy" (Jackman 1987, 419).

Second, there is a class structure to participation; lower social classes are disproportionately left out of the electorate. Put another way, there is a strong correlation between demographic variables and voter turnout, with those scoring higher on economic and class indicators being overrepresented among voters, a condition Powell argues is abetted by structural factors (Powell 1986).

As examples, in the 1988 presidential election, the working class; those with the least education, the lowest status occupations, and the smallest incomes; and the unemployed are more likely to be found among the nonvoters than those at the higher end of the socioeconomic (SES) scale (table 1.1).

The class bias to voting has political consequences. Candidates for elective office confine their appeal and the policy options they support to the better-off half of the electorate. The policy consequences that result from such an economically skewed electorate are not difficult to predict, as those who followed the budget controversy (or debate on any policy issue for that matter) that engaged the Congress, the president and both parties during the fall of 1990 are aware. The proposals in the compromise agreed to by the White House and congressional leaders (and later rejected by the House of Representatives) cut social services (and especially Medicare benefits) and disproportionately increased taxation on the middle to lower income categories. This included those earning less than $10,000 and groups such as welfare recipients, the elderly, and even the homeless. It was a curious political gamble for an election year, understandable only in terms of whom the congresspeople facing re-

Table 1.1
Selected Demographic Indicators and Nonparticipation (in Percent)

Variable	Vote	Not Vote
Race		
White	72	28
Black	60	40
Age		
45 and over	77	23
Under 45	63	47
Education		
Less than high school	49	51
High school or better	75	25
Social Class		
Working class	61	39
Middle class	79	21
Income		
Over $25,000	80	20
Under $25,000	57	43
Occupation		
White collar	81	19
Blue collar	57	43
Employment Status		
Employed	70	30
Unemployed	46	54

Source: Data are from the Center for Political Studies, 1988 National Election Study.

election believed they had to please and whom they could safely ignore. If numbers alone determined outcomes in a high participation electorate, or if turnout (or nonparticipation) was evenly distributed among classes, the likelihood of any such budget proposals being put forward by the congressional leadership or the administration would be minimal.

Third, if a person does not vote, that person does not count politically. In the real world of politics, if you fail to vote, which is an entry-level form of political influence, you will not have much, if any, impact on what political decisionmakers do. The odds are enormous against perpetual nonvoters' needs being identified and addressed or of such individuals or groups receiving their fair share of society's policy gains. Nonvoting has profound consequences for representation and decision-making in a democratic society (Crotty 1990).

These contentions reflect value assumptions and verge over into the rather contentious mainline arguments over participation. On the one hand, it is asserted that broad participation is necessary within a democratic system to insure legitimacy to the government, stability to the system and equity in its policy allocations. This would be the high participation school. In contrast, there is a school of democratic thought that argues that high levels of participation reflect an instability and insecurity within the system and pose a threat to the democratic order itself. The debate rests on different assumptions as to what a democracy should be and on the tolerable limits as to the numbers of individuals and interests it can accommodate while still retaining its cohesion and an intelligent sense of direction. Qualitatively, the issue becomes whether the involvement of unprepared, ignorant, and least interested in the society should be facilitated. Are there dangers in large numbers of people casting an uninformed vote? Should the vote be restricted to those qualitatively (morally, intellectually or by some other barometer) best suited to guide the society? Most pointedly, the questions become who and how many should participate.

The assumption in this chapter is that high levels of participation are a "good" and that they enhance stability, increase political interest and commitment, and lead to more inclusive and therefore "better" representation. It should be a matter of fundamental significance to a society who participates and who does not and what is the proportion of its eligible electorate included in its political decision-making.

PROFILING THE NONPARTICIPANTS

There are differences between those who vote and those who do not. They are predictable. An analysis of data from the 1988 presidential election, in distributions not significantly different from the other presidential elections of the decade, shows that those with stronger roots within the society and the community (the older, married, working people who attend church on a regular basis) vote more regularly; and that those better-off economically and of middle- and upper middle-class status (the better educated, higher income respondents living in nonrural areas and with higher status occupations) participate more. Blacks, the young, the unemployed, manual laborers, those with the least formal education, the less well-off financially, and those living in the South participate less in elections. These differences should be familiar to any-

Table 1.2
Political Attitudes and Nonparticipation

Political Efficacy Index		Vote	Not Vote
High	1	84	26
	2	78	22
	3	67	33
Low	4	55	45

Political Trust Index		Vote	Not Vote
High	1	74	26
	2	71	29
	3	65	35
Low	4*	44	66

* There were a total of only 27 respondents in this category in a sample of 1,775.

Source: Data are from the Center for Political Studies, 1988 National Election Study.

one conversant with the research in the field. (Conway 1985; Milbrath and Goel 1977; Kleppner 1982; Wolfinger and Rosenstone 1980; Nagel 1987; Teixeira 1987; Cavanagh in this volume).

In terms of political attitudes (table 1.2) those who feel politically efficacious (that is, those who believe that they can have an impact on politics and government) and those whose levels of trust in government are higher are more likely to take part in elections (Uhlaner in this volume). These findings are again consistent with those uncovered since such measures were first employed in voting studies (Conway 1985). It is less clear whether people with weak feelings of efficacy and trust in government see little point in voting, or whether the failure to participate lends itself to a belief that elections and voters have little impact on how the country is run. More than likely, feelings of political distance and impotency encourage a withdrawal from the electorate, and such beliefs in turn are fed by a continued nonparticipation.

Finally, institutional and structural factors contribute significantly to nonparticipation (Rusk and Stucker; Engstrom and Caridas, both in this volume). The registration system used and the extent to which it facilitates involvement correlate strongly with turnout, and it may be the factor that best distinguishes (that is, depresses) participation in the United States as compared with other nations. It is likely that a government-sponsored and -funded person-to-person registration system maximizes the eligible electorate. Powell, in fact, argues that the "American attitudinal environment is . . . rather favorable to citizen participation of all kinds, including voting" but that the legal and institutional environment is a more important influence and this acts to depress turnout in the United States (Powell 1986, 36). Powell also contends that institutional arrangements, and most specifically, registration laws, "are responsible for the unusual degree to which education and other socioeconomic resources are directly related to voter turnout in the United States" (Powell 1986, 36). The procedures for qualifying to vote, while better systemized nationally and less onerous in recent decades, are the most restrictive of any democratic nation and contribute directly to the class and social bias found in American electorates (Crotty 1980; Crotty 1977).

Ideology, Issues, and Nonvoting

The assumption is often made that major issue differences, as well as candidate and ideological preferences, divide the washed from the unwashed, the voters from the nonvoters. This is one reason advanced for the failure of politicians to substantially reduce the barriers to registration and voting. Everyone is aware of the demographics of involvement and the assumption is made that the class structure inherent in nonparticipation would lead to a markedly different issue agenda if the electorate were expanded to include much of the disadvantaged groups now excluded. There is a threat implicit in such a change (Tucker and Vedlitz 1986; DeNardo 1986, 1980). A fear of the unknown is strong enough to keep politicians, Republicans and Democrats alike, from championing fundamental change. In addition, and not insignificantly, an enlarged electorate could change the political calculus of who receives the policy awards; the position of many now advantaged by the system could be eroded.

The heart of this dispute revolves around the policy preferences of the nonparticipants. John Petrocik and Daron Shaw, in this volume, in examining both the congressional and presidential vote, find that attitudinal and policy differences between voters and nonvoters, while statistically significant, are relatively narrow, yet they do have a discernible effect on turnout. Voters as compared to nonvoters are more likely to see important differences in policy positions between the candidates and parties in an election, another factor which can influence turnout.

Table 1.3 examines such concerns by comparing voter and nonvoter attitudes as to ideology, social welfare, foreign policy, and life style concerns. There is a difference in ideological affinity between voters and nonvoters, but possibly not as marked nor as radical as many might have expected. Nonvoters are slightly more liberal and centrist and are more evenly balanced between those holding moderate positions and

Table 1.3
Issue Positions of Voters and Nonvoters (in Percent)

Ideology			Voters	Non-Voters
Liberal			8.0	9.3
Slightly Liberal			13.4	21.7
Moderate			27.6	23.7
Slightly Conservative			25.6	28.5
Conservative			21.5	11.7
<u>Social Welfare Policy</u>			Voters	Non-Voters
Government Services				
Fewer	1		16.6	10.2
	2		18.6	14.7
	3		29.9	28.3
	4		18.2	16.6
More	5		16.8	30.2
Guaranteed Job				
Yes	1		13.2	24.8
	2		10.7	10.5
	3		21.6	20.5
	4		20.2	14.8
No	5		34.3	29.5
Health Insurance				
Government		1	16.1	24.9
Plan		2	21.6	28.9
		3	21.1	15.5
		4	27.5	20.0
Private Plan		5	13.7	10.6
Social Security Spending				
Increase			54.0	69.1
Same			43.0	28.3
Decrease			3.0	2.1
School Aid				
Increase			63.8	69.0

Table 1.3 (continued)

Ideology		Voters	Non-Voters
Same		31.4	29.3
Decrease		4.8	1.7
Food Stamps			
Increase		18.3	29.0
Same		47.0	44.2
Decrease		34.7	26.8
Spending on Homeless			
Increase		64.2	71.5
Same		29.5	25.1
Decrease		6.3	3.4
Minority Aid			
Government Help	1	13.7	18.8
	2	11.8	10.8
	3	26.2	21.9
	4	17.1	14.1
On Their Own	5	31.3	35.3
Affirmative Action			
Increase		17.5	26.3
Same		24.8	23.7
Decrease		57.7	51.0
Taxes to Reduce Deficit			
Willing		24.2	18.5
Perhaps		12.6	5.8
Not Willing		63.2	75.7
Lifestyle Tolerance			
High	1	13.6	15.2
	2	22.2	32.3
	3	22.6	26.5
	4	19.4	14.4
Low	5	22.3	12.2

Table 1.3 (continued)

Ideology	Voters	Non-Voters
Most Important Problem		
Economy	9.3	12.3
Budget	34.0	19.9
Social Welfare	19.5	28.0
Environment	5.6	3.3
Drugs	11.5	16.5
Other Domestic Issue	10.3	10.0
Foreign Policy/Defense	9.7	9.8
Party Best Able to Deal With Problem		
Republicans	25.4	12.9
No Difference	49.8	65.3
Democrats	24.8	21.8

Source: Data are from the Center for Political Studies, 1988 National Election Study.

those leaning right or left. There are also considerably fewer self-identified pure conservatives. Voters self-identify themselves as more conservative. Three out of four voters locate themselves from moderate to conservative on the scale.

There are few basic differences on foreign policy between participants and nonparticipants. In data not included in the table, both groups are found to have broadly comparable views on defense spending, on cooperation with the U.S.S.R., and on indicators of attitudes towards national security. On more specific items relating to South Africa and funding for Star Wars and the Contras, both issues of national debate during the 1980s, the groups are close in their preferences. Only on negotiating an arms agreement with the Soviets do the groups diverge: voters are more in favor of such a treaty, nonvoters are more wary.

It may not be surprising that on foreign policy issues, unlike domestic choices, both voters and nonvoters are likely to follow the national leadership, and consequently their views are more likely to converge. People have less information on such questions; there is a tendency to defer to authority and to accept the explanations it advances; and the policies being debated seem to have less immediate consequence for observers. They do not tie into well-developed basic attitudinal commitments for most Americans. This cannot be said for domestic policy issues.

As table 1.3 shows, there are observable differences in policy emphasis among voters and nonvoters. The nonvoters are more likely to support an increase in government-sponsored social welfare services, guaranteed job programs, social security spending, food stamp eligibility, and federal health insurance. They also favor more aid for the homeless. There is little difference between the groups on federal aid to education or on increased government support for affirmative action or minority aid. Nonparticipants are somewhat less willing to support an increase in taxes to reduce the deficit, but neither is much in favor of the idea.

A listing of the problems considered most significant by respondents reflects the differences observed; nonvoters are more likely than voters to consider social welfare issues more important. Voters clearly see the budget as their number one priority.

Finally, nonvoters are more likely than voters (almost one-half score higher on the index) to show a tolerance for less conventional life styles, although there is little to separate the groups in their views on specific issues such as AIDS, abortion, school prayer, the death penalty, gays, the war on drugs, and the role of women in society.

The greatest differences that do emerge then relate to social policy and directly reflect the predominately class-based cleavage structure in society between the political parties. Such issues have the greatest personal immediacy and impact for the individual: the parties take clearly identifiable and contrasting stands on them; the issues are subject to extended treatment in campaigns and media reports; there is considerably more information available to the individual on such questions; and the Congress, as well as the political parties, and unlike foreign policy, continuously debate and maneuver to position themselves favorably on such matters. These are the lifeblood of American politics. It is quite likely that should a *significant* proportion of the nonvoters become involved in politics and should they *vote their preferences* on domestic issues, they very well might make a substantial impact on the direction American politics takes. These are big "ifs." Even then, it might well be a matter of degree and emphasis, yet enough to institute different program allocations and priority emphases. It would not likely constitute a totally new direction for American politics nor would it be the fundamental political realignment many have yearned for. It is important to note that many similarities exist in issue views among participants and nonparticipants, and when differences do emerge, they are often incremental in nature.

Issue comparisons, however, are far from the whole story. When asked to choose which party would best be able to deal with the problem, voters are more likely than nonvoters to pick the Republicans. One-half of the voters and two-thirds of the nonvoters could see no difference between the parties. This last figure may suggest one of the principal keys to the large number of nonparticipants. Political ignorance and a lack of information may well be major contributors to nonparticipation.

This may be one of the more fundamental attitudinal distinctions between voter and nonvoter.

Levels of Influence: The Winning Coalition, the Losing Coalition, and the Noncontributors

Another way of looking at the relative position of nonvoters and their needs, views and potential for influencing the nation's political agenda is to compare the policy views of the winning coalition (George Bush and the Republicans), the losing coalition (Michael Dukakis and the Democrats), and the nonparticipating bloc. A few selective issues can illustrate the comparative positioning of the three groups (table 1.4).

In domestic issue positions, with few exceptions, the nonvoters are significantly closer to the losing coalition's views, and therefore the Democratic Party supporters' views, than to the winning coalition and the Republican Party voters' stands. These results would suggest that, as it has been argued, the Democratic Party, its candidates, and its policy commitments would benefit significantly and possibly overwhelmingly if the nonparticipants were brought into the electorate.

If the data are accurate (and there is every reason to believe that they are), they suggest also the power of the winning coalition to set the national agenda and to dictate policy considerations. The coalition that prevailed during the 1980s may well have represented minority views on the most important social and domestic issues of the day, yet it was powerful enough in the Reagan years to challenge the very foundations of the welfare state. Both Democrats and those who contend that a low-participation electorate is inherently unrepresentative might have an argument based on the domestic policy positioning of the three coalitions. However, once the examination is extended to social issues such as the death penalty or abortion and to foreign policy and defense spending, the matter is considerably less clear. Nonvoters as a group are more likely to fall between the two coalitions and the two political parties on such policy questions and somewhat closer to the Republicans on a number of issues. At a minimum, they would provide the Republican party a fertile ground for recruitment and might even add to the margin of its impressive electoral victories in presidential races manifested during the 1980s. That could provide the basis for a renewed competition with the Democrats for control of the Congress, a position a number of Republican leaders have argued.

To a degree, both sets of arguments are speculative (Lyons and Gant 1989). The results of the issue positioning among winning, losing, and nonvoter coalitions, while not clearcut, do demonstrate marked tendencies. How these manifest themselves in actual campaigns is prob-

Table 1.4
Issue Positions of Winning Coalition, Losing Coalition and Nonvoters, 1988 Presidential Election (in Percent)

	Winning	Losing	Non-Voters	Support Tendency of Non-Voters
Government Services				
Increase	20.7	51.5	46.8	Dem.
Same	30.4	28.8	28.3	
Decrease	48.9	19.7	24.9	
Guaranteed Job				
Favor	12.2	37.5	35.3	Dem.
Center	18.1	25.9	20.5	
Oppose	69.7	36.6	44.3	
Government Health Insurance				
Favor	25.2	51.7	53.8	Dem.
Center	19.8	22.6	15.5	
Oppose	54.6	25.8	30.6	
Social Security				
Increase	44.0	65.5	69.1	Dem.
Same	52.3	32.6	28.8	
Decrease	3.7	2.0	2.1	
Food Stamps				
Increase	8.7	29.2	29.0	Dem.
Same	46.5	48.0	44.2	
Decrease	44.7	22.7	26.8	
Spending on Homeless				
Increase	48.5	82.1	71.5	Dem.
Same	41.4	15.9	25.1	
Decrease	10.0	2.0	3.4	
School Aid				
Increase	52.2	76.4	69.0	Dem.
Same	40.7	21.6	29.3	
Decrease	7.1	2.0	1.7	

Table 1.4 (continued)

	Winning	Losing	Non-Voters	Support Tendency of Non-Voters
College Aid				
Increase	32.5	58.3	48.2	Dem.
Same	52.6	34.9	43.3	
Decrease	15.0	6.8	8.5	
Child Care				
Increase	45.6	68.5	61.0	Dem.
Same	37.4	24.4	32.6	
Decrease	17.0	7.1	6.4	
AIDS Spending				
Increase	66.5	79.8	75.8	Dem.
Same	25.6	16.6	18.4	
Decrease	7.9	3.6	5.9	
Abortion				
Always Permitted	30.5	42.3	34.7	In-Between
Selected Cases	46.9	47.0	50.3	Reps.
Never Permitted	11.2	10.8	15.0	
Death Penalty				
Favor	91.8	67.0	79.4	In-Between
Oppose	8.2	33.0	20.6	
Minority Aid				
Help	13.4	39.9	28.8	In-Between
Same	27.7	25.0	25.2	
On Own	58.8	35.1	56.0	
Affirmative Action				
Favor	7.4	29.8	26.3	Dem.
Center	24.1	25.3	22.7	
Oppose	68.5	44.9	51.0	

13

Table 1.4 (continued)

	Winning	Losing	Non-Voters	Support Tendency of Non-Voters
Equal Jobs for Blacks				
Favor	44.4	70.0	59.6	In-Between
Oppose	55.6	30.0	40.4	
Defense Spending				
Increase	43.7	20.5	34.3	In-Between
Same	38.1	30.7	29.6	
Decrease	18.1	48.8	36.2	
Star Wars				
Favor	26.7	9.0	15.5	Dem./In-Between
Center	44.8	22.6	33.0	
Oppose	28.4	68.4	51.5	
Aid to Contras				
Increase	19.7	5.5	9.9	Dem./In-Between
Same	35.5	19.6	28.8	
Decrease	44.8	79.4	61.3	
Policy Towards U.S.S.R.				
Cooperate More	36.5	53.8	42.8	Reps./In-Between
Same	27.0	20.5	25.3	
Be Tougher	36.6	25.6	32.0	
Policy Towards South Africa				
Pressure	44.1	73.8	60.9	Dem./In-Between
No Pressure	55.9	26.2	39.1	
Use of Military Force in Mid-East				
Favor	77.8	50.0	63.7	In-Between
Oppose	22.2	50.0	36.3	

Source: Data are from the Center for Political Studies, 1988 National Election Study.

lematical, given the weak levels of information of the nonvoters and their difficulty in matching their views with those of the candidates. All sides might have something to gain, or at least the potential for gain, from an expanded electorate. One thing is clear: the power of the winning coalition to dominate policy outcomes and consequently the critical importance of the election in setting a society's reward structure is reaffirmed. Elections do matter. In a political event of this magnitude the normative argument can be made that all should have a voice.

Political Information and Political Apathy

It is reasonable to expect political ignorance to correlate strongly with political apathy; that is, those with the least interest in or information about politics are those most likely to avoid exercising the franchise. There is some evidence that such is the case (see Junn in this volume). Two-thirds of the nonvoters indicate that they follow political affairs "little" to "very little." Conversely, two-thirds of those who voted say they follow politics "some" or "most" of the time. Almost one-half of the nonvoters (as against one-seventh of the voters) report having a minimal interest in the campaign.

When respondents are asked the sources from which they acquire political information and the extent to which they relied on these, the differences are stark (table 1.5).

Television was the most common source of political information; close to one-half of the nonvoters (compared to one-fifth of the voters) relied on it little to not at all. If the vast majority of nonvoters did not get the information from television, the likelihood was that they did not get it at all. Over 80 percent (compared with 60 percent of the voters) received little to no information concerning politics from alternative media sources. This reaffirms the pivotal role of television as *the* campaign medium.

A somewhat different indicator of political interest and knowledge can be found in the opinions people have on issues of contemporary relevance. More specifically, nonvoters approach (while still falling below) voters in the proportion having a position on policy questions and therefore presumably some information on, or at least concern with, the problem. More significant discrepancies emerge when both groups are asked their views on the candidates' stands on these issues. When nonvoters are questioned as the extent they agree or disagree with the candidates' positions, the proportion of nonvoters not answering or having no opinion increases substantially. The same pattern is evident for voters, but not to the same degree. Fitting an individual's view to a candidate's position is a more demanding test of political knowledge. The fall-off among nonvoters in response to such items relates to their

Table 1.5
Reliance of Voters and Nonvoters on Media Sources for Political Information (in Percent)

	Voters	Non-Voters
Television		
Some or Much	78.6	53.0
Little or None	21.4	47.0
Newspapers		
Some or Much	51.8	17.8
Little or None	48.2	82.2
Magazines		
Some or Much	17.6	9.7
Little or None	72.4	90.3
Radio		
Some or Much	36.0	21.6
Little or None	64.0	78.4

Source: Data are from the Center for Political Studies, 1988 National Election Study.

weak interest in the campaign, their failure to follow events, and their restricted use of the media.

The pattern can be illustrated (table 1.6). In the most ideological of times, 40 percent of the nonvoters (compared to an average of 16 percent of the voters) do not have an opinion as to whether George Bush is conservative or Michael Dukakis is liberal or if the Republican Party is conservative or the Democratic Party liberal. When asked their opinion on policy matters, most respondents are willing to advance one, although the discrepancy between voters and nonvoters continues. When asked the candidates' positions on the same issues, the fall-off among nonvoters is substantial, decisively greater than for voters, and approaching twenty percent or better on some issues. The gap between voters and nonvoters also widens, again approximating 20 percentage points, in selected policy areas. Overall, an average of 44 of every 100 nonvoters can offer no opinion as to the candidates' policy on the items examined. The pattern appears to be that on general items—the individual's own views or personal qualities associated with the candidates

Table 1.6
Proportion of Voters and Nonvoters Having No Opinion on Selected Topics (in Percent)

Ideology	Voters	Non-Voters
Bush-Liberal/ Conservative	14.8	36.6
Dukakis-Liberal/Conservative	17.3	39.0
Republican Party-Liberal/Conservative	17.0	40.5
Democratic Party-Liberal Conservative	16.7	39.4
Policy Positions		
Expand Government Services		
Have No Opinion	15.0	32.9
Don't Know Bush Position	22.4	46.7
Don't Know Dukakis Position	24.0	49.3
Guaranteed Jobs		
Have No Opinion	12.0	18.2
Don't Know Bush Position	19.2	35.1
Don't Know Dukakis Position	20.9	36.2
Federal Health Insurance		
Have No Opinion	13.3	21.0
Don't Know Bush Position	26.3	44.2
Don't Know Dukakis Position	28.3	46.8
Minority Aid		
Have No Opinion	10.0	16.7
Don't Know Bush Position	24.9	39.6
Don't Know Dukakis Position	26.6	44.4
Role of Women		
Have No Opinion	4.1	10.2
Don't Know Bush Position	22.8	45.5
Don't Know Dukakis Position	28.2	48.1
Defense Spending		
Have No Opinion	9.3	21.4
Don't Know Bush Opinion	16.4	37.4
Don't Know Dukakis Position	20.6	41.8
Cooperation With U.S.S.R.		
Have No Opinion	10.9	25.7
Don't Know Bush Opinion	21.7	44.4
Don't Know Dukakis Position	31.3	50.2

Source: Data are from the Center for Political Studies, 1988 National Election Survey.

(as to whether they are intelligent, compassionate, inspiring, strong leaders, knowledgeable, and honest)—the balance of both voters and nonvoters can offer an evaluation. (For example, only 4 percent and 6 percent of the voters and 13 percent and 16 percent of the nonvoters could not assess Bush's or Dukakis' personal attributes.) The more specific the question, the more substantive the demand in the evaluation, and the greater the possibility of a right/wrong response (Bush and Dukakis, as examples, do have policy positions on crime or the environment), the less likely the nonvoter is to have the necessary information to make the needed connections. As an example, one-quarter (against one-tenth of the voters) could not evaluate as broad an item as to whether the Congress was doing a good job.

It could be argued that these results reflect a failure of the campaign to reach and inform prospective voters and that they may be in part a by-product of the television age and the 30-second sound byte. There may be justification in such contentions but the impact would have to be assessed in terms of the electorate as a whole and its comparatively weak rates of political participation. The problem is even more accentuated for those who do not now vote; the differential impact of information flow on nonparticipants is considerably more severe than for participants, and the correspondence between political ignorance and noninvolvement more substantial. Not surprisingly, of potential concern to the political system, 70 percent of the nonvoters score low in political efficacy: 55 percent believe that people have no say in government; 62 percent feel public officials do not care about what people think; and 78 percent say that they find politics too complicated. The dimensions of the informational problem and its consequences are clear enough. Less obvious is what to do about them.

Conclusion

The patterns found in this analysis and, more specifically, those relating to demographic tendencies and, more subtly and more contentiously, those concerning issue representation and the lack of political information are not generally dissimilar to those uncovered in related studies. One election has been used to exemplify the problem. The contours described would hold for any of the three presidential elections of the 1980s and, for that matter, for elections of the last several decades, differentiated in these terms primarily by succeedingly greater numbers of nonvoters.

The nonvoters can be isolated and the traits that characterize them identified. A laundry list of reasons can be advanced to explain the decline. These include such factors as technological developments in communication and the depersonalization of the campaign; the weakening of political parties; the quality of choices offered and the failure of campaigns to address issues of societal significance; the frequency of contests and the demands they make on the interest, time and knowledge of the prospective voter; and the continuation, despite modification and improvement, of what has to be the most onerous voter certification system employed by any democratic nation. Whatever the reasons, the results are clear: among democratic nations, the United States ranks at the bottom, or just above last place, in voter involvement (Wolfinger, Glass and Squire 1990).

The low level of participation is not in question nor are the natures of the individuals least likely to turn out. The real question is the significance of the findings. What does it matter?

The argument over participation may be over power and political influence, the usual context in which the issue is debated. Or it may be over the stability of a democratic order and its ability to protect itself from both external threats and internal impulses that push towards disorder, irrationality, and, in the extreme, chaos and potential totalitarianism. To summarize, in the words of Carole Pateman, an advocate of a quite different model of political commitment, many democratic theories believe that "limited participation and apathy have a positive function for the whole system by cushioning the shock of disagreement, adjustment and change" (Pateman 1970, 7). Such concerns, it would seem, dominated the thoughts of a previous generation of political theorists (Berelson 1952; Schumpeter 1943; Eckstein 1966; Dahl 1956; see the discussion in Pateman 1970). Embedded in the equation at some level should be the accountability of those in office to the public they purport to represent and the vitality and power of a democratic society to regenerate itself. How much nonparticipation can a democratic system tolerate? Does participation fundamentally affect the quality of representation?

The importance of elections is universally affirmed. The importance of full participation in elections, or something approaching this, is less clearly understood. Robert A. Dahl contends that "a key characteristic of a democracy is the continuing responsiveness of the government to the preferences of its citizens" (1971, 1). This would appear reasonable. It would also appear reasonable that an electorate approaching the standards of turnout common in other democratic nations would yield a greater variety and subtlety of preference orderings and intensities and a greater confidence that the citizenry's wishes had been included in the electoral decision-making than a turnout struggling to remain at fifty percent of the voting age population (and producing something substantially below this level of involvement in other than presidential races). Gary Orren (1987) points out that a fuller electorate provides a balance and counterweight to the more specialized issue activists whose views dominate presidential selection. In making a related argument advocating fuller participation, Stephen Earl Bennett and David Resnick argue that "if voting makes elites attend to citizens' opinions, its fundamental value to democracy is firmly established" (Bennett and Resnick 1990, 800). They add: "A ballot may be, as some contend, a very blunt instrument for tying elites' behavior to ordinary people's wishes. But ... elections have occasionally been successful in refocusing public officials' attention to the electorate's desires" (ibid.). This would seem to be a minimalist argument on behalf of a broader involvement.

In a study of black political participation Lawrence Bobo and Franklin D. Gillian, Jr., found that "where blacks hold positions of political power, they are more active and participate at higher rates than whites of comparable socioeconomic status" and that "black empowerment [measured as black control of the mayor's office] is a contextual cue of likely policy responsiveness and encourages blacks to feel that participation has intrusive value. . . . Empowerment leads to higher levels of political knowledge and . . . it leads to a more engaged [i.e., trusting and efficacious] orientation to politics" (Bobo and Gillian 1990, 307). These findings, in turn, would lend support to contentions made by theorists such as Pateman in favor of "participatory democracy" who, building on the views of J. S. Mill and Rousseau, believe that participation "is central to the establishment of a democratic polity, the latter being regarded not just as a set of national representative institutions but [as] . . . a participatory society" (Pateman 1970, 20). Pateman's views are, of course, at the polar opposite from those that have dominated in the social sciences in the debate over participation.

The significance fuller participation can have for the political system was compellingly developed by E. E. Schattschneider a number of years ago. Schattschneider, in his now famous dictum, contended that "the scope of conflict determines its outcome" (1960, 60). He believed that "a tremendous amount of conflict is controlled by keeping it so private that it is almost completely invisible" (ibid.). Variations in patterns of participation have an impact on the outcome: "Every change in the scope of conflict has a bias; it is partisan in its nature. . . . It must be assumed that every change in the number of participants is about something, that the newcomers have sympathies or antipathies that make it possible to involve them. By definition, the intervening bystanders are not neutral. . . . In political conflict every change in scope changes the equation" (ibid., 4–5). And finally, "it is hazardous to assume that the spectators [those not participating in an election or a political decision] are uninterested" (ibid., 5). Everyone has a stake in the outcome and a direct concern with the decisions made. This is particularly true in elections.

One final point: voting represents only the most rudimentary and indirect means for influencing political outcomes. While clearly a fundamental act in democratic governance and possibly the most critical behavior of all, it is, nonetheless, only the most preliminary of steps in democratic decision-making and influence-wielding. It is the entry-level stage of involvement. If people do not participate at that level, how do they participate? What is their role in and contribution to the democratic society?

The questions can be raised and the issues implicit in the controversy can be outlined. Any generally accepted answers as to the level of participation necessary to sustain a democratic government or the true meaning of the effects of nonparticipation remain far off. Studies such as those in this volume can only contribute to a modest extension of the knowledge available and a clarification and reexamination of some of the basic issues that fuel the debate.

REFERENCES

Bennett, Stephen Earl, and David Resnick. 1990. "The Implications of Nonvoting for Democracy in the United States." *American Journal of Political Science* 34:771–802.

Berelson, Bernard R. 1952. "Democratic Theory and Public Opinion." *Public Opinion Quarterly* 16:313–330.

Bobo, Lawrence, and Frank D. Gillian, Jr. 1990. "Race, Sociopolitical Participation, and Black Empowerment." *American Political Science Review* 84:377–393.

Conway, M. Margaret. 1985. *Political Participation in the United States*. Washington, D.C.: Congressional Quarterly Press.

Crotty, William. 1977. *Political Reform and the American Experiment*. New York: Thomas Y. Crowell.

Crotty, William. 1980. "The Franchise: Registration Changes and Voter Participation." In *Paths to Political Reform*, ed. William Crotty. Lexington, Mass.: Lexington Books/D.C. Heath. Pp. 67–113.

Crotty, William. 1990. "Setting Forth Premises: The Politically Invisible." *Policy Studies Review* 9:505–515.

Dahl, Robert A. 1956. *Preface to Democratic Theory*. Chicago: University of Chicago Press.

Dahl, Robert A. 1971. *Polyarchy*. New Haven, Conn.: Yale University Press.

DeNardo, James. 1980. "Turnout and the Vote: The Joke's on the Democrats." *American Political Science Review* 74:406–420.

DeNardo, James. 1986. "Turnout in Presidential Elections." *American Political Science Review* 80:1298–1304.

Eckstein, Harry H. 1966. *Division and Cohesion in Democracy*. Princeton, N.J.: Princeton University Press.

Jackman, Robert W. 1987. "Political Institutions and Voter Turnout in the Industrial Democracies." *American Political Science Review* 81:405–423.

Kleppner, Paul. 1982. *Who Voted?* New York: Praeger.

Lyons, William, and Michael M. Gant. 1989. "Non-Voting and Public Policy:

The 1972–1984 Presidential Elections." Paper prepared for the Midwest Political Science Association Meeting, Chicago.

Milbrath, Lester W., and M. L. Goel. 1977. *Political Participation*, 2d ed. Chicago: Rand McNally.

Nagel, Jack H. 1987. *Participation*. Englewood Cliffs, N.J.: Prentice-Hall.

Orren, Gary. 1987. "The Linkage of Policy to Participation." In *Presidential Selection*, ed. Alexander Heard and Michael Nelson. Durham, N.C.: Duke University Press.

Pateman, Carole. 1970. *Participation and Democratic Theory*. Cambridge: Cambridge University Press.

Powell, G. Bingham, Jr. 1986. "American Voter Turnout in Comparative Perspective." *American Political Science Review* 80:17–43.

Schattschneider, E. E. 1960. *The Semi-Sovereign People*. New York: Holt, Rinehart and Winston.

Schumpeter, Joseph A. 1943. *Capitalism, Socialism and Democracy*. London: George Allen and Unwin Press.

Teixeira, Ruy A. 1987. *Why Americans Don't Vote*. New York: Greenwood Press.

Tucker, Harvey J., and Arnold Vedlitz. 1986. "Does Heavy Turnout Help Democrats in Presidential Elections?" *American Political Science Review* 80:1291–1298.

Wolfinger, Raymond E., and Steven J. Rosenstone. 1980. *Who Votes?* New Haven, Conn.: Yale University Press.

Wolfinger, Raymond E., David P. Glass, and Peverill Squire. 1990. "Predictions of Electoral Turnout: An International Comparison." *Policy Studies Review* 9:551–574.

2 Theories of Turnout: An Empirical Comparison of Alienationist and Rationalist Perspectives

Jack Dennis

A recurring nightmare among those who hold that democracy depends upon the strongly institutionalized presence of free, fair, frequent and meaningful elections is that we will hold an election in this country someday soon and no one will come to cast a ballot. We are still far from that unhappy state. But since 1960 there has been a substantial erosion in American electoral participation—which in world perspective was already low. Political science research thus needs to give a better account of the origins and meaning of such low and declining levels of voter turnout.

Political scientists have been concerned with this low level of participation for additional reasons, however—beyond simply understanding the lack of enthusiasm that our citizens have for elections or speculating about the health of American democracy. We also connect voting to major matters such as who holds power and what the holders of that power are able to do with it. Despite their limitations as mechanisms of popular control of rulers and policies, elections do have both tangible and symbolic effects on the processes of government. The wider social scientific concerns of political scientists are also served by studies of turnout and of nonvoting. Voting has some special advantages for generalizing about the political aspects of human behavior. People who vote are many and diverse. While voting in popular elections is a limited political activity, it is a highly standardized one. There is considerable uniformity of situation and role surrounding voting, which makes it easier for scientists to assess psychosocial processes in voting than in more specialized, less constrained political participation. Understanding voter participation is therefore important on a variety of grounds.

Despite such significance, we do not as yet have available a body of well-ordered generalizations about turnout and nonvoting. Empirical studies began at least as far back as Merriam and Gosnell's *Non-Voting* (1924). But we still have no widely accepted theory regarding voters' decisions to participate in elections or to stay away from them. Thus, the very rich accumulation of empirical findings gathered over more than sixty years is not easily assimilated or interpreted. Such findings constitute instead an unusually hyperfactual state of the art—in comparison to other areas of political science research. Indeed, one must make a relatively diligent effort to detect anything approaching a sustained treatment of broader theoretical themes and concepts that are matched in empirical findings. Such theory as exists in connection with most of the research is both vague and fragmentary. The theories that have been widely operationalized are often perfunctorily laid out, so that the the operationalizations that supposedly follow from them are shrouded in mystery. The lack of clear lines of theoretical parentage has meant that our empirical observations of the phenomena of voting and nonvoting often lead us to unresolvable puzzles and paradoxes—given the lack of any well-conceived, compelling general account of the most important features of the phenomena (Brody 1978).

The present empirical essay tries to stem the natural flow of hyperfactualism in this area by making more explicit some theoretical alternatives of relevance. It also attempts to recast some of our familiar measurements in terms of these more explicitly theoretical options, to add some new measurements, and then to confront such theories with empirical evidence—to see which might have in some sense more scientific "cash value."

What is being assumed from the outset is that we need a more self-conscious consideration of our theories of voter turnout and nonvoting. Only when we make clear that we are comparing more general interpretative paradigms in our confrontation of evidence will such efforts at measurement and data analysis take on truly scientific meaning. We need therefore to reverse the usual practice of this area—which is to focus mainly on new ways to measure the variables of possible interest or to use new electoral situations in which to measure them. We should instead be more explicit about the nature of our theoretical interpretations and indeed, where possible, confront and contrast the relative utility of alternative general accounts of the phenomena.

If we are to construct theories of voting/nonvoting, where should we look for promising building blocks? It may seem strange to some, but I would argue that some older works from the 1950s are a good starting place. Given the predominance in subsequent research of the use of variables of a psychosocial variety, introduced originally in *The Voter Decides* (1954) and *The American Voter* (1960), I think one has to begin with the work of Campbell, Converse, Miller, and Stokes. What will be argued, however, is that the theoretical value of these authors' approach to turnout may not lie with what little they lay out explicitly as their theoretical core. The theory is contained rather in their original list of explanatory variables and how these variables have been used in later work on voting and related areas—both by these authors and by a variety of others influenced by them.

We might thus begin our exploration with the observation that the theory of turnout in *The American Voter* and *The Voter Decides* is mostly implicit rather than explicit. Indeed, if one's criteria for a theory include such things as being explicit, general, unambiguous, internally coherent, parsimonious, testable, distinguishable from other theories, providing a good account of the causal processes involved, and being stated in the form of interlinked propositions about empirical reality, rather than being merely a collection of definitions and concepts, then their approach might qualify as theory on some of these grounds, but not on all. What is said about turnout in *The American Voter*, for example, probably qualifies best on the grounds of testability or operational explicitness, but less so on other criteria. It is actually a quite daunting task to reconstruct the core of *The American Voter*'s theory of turnout, given that there are not many explicit theoretical discussions of relevance contained there. Nor is it possible to do this well from the trailing literature, authored by those who have followed in the wake of *The American Voter*.

What is remarkable in all of this subsequent work is that the original theory has remained more inarticulate, indistinct, and fragmentary than might seem possible given the large volume of empirical studies that have replicated the measures originated by these authors. The landmark status of the original studies indeed persists despite these studies not having any elaborated, unambiguous presentation of their theoretical assumptions. One may be quite sympathetic to the general drift of this approach—as is the present author—without having any precise guidelines for where the theory is headed and what its scope and limits might be. As one may easily demonstrate, the measurements originated in *The Voter Decides* and *The American Voter* have robust empirical relationships with turnout; but one is never quite sure what should be the wider explanatory meaning attached to such demonstrable relationships.

My own analysis would reveal at least three different types of general theoretical emphases present in *The American Voter*, which bear on one's interpretation of turnout. Discovering these three different kinds of theoretical focus depends on how broadly or narrowly one construes what is said there, what is measured, and how these themes get either reproduced or dropped in subsequent work—or in a few cases become amplified beyond what was contained in the original work.

The first kind of theory specification one might be led to make—and this is the most conservative interpretation of the central elements of theory in *The American Voter*—is simply that people bring to an election some sense of personal political involvement that can be translated into a probability of participating or not. An election thus provides a suitable situation for the manifestation of an underlying sense of political involvement. There are long-term aspects of political involvement, such as in one's sense of political efficacy; and there are short-term components, such as concern for the outcome of the election at hand. But for practical purposes such different aspects of political involvement may be treated together. At heart, this theory is simply that psychological involvement is the basis for overt behavior in the presence of stimulating circumstances—that is, the stimuli of an election.

One may readily agree that such a theory is correct so far as it goes. But that is not very far. Such a relationship indeed comes close to being true by definition—in that the operative explanatory hypothesis could be restated as "psychological involvement leads to (or is part of?) behavioral involvement." We could imagine that these authors might have chosen to pursue this further if they had wanted us to have a more explicit explanatory paradigm. For example, they might have hypothesized some deeper psychic sources of such involvement, as in a theory of political motivation. Studies of political elites, beginning at least with Lasswell (1930, 1936, 1948) have often assumed, and sometimes tested, the idea that particular configurations of motives, such as those associated with high or low self-esteem, have major effects on a person's sense of political involvement, as both psychically and behaviorally defined. Had our attention been drawn to processes involving the origins, types, and conditions for expressions of such motivational patterns, then we might have a more secure sense that there is an explanatory theory being provided. But *The American Voter* and its trailing literature do not give us an explicit theory of political motivation that could serve to account for voter turnout/abstention below a surface level.[1] Nor indeed is there presented any other well-worked-out, explicit, and general explanatory theory of an equivalent nature.

One could simply stop at this point and admit that this approach does not take us very far, but that it is what we have for the time being as the dominant approach to these studies. But if we are unsatisfied by such an admission, then one alternative strategy is to look harder in what has been said and done and thus to discover what kind of theoretical elements satisfying as explanations might be driving this research. Surely there must be something more than what in retrospect seems to be a rather superficial observation that involvement leads to behavior.

A fainter, but possibly more illuminating second theoretical theme that is present in *The American Voter* concerns the possibility that political involvement could arise and be sustained via certain social processes of communication. The authors suggest, if tersely and offhandedly, that there are small group dynamics and reference group behaviors that stand behind one of the major components of political involvement, intensity of political party identification (Campbell et al. 1960, 121). To take this route we would need to expand these suggestive remarks to include the other specific components of political involvement. We would perhaps want to employ more of the content of explanation from small group dynamics (e.g., Verba 1961) or from reference group theory (e.g., Hyman and Singer 1968). More satisfactory general accounts of the origins and expressions of political involvement might derive from the frequent, if not universal, stimulation that people receive from others in the form of directing and reinforcing communication of group standards, concerns, and sense of common purpose. Group consciousness, the processes of forming group identifications, and social comparisons may all be part of what gives rise to, and sustains, a sense of political involvement under many circumstances.

But the authors of *The American Voter* and the vast majority of those whose efforts flow from their original formulations do not really spell out a theory of the social sources of political involvement. Indeed, it is a quite different tradition, that of political sociologists, especially of the Lazarsfeld/Columbia tradition, that came closest to doing so. The general thrust of the Michigan NES (National Election Studies) authors has been to downplay such sources of variation. With only a few recent exceptions, there has been no follow-through of these suggestions in subsequent research efforts by the people who have worked mainly with the NES data.[2] Thus, one is left in some doubt about the theoretical status of group-process approaches in these studies.

A third possibility—but one that requires even more stretching of the actual words of the "sacred texts"—is what I would term an alienationist approach. There is not much said in *The American Voter* about political alienation or support. But one does get an impression that people's sense of political involvement may be related to prior political experience or to learning about electorally related aspects of politics and government, as in the very brief discussion of political socialization in *The American Voter* (Campbell et al. 1960, 146–149, 155, also see 24 ff.). If people come to regard political policies and leadership, as well as the processes and institutions of politics, in a more or less favorable light through their longer term, direct or indirect experiences with how well these things have operated, then the observer has a theoretical basis for assessing the causes of political involvement or detachment. One's sense of political efficacy, for example, may be more than simply a way of expressing a more general sense of political involvement. And it may be more than simply a registering of group norms about the worth of personal participation in politics. The alienationist approach presumes rather that an individual's observation (or learning from others) about how well the system, its leadership, and policies respond to her or his needs and concerns is tied to that individual's level of (sense of) political efficacy. People respond, therefore, in significant ways to political reality. This species of theory says inter alia that people's psychological political involvement, and thus their resulting participation in elections, is a function of interpreting how well major actors, processes, programs, and institutions meet their demands over the long term. And it may not be simply the definition of the general character of the system that is operative, but more particularly, those aspects of government and politics that have special meaning for one's electoral actions.

Past work on participation in politics (for useful summaries, see Lane 1959; Milbrath and Goel 1977; Conway 1985) suggests that persons whose long-range experience with government and politics is positive will participate with fair regularity. But more complexly, those who may see leaders and government actions less favorably—but whose sense of political efficacy is high—should tend to vote more consistently and also to engage in political acts more difficult than voting (see Gamson 1968; Finifter 1970).

Can one make the case successfully that such a theoretical alternative is present, if implicitly, in the work of Campbell et al. and subsequently in the so-called "Michigan School"? To do so probably depends more on reinterpreting what is contained in the measurements used in connection with indexing a sense of political involvement, as in *The American Voter*, and in subsequent uses of these measurements in voting and related research (see, for example, Abramson 1983), than from explicating what is in the text of their presentations.

Let us review briefly the nature of these operations. The three longer-term political orientations most closely connected to the index of "intensity of political involvement," and thus to voter turnout, are sense of political efficacy, sense of citizen duty (to vote), and intensity of partisan identification (Campbell et al. 1960, 107). As we have learned, post-*American Voter*, from studies of socialization (e.g., Easton and Dennis 1967, 1969; Jennings and Niemi 1974), these broadly focused political orientations typically arise during the preadult and young adult phases of the life span of Americans. They are all part of how one comes to be committed to the institutions and processes of democracy. Each bespeaks a basic commitment to participation-relevant norms of conduct of special relevance to elections.

Such commitments arise usually in circumstances that substantially predate those of a present campaign. While each type of attitude may be more or less subject to short-term fluctuations due to particular events, issues, candidates, or other phenomena of an election—as Brody demonstrates is true in certain circumstances for intensity of partisan identification (1977), they are probably nonetheless best thought of as long-term, traitlike aspects of the political psychology of individuals, given their relative stability compared to most political orientations. This applies even in an era in which both partisan intensity and high efficacy have declined as attributes of Americans, taken collectively (Abramson 1983).

One does not need a very long leap of imagination, I would argue, to suggest that such highly relevant forms of general political orientation may operate from a basis of long-term learning about, and experience with, the political system at various levels. These long-term orientations therefore reflect in a quite direct way—for most people, most of the time—a sense of integration into, or alienation from, the wider institutional context in which elections are held.

This is not to say that such orientations reflect only this kind of content or that they do so in every kind of electoral context. It is only to argue that they are likely to have a strong political alienation/support component. Nor is it to argue that all of the long-term general orientations that seem to measure political alienation—such as political trust/cynicism—suggested in *The American Voter* and in subsequent work of a related nature, are necessarily related except in special circumstances to turnout. One of the virtues of the alienationist approach as it has developed within the context of election studies is to suggest that not every measure of political alienation may have relevance for understanding voting. Of course, in the case of the popular measure of political trust used in the National Election Studies, this may have as much to do with ambiguities in the wording of the questions as with anything substantive (Miller 1974; Citrin 1974).

Now Campbell, Converse, Miller and Stokes might well be surprised (and even a bit alarmed) that in a mostly latent sense they provided the beginnings of a theory of political alienation of relevance to the study of turnout. At least their practices or operations, if not their descriptions of what theoretical concepts were being offered, could lead us readily in that direction. Such an interpretation could be connected, moreover, even to the two short-term (and less complexly measured) orientations included in the composite index of intensity of political involvement (Campbell et al. 1960, 107). Interest in the election at hand and concern about which party wins the election also may suggest a degree of longer-term based readiness to immerse oneself in, or distance oneself from, the present proceedings. Indeed, campaign interest is highly related to more long-standing aspects of political involvement, and concern about the (party) outcome is quite related to how one feels about the parties more generally (Dennis 1988). Thus, these variables may have important longer-term components that are based upon alienating or integrating prior political experience as much as present election circumstances.

THE PRESENT STUDY

In what follows, I have focused upon the political alienationist interpretation of these variables. This may seem at first glance to be a choice for the most far-fetched reconstruction of the theoretical basis of the dominant explanatory approach to the study of turnout and nonvoting. But I believe that it accords reasonably well with the meaning of the measures actually employed and with the subsequent history of their use—in so far as investigators have sought to give a deeper account of the forces giving rise to these general political orientations. I would also argue both that it is more intuitively interesting as a theoretical alternative than are the other two interpretative theories that seem to be present in this work and that it seems to have greater subsequent currency in the research community. Thus, this interpretative strategy offers perhaps greater promise as a focus of cumulative generalization about the phenomena of voter participation than do the other two.

ALTERNATIVE THEORETICAL APPROACHES

What I am thus suggesting is that we try to build upon the kinds of operationalizations and the theory implicit in *The American Voter* and in its trailing literature. I simply propose to widen the theoretical meaning of such operationalizations in order to have a basis of theory comparison for the study of turnout. But in order to explore the value of such a theoretical alternative, it is useful to have something to compare it with. Two other major modes of interpretation of turnout seem to me to have some currency in the literature on turnout/nonvoting; and they might thus serve as bases for such a comparison.

One of these I would term "the demographic approach." I so identify it because of the prominent use that demographic variables such as race, gender, age, and education have had in turnout studies. One of the most noticeable features of such applications is how close most of such studies come to being *atheoretical*. That is to say, the studies that focus most of their attention on these sociodemographic differences in voter behavior either typically do not have a theory of what causal processes are at work to produce such differences, or else they need to seek their causal explanations in forces that lie behind such observed differences. Thus the vast majority of such studies end up being descriptive rather than explanatory. Most of such social categories are very broad and thus ambiguous in terms of their theoretical meaning.

For example, let us take the two demographic variables that are most consistently demonstrated as having a significant relationship to turnout and nonvoting—age and education. One might suppose that such variables represent major differences in the kinds of roles and statuses that

Theories of Turnout   31

people come to occupy—and that they thus help us in some way to account for people's voting behavior. But to put the matter thus does not really take us much further than we were already. Can such a vague and static rendering of what age and education are about—that is, as measures of social status—indeed capture the complex of forces buried in each? I would suggest not.

Age categories, for example, may be convenient groupings of people on the basis of any or all of the following:

1. Differences in the rate of geographical mobility that affect the probability of registration and voting—for younger potential voters in particular. Young adults are generally less settled in a given location and thus are affected more by voter registration requirements and the like.
2. Younger adults may also have fewer meaningful community ties or a lesser feeling of belonging to social units with political meaning.
3. Younger adults have usually also a smaller tangible stake in the community in which they reside, or in society more generally, given their higher probability of being in transitional roles and statuses.
4. But differences among age groups may reflect instead the relative extent of past political learning and experience, which may include, for example:

    (a) differences in degree of internalization of participation-relevant orientations as they have matured

    (b) facilitating or obstructing personal attitudes

    (c) habits of participation in general

    (d) the development of participation-relevant skills, such as learning the rules and procedures governing the electoral process

    (e) extent of general involvement in politics and thus extent of political motivation

    (f) longer or shorter experience with leadership, policies, and government performance

    (g) practice in the collection and processing of decision-relevant political information

    (h) other life-span-related learning and experience

5. Differences that appear because of cohort specific, or generationally defined events and processes—such as coming of age in a period of high collective politicization and/or mobilization.
6. Differences in levels of group membership, consciousness, identification, communication, and social support.

Education, to take the other most prominent demographic correlate of voter turnout in the literature, has an equally ambiguous explanatory status. It may refer, for example, to any or all of these:

1. Differences that arise in connection with one's social origins. Thus, on these grounds, one's socioeconomic origins simply are reflected in, and perhaps magnified by, one's schooling. Thus, education may be a measure of not simply one's current social status but, more importantly, where one has come from. It also thus reflects family, peer, or other social milieu influences that affect one's recruitment to, and thus socialization by, educational institutions.
2. Differences that have to do with the content of what is learned—knowledge, skills, interests, motivations, self-confidence, or practice in participation that comes with greater exposure to schooling or from greater educational attainment.
3. Differences connected to other inputs of schooling: from teachers, curriculum, the climate of learning, or school-related other activities and qualities.
4. Differences arising from more severe habituation, reinforcement, or internalization—as a function of longer or more comprehensive school-related political communication and observation.

Measuring respondents' ages and levels of educational attainment and demonstrating significant empirical relationships of these antecedents with turnout may be easy. *What is difficult*, however, is knowing precisely what such relationships reflect about causal processes. To show an empirical relationship for such broad categories of individuals is but a first step in theory construction and a relatively descriptive one. One still needs either considerable theoretical imagination to know what lies buried there, or else fairly complex auxiliary evidence—as in studies of political socialization—to find what such variables mean causally.[3]

This is also true for such commonly included demographic variables as gender and race. Demonstration of these (declining) bases of differences in voter participation often involves considerable interpretative debate and uncertainty about the relative effects of such causal forces as role socialization (and thus wider cultural biases), social status inequalities of various kinds, or political structural barriers to equal participation (see, for example, Baxter and Lansing 1983; Carroll 1985; Sapiro 1983; Abramson 1983; Walton 1985). Without something further attached to them, therefore, demographic categories do not constitute an explanatory theory of turnout. To understand the meaning of social categorical differences, one must designate which particular social, psychological, political, or other causal processes are of greatest relevance—and thus overcome the implicit diversity of interpretation contained in each. I therefore designate such inquiries as constituting what is, relative to the two kinds of theories I try to compare below, essentially an atheoretical/descriptive alternative.

RATIONALIST THEORY

There is another currently lively candidate for an alternative general explanatory perspective on turnout and nonvoting. This is what I would term "rationalist theory." This approach derives mainly from economics, with some contributions from other disciplines such as mathematics. Rationalist theory applied to voting stems originally from the work of Anthony Downs (1957). Such theory has been expanded, elaborated, and refined in various efforts of the "positive theory" school, centered especially at the University of Rochester. Rationalist thought begins with the supposedly simple assumption that people act in accordance with their definition of what is best for them—that is, they seek to maximize their own utility. For voting or abstaining, this means that they must evaluate the expected benefits versus the expected costs of voter participation. When deciding whether to vote, what is therefore at issue is not one's emotions about government per se, nor one's feelings about political elites. One could be either very positive or very negative in one's affective orientations to the structure, personnel, or general performance of government and still not be much affected by any of these things in deciding about the personal relevance of voting. The motivation to vote comes not from attitudes toward the system, but rather from the perceived personal relevance of government policies that have been implemented versus those that may be expected to be put into place in the future—when one or another of the contesting parties wins the election.

Downsian and post-Downsian rationalist theories have provided a widening array of concepts to use for analyzing the situation of electoral choice. If one starts with the assumption that people are capable of, and inclined toward, a deliberative, conscious weighing of alternatives in connection with voting decisions, then concepts such as "utility-maximization" and "minimax-regret" have been proposed as relevant to such deliberations. Motivations to participate become a function of the tradeoffs between expected costs versus expected gains, for the alternatives available. Such motivation need not be affected by one's emotional reactions to who is in power or to the general worth of the political system. Rather, one attempts to act within the system in such a way that one's own interests will be promoted or at least not harmed.

There is a strong theme of individualism assumed in this approach, even though what a person seeks to maximize may be values that are in part group-centered or derived. One seeks just the things that bring oneself happiness, and these desiderata may be sought even in elections. There is also a strong emphasis upon cognition in this approach—in characterizing human response in terms of information-processing, alternative-weighing, goal-maximizing, uncertainty-diminishing, risk-estimating decision-making.

This is in several important respects quite different from the alienationist perspective. In the latter, one finds a more group-centered, emotive, social-psychological portrait of how humans behave. While in this approach individuals are still primary actors who "decide" to vote or not, the major analytical focus is not as much upon highly conscious, deliberate, cognitive, personally centered, explicit weighing of costs and benefits. Rather, a more diffuse set of emotional responses to the political process is usually assumed by alienationism instead of a direct, one-to-one connecting of personal states of well-being to the recent actions and structures of government. In alienationism, much of the impetus to participation or indifference with respect to elections comes from an earlier derived sense of political obligation, as via preadult political socialization, or from experiences that have accumulated over a longer period than the incumbent presidential administration's period in office. General sets of reactions to government or to other aspects of the political system, or even a more global sense of satisfaction with the overall structure of government, its long-term performance, or feelings toward salient levels and institutions of government thus count for more. From the alienationist theorist's perspective, it is not mere short-term, individual self-interest that is at stake in elections, but the broader interests of the groups with which one identifies, and the character of the political system itself. Motivations to participate or to abstain spring from more diverse, diffuse, and complex sources therefore than simply any expected personal gain or loss connected to specific acts of voting. Motivations and emotions relevant to turnout derive instead from the social group, system, and other long-term sources that are activated again by the election at hand.

In contrast, the rationalist perspective presupposes a kind of single global motivation for individuals, as does conventional economics. This motivation is at base the pursuit of individual self-interest; and the consequences of greatest analytical interest are relatively short-term and specific to the action being taken, relative to benefits or losses that result from that action. If each person inevitably seeks his or her own utility as primary, then longer-term, larger societal purposes come into play only consequently and indirectly. The collective context of individual action comes to be of interest only as it sets limits upon individual action, rather than as the cause or major focus of such action. The implicit view of such rationalism is that individual actions in the aggregate will provide and maintain the collective context of action automatically, without individuals needing to direct their thoughts or actions toward its construction or preservation.

Given how long such an approach has been available (Downs 1957), a number of criticisms have been made of such theoretical thinking, some of which apply to rationalist concepts of interest in the study of turnout. A most visible criticism that arises within the rationalist camp itself is the so-called "paradox of not voting." This argument, very simply put, is that the potential voter stands to gain very little as an individual from expending resources to vote, given the difficulty in a large potential electorate of making any significant difference in the outcome. Thus, virtually any expenditure of time, money, or effort will be wasted, given the low probability of an individual's affecting the result. It is therefore irrational for any individual voter to cast a ballot. Yet, millions of people are observed to troop to polling places in national elections. And a higher proportion of voters turn out in national elections than in most local ones, despite the individual's chances of affecting the outcome being much greater in local contests. People thus vote in relatively large numbers despite the logical argument that as individuals they have only an infinitesimal chance of making any difference in the election results. This is the paradox of not voting.

Can millions of people simply be mistaking their own potential weight in elections? Or could it be that the voting act is a virtually costless one? How does one explain such large-scale "irrationality" of individual voters? One can tender a variety of solutions to this paradox; but the ones proposed so far do not seem to be universally convincing. For example, one might borrow elements from alienationist theory, as I have defined it, to give an explanation of why people nonetheless participate when the chances that their votes will make a difference are so small. Riker and Ordeshook (1973), for example, suggest in their version of the rationalist approach that the solution might lie in there being present among voters a strong sense of citizen duty to vote. Thus the voter gains a sense of positive satisfaction or utility from casting a ballot, since such voting fulfills one's sense of obligation learned at some earlier point. In the present context we cannot opt for that solution, however. In a contest between alienationist and rationalist accounts of voting/nonvoting, this strategy would give away the game to the alienationists.

Another noteworthy attempt to save the rationalist structure, by changing some basic Downsian assumptions, is by Ferejohn and Fiorina (1974). Their substitution of the "minimax/regret" principle essentially reassesses the size of the stakes involved for voters. Ferejohn and Fiorina assume that people are especially unwilling to take the risk that in a close election, their side could lose narrowly if they failed to vote. Thus, they would find themselves conscience-stricken once they realized that their own efforts could have saved the day. Whether many people conceptualize the risks in such a manner has not been demonstrated, however. Such a principle may indeed apply. But it may well be that only a few people in a few elections that are generally recognized as being very close (before the fact) show any realistic minimax/regret impetus. Thus, while such a principle, or logical possibility, is certainly worth looking at, it may turn out empirically to account for only a small proportion of the variation in turnout.

THE PRESENT APPROACH TO COMPARING THEORIES

In what follows, I have tried to take seriously the possible contributions to our understanding of these two general theoretical approaches. Despite some indistinctness in how each has been formulated to this point, and despite some obvious, if different, limitations of each type of theory for empirical applications in this realm, I have tried to devise a fair test of each of them in relation to turnout/nonvoting. I am indeed entertaining the hypothesis that each of these approaches explains correctly some part of the voting/nonvoting phenomenon. Thus, potentially, they may complement each other. But we need to be mindful of their differences in basic assumptions about human nature, as well as possible areas of conceptual or empirical overlap. Our problem here is to devise ways of measuring major elements of each that will give us a basis of relative assessment when they are used in contrast.

The argument to be made is that neither theory is as general as usually assumed by its proponents. Rationalist thinking in particular has a kind of single, global motivational presumption which makes it seem dubious from the outset to most students of political psychology. This assumption is that, left to their own devices, people invariably seek to maximize their own utility by weighing alternative expected outcomes relative to some set of well-ordered personal preferences. But social-psychological theories generally reject such an account of human motivation as too simplistic. Indeed, it is more reasonable from a social-psychological perspective to assume that people may or may not seek only, or primarily, their own ends, particularly if such ends are defined in materialistic terms. And such ends may not be simple or easy for people to address at a conscious level. Rather, such deliberate, conscious, goal-seeking, utility-maximizing behavior is only one possible scenario or human subtype. There may indeed be required a rather special set of conditions for "economic persons" to emerge fully, especially in connection to tasks that are so infrequent and low in salience to the average person in settled democracies as participating in elections. Indeed, it may be more reasonable to assume that most people's perceived options and likely actions will be highly constrained by social contexts—both in the initial formation of voting-relevant attitudes and motives, and in their maintenance and timely expression. Thus, it is more reasonable to assume that rational behavior as related to turnout is more likely to operate in a restricted fashion. We may indeed hypothesize in general that:

1. Nearly every potential voter or nonvoter has both rationalist and alienationist tendencies. Depending on the circumstances, extent of participation will derive from a complex mix of motivations, beliefs, preferences, and norms—both cognitive and affective, group-derived and individually derived, self-interested and other-directed, which thus will be, in general, both rational and nonrational.
2. Under some sets of conditions, rationalist aspects of turnout/abstention behavior may come to predominate; whereas under other conditions (both personal and societal), alienationist/supportive dimensions of orientation will emerge more strongly—both for individual persons and for aggregates of individuals, relative to voting.
3. Thus, neither alienation/support nor rational decision-making is likely to be universal in application (Simon 1985). Even when one or the other predominates, it will likely do so only for a given period of time. The assumption of conventional economics that people seek to maximize their own anticipated benefits and minimize their costs probably does work some of the time—at least in those situations, perhaps less common than often assumed—where there are many sellers and many buyers; where information is good, complete, and inexpensive; and where there are already in place well-organized, convenient, unfettered mechanisms for effecting exchanges. This set of conditions may even apply to the act of voting. But such situations may be considerably more special than rationalist thinkers have been willing to recognize. In most instances, the average person will exhibit a complex set of emotions and understandings that apply even to behaviors as mundane as voting. Whatever impetus to vote may be present for an individual therefore springs from diverse sources that encompass, but may also surpass, the causal forces usually given prominence in rationalist approaches.

On the other side of the coin, global alienationism may be equally misleading and simplistic, if taken too literally. There is no reason to expect that everyone in a democracy will be moved only by their negative or positive feelings about the political system in general or about its chief actors and policies. Generalized attitudes of this kind may often be difficult to connect to the limited role of voting or to translate into any actionable political terms. In this country we seldom have the opportunity to vote, for example, on whether we should transform fundamentally the political system or its major constituent institutions. Most of such opportunities were exhausted immediately before and after the American Revolutionary War, or around the time of the Civil War. Thus, if political alienation or support is to become operational for the average person, it will need to be geared directly to relevant political objects. In the case of elections, one thus needs to focus most directly upon the major institutions, processes, persons, and policy content of campaigns for office to see significant impacts of politically alienated or supportive feelings. For example, we would expect that orientations toward the political parties, the candidates, and other well-defined aspects of the electoral process will hold more relevance than a general sense of political trust of political authority or of one's relative confidence in the national governmental system.

OPERATIONAL COMPARISONS OF THESE THEORIES

A number of these ideas were explored in connection with the 1984 election. Questions for use in telephone surveys in Wisconsin were devised to operationalize aspects of each of these two theories. These items were developed in stages, moving from more open-ended to closed-ended versions. In so far as possible, interview items from earlier surveys, both those used since 1964 in Wisconsin in the author's series on institutional support and alienation and items relevant to turnout from the NES surveys, were utilized. Those most pertinent to the electoral process, such as questions measuring support for or alienation from the political parties were given special attention. Special notice was also given to attitudes focused upon the major norms and relationships surrounding the processes of democratic elections.

One is immediately struck by how many more useful items are available from past studies on the alienationist side of the analysis than is true for the rationalist side, however. For the most part, new measures of rationalist orientations relevant to turnout had to be developed in the present study. They included mostly attempts to operationalize some central elements of Downsian utility maximization theory, with some lesser attention to alternative aspects of rationalist orientation, particularly orientations suggested by Ferejohn's and Fiorina's explication of "minimax/regret" (1974).

With few exceptions, those proposing the relevance of rationalist concepts to the understanding of individual voting behavior have not developed incisive survey items useful for testing whether such concepts have any individual-level empirical validity. In part, this stems from the more deductive, formal-modeling cast of mind among proponents of such ideas. This lack of serious empirical treatment is the result of assuming that if the postulates derived from one's original axioms have putative empirical applications, then it is not necessary to examine the axioms themselves through empirical measurement.

I should emphasize that the opposite is assumed here. Not only do the basic assumptions of rationalist theory need closer theoretical examination, but more importantly, they need to be translated into empirically testable form if they are to provide the basis for illuminating voter turnout and nonvoting. If the people seldom apply rationalist modes of orientation to their consideration of political actions, then there is probably little point in drawing out elaborate series of postulates from axioms of rational behavior—except as a purely normative exercise. Nor will connecting citizens' rational orientations to their voter behavior prove fruitful.

Thus, a central purpose in the present research has been to attempt to devise ways of testing whether rationalist concepts have any empirical "cash value" in this context. Given the exploratory nature of these efforts, one should expect only a crude set of indicators of rational behavior to emerge. This is necessarily a preliminary stage of development, in which we can begin to see whether rationalist ideas might have operational value in accounting for voting/nonvoting, or whether they are more likely to lead us up an empirical blind alley. What is attempted here, therefore, is not another purely theoretical critique of rationalist theory (see, for example, Hardin and Barry 1982). Rather, I take seriously the possibility that a rationalist approach may add something important empirically to our attempts to account for these phenomena, if we can give this approach more precise operational meaning.

THE MEASURES

What was done thus far in developing indicators could be simplified as follows. First, several measures of political alienation and support, originally developed for use in earlier Wisconsin surveys and which seemed most appropriate to the explanatory task at hand, were used. In addition, I added a number of items to fill out earlier series on such dimensions as party system support, support for the system of elections, and feelings about interest group participation in politics, political efficacy, and citizen duty to vote. Some questions were added concerning more general feelings related to democracy and to its operation through elections. Thus, I designed a number of new questions to tap general beliefs about majority rule and the wisdom of voters, the necessity for popular participation in choosing and restraining elites, and the like. As indicated above, some questions that the National Elections Studies included were repeated and reconceptualized, such as those on interest in the election and concern for the outcome—as part of a more general dimension of orientations entitled "electoral alienation."

On the rationalist side of the argument, I tried to operationalize a number of what I took to be more basic concepts of Downs and post-Downsians. For example, several different Downsian indexes were developed—to tap some central ideas provided by Downs in *An Economic Theory of Democracy*. Measures inspired by the approach of Ferejohn and Fiorina in their minimax/regret principle, as applied to turnout/abstention, were added. What was attempted substantively was to compare how well sets of rationality and alienation/support variables contribute (significantly and independently) to an analysis of turnout/abstention.

A variety of multi-item indexes was developed to measure each of the antecedent variables of both types. In developing the specific indexes to be explicated below, a series of factor analyses and item analyses (Cronbach's alpha) were used primarily to test for discriminant validity and internal cohesion. The resulting indexes were then related to each other in various ways and to the dependent variable.

The dependent variable—the turnout behavior index—included not only self-reported voting or not voting in the 1984 elections, but also respondent recollection of behavior in a series of previous elections. This was believed to be a better method of indexing the behaviors of interest than to use only the November 1984 election turnout. First, such an index refers to a pattern of behavior more general than that attached to a particular recent election. Second, one faces a special problem in using the Wisconsin potential electorate relative to the populations of most other states, given the high rate of turnout in Wisconsin. Third, for the American population as a whole, there is the well-known problem of some overreporting of having voted. Finally, one prefers an index for the kind of multivariate analyses to be undertaken that will give a reasonably wide dispersion of observations and something approaching a normal distribution.

ALIENATIONIST MEASURES

What I begin with is the index of the intensity of political involvement found in *The American Voter*. I take the subcomponents of this index to be mostly measures of the extent of political alienation from, or support for, the electoral process. Sense of citizen duty to vote is particularly crucial to an understanding of the operational difference between alienationist and rationalist approaches. What is central to such a sense of personal obligation to participate, from an alienationist perspective, is that the terms of such obligation are couched in terms of the lack of anticipated personal payoffs from such action. The wording of the Michigan items—which have been repeated in the series of National Election Studies since 1952—emphasizes the idea that one should vote even when the payoffs are expected to be low. As I showed in a Wisconsin study of public support for elections in 1966, the tendency of many voters to be strongly focused on voting duty has been pronounced for some time (Dennis 1970). Voting duty may indeed be one of the major antecedents that keeps turnout from dropping below the low levels it presently shows—in a time when intensity of partisanship and political efficacy have dropped significantly and thus have helped to undermine turnout. The sense of duty to vote is probably the general orientation most opposite to prospective Downsian variables of any of these alienation measures—in that one should rationally abstain if there is not much in it for oneself, according to Downs (1957, 260). A person with a strong sense of voting duty would be unaffected by such personal utility calculations.

But partisan intensity and political efficacy are also counter to the spirit of Downsian theory. One needs to be nonpartisan or very flexibly partisan to behave rationally according to Downs (1957, 38). "Brand loyalties" at the level of parties and candidates serve to obstruct one's capacity to reward or punish the performance of those being put forward as the next set of prospective incumbents.

Political efficacy is perhaps in Downsian terms more debatable, given that there is an implied value being put on one's potential participation in an election. People who have an enduring low sense of their own political weight, for example, may well calculate that voter participation is not worthwhile. Yet such an enduring sense of powerlessness would serve to cut off consideration of those instances in which one's vote might (at relatively low cost) serve to make an important difference. Probably a low sense of political efficacy could thus serve as a rigidity in one's voting calculus that prevents the full operation of rationalist principles. Indeed, if low, political efficacy could cause a miscalculation of one's true utilities. Thus, the more reasonable theoretical context is probably that of a species of political alienation and support that taps the essential immersion of powerlessness/potency.

The supposedly short-term orientations of interest in the election and concern for the outcome are taken here to be as much likely indicators of a general orientation to the electoral process, as they are indications of just how exciting and fraught with potential significance the present contest might be. Dimensional analysis shows that they are part of a wider component that is called here "electoral alienation"—the interview questions which will be detailed below. This has some of the immediate situation of a particular election contained within it. But it also reflects longer-term elements. For example, one can show that the item on caring which party wins the election is quite related to more general feelings about the worth and performance of political parties, both in Wisconsin data and in the 1980 NES evidence.

INDEXES USED IN WISCONSIN IN 1984

For measuring political alienation of relevance to turnout, the following indexes were used:

1. *Citizen duty to vote*
   a. "It isn't so important to vote when you know your party doesn't have any chance to win."
   b. "So many other people vote in the national elections that it doesn't matter much to me whether I vote or not."

c. "How worthwhile is it to you personally to try to vote in every election, including primaries and elections at local, state and national levels—very worthwhile, worthwhile, not worthwhile, or a waste of time?"

   d. "A good many local elections aren't important enough to bother with."

   All of these citizen duty items except *c* have an option format that consists of strongly agree, agree, disagree, and strongly disagree. A few people also volunteered that they both agreed and disagreed on each item, which was treated as a middle category in the scores for each item. The index simply added up the scores on the individual items (1–5 on most items; 1–4 on item *c*).

2. *Sense of political efficacy*

   a. "I don't think public officials care much what people like me think."

   b. "People like me don't have any say about what the government does."

   c. "Sometimes politics and government seem so complicated that a person like me can't really understand what's going on."

   d. "Voting is the best way that people like me can have a say about how the government runs things."

   e. "I vote primarily because I feel that voting is the most effective way to participate in government."

3. *Partisanship*

   The measure of the partisanship of respondents was the Partisan Supporter Typology developed earlier in connection with the 1980 National Election Study to supplement the traditional party identification index of SRC/CPS/NES (Dennis 1988). This measure is constructed as a six-point classification scored for involvement. It ranges from the Unattached (who are neither partisan nor independent), scored as 1, through Independent Republicans, who are scored 6. These questions were used: "Next we have a few questions about political parties. In your own mind, do you think of yourself as a supporter of one of the political parties, or not?" (If yes) "Which political party do you support?" "Do you ever think of yourself as a political independent, or not?"

4. *Electoral alienation*

   a. "Would you say that you are very much interested, somewhat interested, or not much interested in following the political campaigns this year?"

   b. "How much do you personally care about which candidate wins the presidential election this fall?"

   c. "How much do you personally care whether the Democratic Party or the Republican Party wins most of the offices being contested in November?" (a great deal, somewhat, very little)

   d. "Are the people running for President and Vice President as Democrats and Republicans offering quite different solutions to our country's problems; or are they pretty much the same?"

5. *General political alienation*

a. "How often do you feel isolated from the people who seem to be making most of the important decisions in this country?" (frequently, sometimes, rarely, never)
b. "How often do you feel that the people in the government are being directed by some small group of powerful individuals who are not usually visible to the general public?" (frequently, sometimes, rarely, never)
c. "How much do you feel that you can trust the people in the national government to do what is right?" (completely, mostly, some, almost none)
d. "The best interests of the general public are usually hurt by the lobbying activities of various interest groups."
e. "Too many special privileges have been obtained from the government through lobbying by various interests."

Items *d* and *e* have a strongly agree to strongly disagree format.

6. *Party pluralism*
   a. "Democracy works best where competition between political parties is strong."
   b. "It would be better if, in all elections, we put no party labels on the ballot."
   c. "The parties do more to confuse the issues than to provide a clear choice on the issues."
   d. "The political parties more often than not create conflicts where none really exists."
   e. "How important should be the role of parties in elections?" (very large, fairly large, fairly small, none)
   f. "How strongly would you favor restricting what the Republican and Democratic Parties can do in elections and elsewhere in American politics?" (strongly favor, favor, oppose, oppose strongly)

   Items *a-d* have a strongly agree to strongly disagree format.

7. *Support for an interest group role in politics*
   a. "Without the participation of organized interest groups in government, democracy would be very difficult to maintain." (strongly agree to strongly disagree)
   b. "Democracy works best where organized interest groups can make themselves heard in government decision-making." (strongly agree to strongly disagree)

8. *Majoritarianism*
   a. "How smart are the voters about whom they elect—are they very smart, fairly smart, or do the voters get fooled fairly often?"
   b. "In general, how well does the idea of majority rule really work in this country—very well, quite well, only so-so, or poorly?"
   c. "How often are the majority of the people able to come up with the best

answers to difficult questions of public policy—all the time, most of the time, sometimes, or almost never?"

d. "Overall, how good a record have the people of this country had in choosing wise, honest, and effective political leaders over the past 25 years—has it been a great record, very good, mixed, poor, or very poor record?"

Rationalist Indexes

Unlike the alienationist variables, where most of the questions used are of a quite familiar variety, the indexes used to measure rationalist orientations are new. Thus, the marginal distributions of the items below are also provided to give the reader a sense of how pervasive or infrequent such orientations are in the Wisconsin population. Comments on these distributions will be held to the end of this section. First, let us consider five indexes that come out of an attempt to identify some central ideas from Downs' theory:

1. *Utility calculation*
    a. "For an election such as the one coming up in November, how hard do you try to weigh the likely costs or benefits to you personally from voting or not voting—extremely hard, fairly hard, not very hard, or not at all?" ($N = 534$)

    | Extremely hard | 22% |
    | Fairly hard | 32 |
    | Not very hard | 24 |
    | Not at all | 17 |
    | Don't know | 3 |
    | Not ascertained | 1 |

    b. "In elections such as the one this November, how hard do you try to compare how well the people in office have done in meeting your needs and concerns versus how well the other side's candidates would do if they were in office? Do you usually try extremely hard, fairly hard, not very hard, or not at all to make such comparisons before deciding how to vote? ($N = 554$)

    | Extremely hard | 27% |
    | Fairly hard | 53 |
    | Not very hard | 14 |
    | Not at all | 4 |
    | Don't know | 1 |
    | Not ascertained | 1 |

2. *Policy demands voting*
    a. "I vote mostly to help the candidates who are most likely to work to take care of my own needs and concerns." ($N = 552$)

Strongly agree	21%
Agree	53
Agree/Disagree	2
Disagree	19
Strongly disagree	2
Don't know	1
Not ascertained	2

b. "I vote mostly to express my opinions on policy issues that are important to me." ($N = 554$)

Strongly agree	18%
Agree	65
Agree/Disagree	1
Disagree	12
Strongly disagree	1
Don't know	1
Not ascertained	1

c. "I usually vote to make sure that the needs and concerns of people like me are heard by government leaders." ($N = 554$)

Strongly agree	23%
Agree	65
Agree/Disagree	1
Disagree	8
Strongly disagree	1
Don't know	1
Not ascertained	2

3. *Self-interest motivation*

   a. "Have you ever felt that there was something you personally might gain by voting in an election?" ($N = 554$)

Yes	46%
No	51
Don't know	3
Not ascertained	1

   b. "Have you ever felt that there was something you personally might lose by not voting in an election?" ($N = 554$)

Yes	57%
No	40
Don't know	3
Not ascertained	1

4. *Rational abstention—low return*[4]

   a. "Whether I vote or not has virtually no effect on who gets elected." ($N = 554$)

Strongly agree	1%
Agree	12
Agree/Disagree	1
Disagree	38
Strongly disagree	9
Always vote	37
Don't know	1
NA	1

b. "My costs in time, energy or money spent in getting to the polls and in deciding how to vote are sometimes greater than any possible benefits voting might have for me." ($N = 554$)

Strongly agree	*%
Agree	8
Agree/Disagree	*
Disagree	43
Strongly disagree	10
Always vote	37
Don't know	—
NA	2

(* = less than 1%)

5. *Rational abstention—high cost*

   a. "Sometimes it is too difficult for me to get to the polling place on election day." ($N = 554$)

Strongly agree	2%
Agree	14
Agree/Disagree	*
Disagree	37
Strongly disagree	8
Always vote	37
Don't know	—
NA	2

   b. "I simply don't have time to keep up with the issues being debated in every election." ($N = 554$)

Strongly agree	1%
Agree	25
Agree/Disagree	1
Disagree	31
Strongly disagree	4
Always vote	37
Don't know	—
NA	1

6. *Minimax—regret orientation*

a. "Have you ever believed that you should vote because the candidate or candidates you support might lose by only a few votes, and you would then be responsible for their losing? Can you remember any specific instances when you felt that way?" ($N = 554$)

Yes, remember instances	28%
Yes, but don't remember	18
No, didn't believe that	54
Don't know	*
NA	*

b. "I often vote to avoid having the wrong people get elected by only a few votes." ($N = 554$)

Strongly agree	13%
Agree	48
Agree/Disagree	1
Disagree	31
Strongly disagree	4
DK	1
NA	1

c. "I sometimes don't vote when the outcome of an election is not going to be close." ($N = 554$)

Strongly agree	1%
Agree	17
Agree/Disagree	—
Disagree	35
Strongly disagree	7
Always vote	37
DK	1
NA	2

7. *Expected election closeness*

"Do you think the vote totals for president will turn out to be fairly close between Mondale and Reagan, or not?" ($N = 554$)

Close	46%
Not close	45
Don't know	7
Not ascertained	1

8. *Candidate differences index*

Two linked questions were used to see how many differences (0–4) respondents were able to articulate in answer to the questions:

a. "Are the people running for President and Vice President as Democrats and Republicans offering quite different solutions to our country's problems, or are they pretty much the same?"

b. "What are the major differences as you see them between Reagan and Mondale?"

48   Jack Dennis

From the standpoint of the questions that have been indexed to form our various rationalist antecedents, we see that a fair portion of the sample could be said to perceive themselves in this manner. Thus, there is a prima facie case for saying that an essential criterion for the application of rationalist concepts is met. If virtually no one agreed to these varied questions about weighing the consequences of one's choices, then we could abandon this approach without further fanfare. On the other hand, we see that significant portions of the same deny doing these things, and thus do not conform to the Downsian positive theory emphasis. If this approach is meant to be more than merely normative, then there is a problem about its universality. By no means everyone can be described as intentionally rational. But enough can be so described, in the terms provided, that further analysis seems warranted—to see how a rationalist impetus, measured thus variously, is related to turnout/nonvoting. Before we turn to that analysis, there is a final set of measures that have been included, which need brief explication.

Measures That Have Mixed Theoretical Standing

There are several measures that were included originally as devices for tapping a rationalist perspective. But upon closer inspection, one can see that the original interpretation may have been more incorrect than correct. One of these is what I have called "political information processing motivation," which had to do with Downs' idea of an information acquisition and processing system that would aid rational decision-making (1957, chap. 11). The following index was used to measure this orientation in the context of the 1984 Wisconsin study.

1. *Political information–processing motivation*
   a. "How often have you made special efforts during election campaigns to find out about the candidates and what they stood for—always, very often, fairly often, or seldom?" ($N = 554$)

      | Always | 20% |
      | Very often | 34 |
      | Fairly often | 30 |
      | Seldom | 15 |
      | DK | * |
      | NA | * |

   b. "How much attention have you usually given to election campaigns as reported on television, in newspapers, on the radio, or in news magazines—a lot, some, not much, or none?" ($N = 554$)

A lot	45%
Some	45
Not much	8
None	2
DK	—
NA	—

This index turns out to be more related to the political alienation indexes than to the rationalist ones. Thus, the original interpretation leaves out the fact that vigorous information processors are people who feel a strong sense of commitment to, and competence in, the wider political system. Thus, I treat political information processing information as an alienist variable below.

I had also presumed that two other prominent concepts used in Downsian and post-Downsian analyses of voting would have an application in this context. One of these is government performance. I assumed that people who disapproved of recent (national) government performance would be more moved to vote than would those who are fully satisfied. As we shall see below, this is almost imperceptibly the case. From an interpretative point of view, one can show, however, that even recent-term government performance affects more basic feelings about political institutions (Dennis 1981). Thus, despite its allocation to the rationalist side, the theoretical status of this variable is probably mixed. The questions used were these:

2. *Government performance*
    a. "In your opinion, how good a job has the Reagan administration done in the past three and a half years to meet the needs and concerns of people like yourself—an excellent, good, only fair, or poor job?"
    b. "How good a job has the U.S. Congress done over the past three and a half years in meeting the needs and concerns of people like yourself—an excellent, good, only fair, or poor job?"
    c. "Do you think that a year from now you and your family will be better off financially, worse off, or just about the same as now?"
    d. "Would you say that at the present time the country as a whole is better off, worse off, or about the same as it was four years ago?"

Another central idea in Downs' approach is the role of liberal/conservative ideology. It is indeed a person's "fixed conception of the good society" translated into left/right terms that allows the necessary candidate/issue position comparisons necessary to make a choice (1957, 96–113). I had thus expected that people with a strong sense of ideological consciousness would be high on rationalism; and that this in turn would relate to turnout. But strong ideological consciousness also means a deeper sense of concern for and commitment to the political process. Thus, we might assume there may also be some elements of alienationism/support associated with ideological identification. In this sense, there is at least some ambiguity of theoretical status of this antecedent. This problem of interpretation is obviated by the finding with these data that those who are middle-of-the road in ideological consciousness are as likely to turn out to vote as are the people at the ends of the continuum. Thus, the relationship of greatest interest is not robust enough to include in further analysis.

DATA ANALYSIS

Having thus set forth the variables to be related to turnout, both from an alienist and a rationalist perspective, what do we find? I have chosen to treat these two sets of variables as separate groups of predictors, in a series of hierarchical multiple regressions reported below. I also add a block of the most significant demographic variables to these equations, to see if we can give a better *empirical* account with them included, despite their theoretical ambiguity. I use them as additions to the main theoretical variables, to help interpret to some degree the residual variation left in the dependent variable—the index of turnout behavior—after the contributions of the two theoretical sets of antecedents have been confronted. The data analysis proceeds first with a presentation of simple bivariate relationships between the Turnout Index and the antecedents. Secondly, I present a series of regressions that took the relative contribution of each type of predictor variables. Finally, a LISREL covariance structure analysis is included for us to look at these relationships from a more general perspective.

Table 2.1 shows the bivariate correlations among turnout and its antecedents. Nine specific indicators of turnout-relevant political alienation/support are included. And there are nine rationalist indicators as well. The three best demographic variables are also shown. What we see is that there are relatively strong specific relationships in each of the three antecedent variable categories. The most robust simple relationship among the alienationist indicators is with citizen duty to vote, which has a Pearson correlation of .53. Next in order of magnitude are electoral alienation and information processing—both about .30. Political efficacy, majoritarianism, and partisanship also show noteworthy bivariate corrections.

Among the rationalist indicators, the two measuring rational abstentionist orientation have the largest relationships, with high cost being related more ($-.46$) than low return ($-.32$). The other indicators in this category do not show particularly strong bivariate relationships. Among

Table 2.1
Correlation of Turnout Index with Antecedent Variables ($N = 275$)*

		r
A.	**Political Alienation**	
	1. Pluralism -- approval or role of interest groups in politics	-.11
	2. Pluralism -- support for political party system	.01
	3. Majoritarianism index	.17
	4. Partisan supporter typology	.18
	5. Citizen duty to vote	.53
	6. Political information processing motivation	.34
	7. Electoral alienation	-.32
	8. General political alienation	.05
	9. Sense of political efficacy	.26
B.	**Rationalist Orientations**	
	1. Rational abstention - high cost	-.46
	2. Rational abstention - low return	-.32
	3. Self - interest motivation	.07
	4. Policy demand voting	.08
	5. Utility calculation	-.08
	6. Minimax - regret orientation	.11
	7. Perceived closeness of presidential election	.05
	8. Extent of perceived candidate differences on issues	.13
	9. Approval of government performance	-.05
C.	**Demographic Antecedents**	
	1. Age	.44
	2. Education	.07
	3. Income	.18

*List - wise deletion of missing cases was used for this table.

them extent of perceived candidate differences and minimax-regret orientation are strongest (.13 and .11).

Among the demographic relationships with turnout in the 1984 Wisconsin study, age has by some margin the greatest one ($r=.44$), with income next ($r=.18$). Age, indeed, comes close to the level of correlation of the two best specific indicators of political alienation and rationalist orientation above (.53 and -.46 respectively).[5]

Table 2.2 shows a comparison of the impact of the alienationist indicators on turnout relative to the impact of the rationalist variables. The alienationist block has a larger overall level of prediction of turnout/nonvoting than do the variables included under the rationalist category: The $R^2 = .35$ for the alienationist variables, versus $R^2 = .26$ for the rationalist ones. Thus, if one's sole criterion of theoretical adequacy were the extent of the variance in turnout behavior accounted for by the measures used, then alienationist theory might be preferred.

On the other hand, we should note that the rationalist variables, even for this crude and preliminary set of operationalizations, do as well as the classic set of the *American Voter* predictors of turnout in the extent of variance accounted for. I applied the set of antecedents in these Wisconsin data that are closest in content and wording to those applied in "the index of intensity of political involvement" of *The American Voter* (Campbell et al. 1960, 1070). I found that the Campbell, Converse, Miller, and Stokes index used in the 1984 Wisconsin data produces an R^2 of .27—which is essentially the same level as the rationalist theory measures used here. And one might further note that this level of variance accounted for is only a little lower than the best recent empirical studies of turnout—which use a wider array of antecedents, less error-prone measures of the dependent variable, and improved methods of parameter estimation. For example, Sigelman, Roeder, Jewell, and Baer (1985, 759) use seventeen demographic and attitudinal predictors with a Kentucky sample to produce an R^2 of .37. While they admit to no particular theoretical orientation in their analysis, their attitudinal variables are essentially alienationist, in the terms used here. But most of the variation they account for is from the demographic rather than from the attitudinal variable. If were to add age, education, and income to the set of rationality measures in the Wisconsin data—as a second block in an hierarchical regression—then we would come fairly close to the Sigelman et al. figure. This would give us an R^2 of .44.

Another recent example which combines nine political alienation and demographic variables, using the 1980 NES evidence, is by Southwell (1985, 666). She tries, within the confines of what was available in the 1980 study, to make explicit use of political alienationist concepts, in conjunction with five of the most important demographic variables. While she is not the first to combine alienationist and demographic variables in connection with predicting or explaining turnout (see, for example, Kagay 1979), she is one of the first to see the usual measures in NES surveys in an alienationist light. And she finds that her nine predictors yield a (probit based) R^2 of .36. This is about the same level therefore as my political alienationist measures *taken alone* in the 1984 Wisconsin data, or the same as the Sigelman et al. seventeen variable R^2 of .37. Obviously, these are not exact comparisons, given the different

Table 2.2
Multiple Regression of Turnout Index on Alienationist and on Rationalist Antecedents ($N = 275$)

		b	Standard Error of b	β	Significance
A.	**Alienationist Block**				
	1. Political efficacy	-.05	.07	-.04	.51
	2. Interest group role	-.06	.09	-.04	.50
	3. Partisan supporter	.04	.12	.02	.77
	4. Party system support	-.04	.09	-.03	.63
	5. Majoritarianism	.11	.11	.06	.32
	6. Information motivation	.36	.15	.14	.02
	7. Electoral alienation	-.32	.10	-.18	.00
	8. Citizen duty to vote	.65	.08	.45	.00
	9. General political alienation	.17	.09	.11	.07

$$R^2 = .35$$

		b	Standard Error of b	β	Significance
B.	**Rationalist Block**				
	1. Government performance	.02	.10	.01	.81
	2. Self - interest motivation	.14	.23	.04	.52
	3. Perceived candidate differences	.18	.10	.10	.07
	4. Policy demand voting	.09	.08	.06	.30
	5. Rational abstention -- high cost	-.70	.11	-.43	.00
	6. Utility calculation	-.31	.14	-.12	.03
	7. Minimax - regret orientation	.20	.10	.11	.06
	8. Perceived closeness of election	.18	.19	.05	.33
	9. Rational abstention -- low return	-.10	.14	-.05	.45

$$R^2 = .26$$

Table 2.3
Hierarchical Regression of Turnout Index on Alienationist and Rationalist Antecedents

Alienationist block	β	Significance
1. Political Efficacy	.01	.87
2. Interest groups	.02	.72
3. Partisan supporter	.03	.52
4. Party system	-.04	.41
5. Majoritarianism	.08	.17
6. Information motive	.11	.05
7. Electoral alienation	-.13	.02
8. Citizen duty to vote	.36	.00
9. General political alienation	.09	.13
Rationalist block		
1. Government performance	-.06	.28
2. Self-interest	-.04	.42
3. Candidate differences	.01	.92
4. Policy demands	.02	.73
5. Rational Abstention -- high cost	-.26	.00
6. Utility calculation	-.12	.01
7. Minimax - regret	.06	.26
8. Closeness of Election	-.01	.79
9. Rational abstention -- low return	-.01	.92

$$R^2 = .43$$

ways of measuring these variables, the differences in times and places of the studies, and the different statistical procedures used in estimating how well such explanatory variables do empirically. But they do provide a rough standard of comparison, and therefore give us some sense of how well we are doing at this early stage in developing our theories of turnout and their empirical applications.

Table 2.3 shows that the two sets of theoretical variables, taken as two blocks of predictors in either order, give us together a better account than previous studies of turnout have done—even in the absence of demographic predictors. The three best predictors in the political alienation/support block are citizen duty to vote, electoral alienation, and political information-processing motivation. On the side of rationalist measures, rational abstention (high cost) and utility calculation are the best specific predictors.

Table 2.4 adds to this hierarchical regression a third block—the demographic variables of age, education, and income. This addition raises the R^2 above .5, which is clearly within an acceptable range for individual level or survey data. Certainly we have some distance to go in devising more incisive and error-free measures of these theoretical concepts. There is still nearly half of the variation in turnout behavior unaccounted for in these terms. But the movement from a little over a third (Sigelman et al.; Southwell) to better than half of the variance accounted for suggests a possible advance in interpretative power—at least on a statistical level.

Where the advance may also be seen in the present effort, however, is in greater explicitness about which theoretical perspectives we are trying to test and how we may indeed confront competing theoretical approaches. In a field where hyperfactualism has thus far reigned supreme, I would argue there is a strong need to make better efforts of this kind. We need to find ways to formulate our analysis of voter behavior in more general explanatory contexts. We should also begin to resolve—both conceptually and empirically—the differences and areas of overlap of the kinds of explanations being offered. In the evidence presented above, we see that both of these substantive theories have something important to offer for giving a better account of voter participation and abstention. We see this only when we formulate and test them as much as possible in parallel, however.

A MORE GENERAL PERSPECTIVE

One further set of issues may be addressed with the present evidence. What we might well ask of these data, given that we have multiple indicators of what could be taken to be major *unobserved* or latent general variables—political alienationist and rationalist orientations—is how they are related to each other within the context of their mutual explanation of turnout. One useful way to approach this question is through some form of covariance structure analysis such as LISREL. LISREL allows one to estimate simultaneously both structural equations and measurement models as well as to permit other forms of data analysis such as confirmatory factor analysis (Long 1983).

In the present context, we can look both at a measurement model that

Table 2.4
Hierarchical Regression of Turnout on Alienationist Rationalist and Demographic Antecedents ($N = 275$)

Alienationist block	β	Significance
1. Political efficacy	-.02	.75
2. Interest group role	.01	.82
3. Partisan supporter	.01	.79
4. Party system support	-.07	.15
5. Majoritarianism	.04	.48
6. Information motive	.07	.17
7. Electoral alienation	-.08	.12
8. Citizen duty to vote	.32	.00
9. General political alienation	.02	.74

Rationalist block		
1. Government performance	-.04	.11
2. Self-interest	-.02	.66
3. Candidate differences	.02	.62
4. Policy demands	.08	.09
5. Rational abstention -- high cost	-.25	.00
6. Utility calculation	-.14	.00
7. Minimax - regret	.05	.27
8. Closeness of election	-.01	.85
9. Rational abstention -- low return	-.02	.78

Demographic block		
1. Age	.35	.00
2. Education	.06	.19
3. Income	.08	.07

$R^2 = .54$

pertains to alienation and rationality and at a structural equation model that estimates their joint effects, along with the most salient demographic variables on turnout. Figure 2.1 presents a measurement model, and figure 2.2 displays a covariance structural model for turnout.

Figure 2.1 shows first how well each of the nine indexes pertaining to alienation and each of the nine for rationality measure the underlying variable in each case. We see that the best indicators of political alienation in this context are X9 (political efficacy), X5 (citizen duty), and X7 (electoral alienation). For rationality, the best measurements of the unobserved variable are X11 (rational abstention—low return) and X10 (rational abstention—high cost).

Figure 2.1 also shows that these two theoretical clusters are not entirely separate (0 = .49), which is to be expected, given the frailties of these measurements and the fact that they have been taken together in the same survey. There is also a problem concerning the mixed theoretical status of some of these indexes, such as information-processing motivation or approval of government performance. There may also simply be some areas of substantive overlap in the two theories that have not been addressed in the explications (e.g., Niemi and Weisberg 1976) or applications of them to this point.

Figure 2.2 presents a LISREL analysis of turnout which assumes a recursive model and includes not only the indexes that estimate alienation and rationality, but also shows the effects of the measured, exogenous variables of age, education, and income. In terms of the direct effects of alienation and rationality on turnout, we see approximately equal impact of the two in this model. Alienation has a marginally larger structural coefficient ($\beta = -.297$ than rationality ($\beta = -.289$. Rationality variables are scored in this context to correspond to rational abstention (Y10 and Y11) being considered positive, and other rationalist variables such as Y14 and Y15 are negative. We also see that age has about the same level of direct impact on turnout as either alienation or rationality. This gives a little different picture than did the regressions of these relationships, in terms of relative magnitude of effects, but in essentially the same order and direction. It shows that both rationality and alienation, despite some possible overlap in measurement, are worth taking into account in the study of turnout.

DISCUSSION

We have seen that it is possible to advance our theoretic *and* empirical capacity to account for the phenomena of turnout and nonvoting. The present effort tries to suggest some possible lines for improvements of both kinds. To overcome the marked tendency toward hyperfactualism that has characterized this area of voting research, we need first to

Figure 2.1
LISREL Measurement Model of Alienation and Rationality

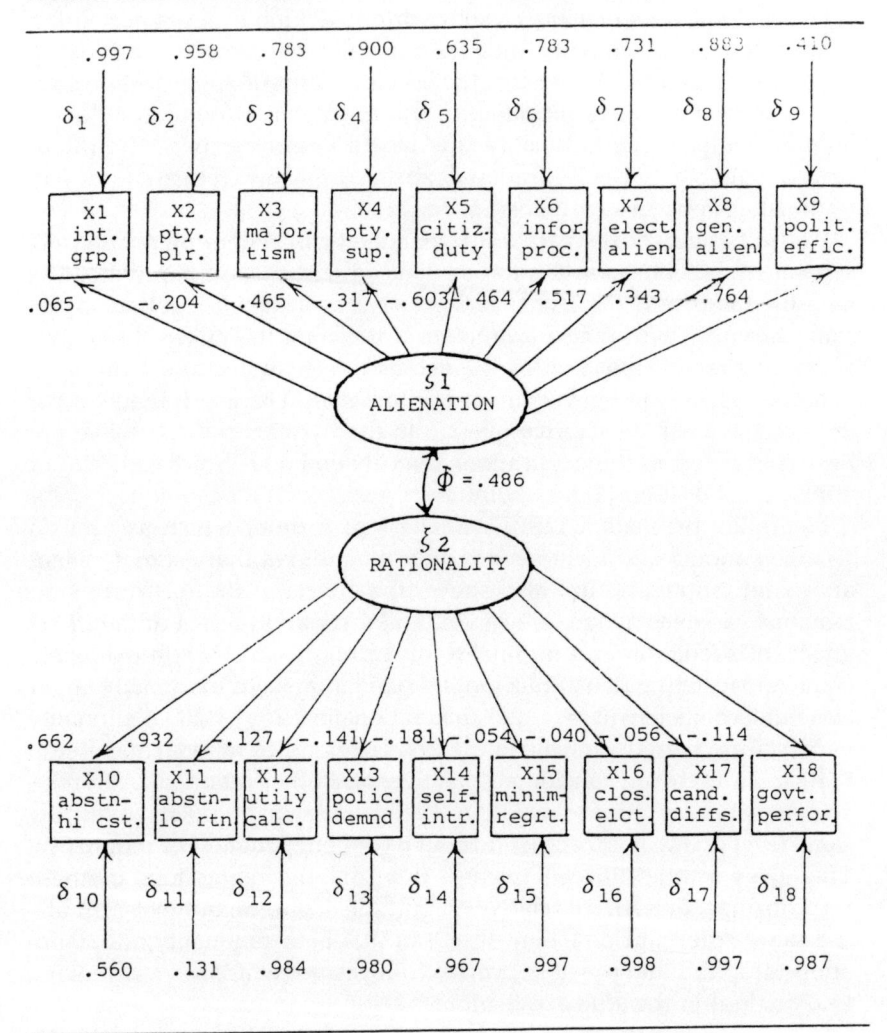

Total coefficient of determination = .876
Chi square = 429.41 with d.f. = 134
Adjusted goodness of fit = .812
Root mean square residual = .087

Figure 2.2
LISREL Structural Model of Turnout

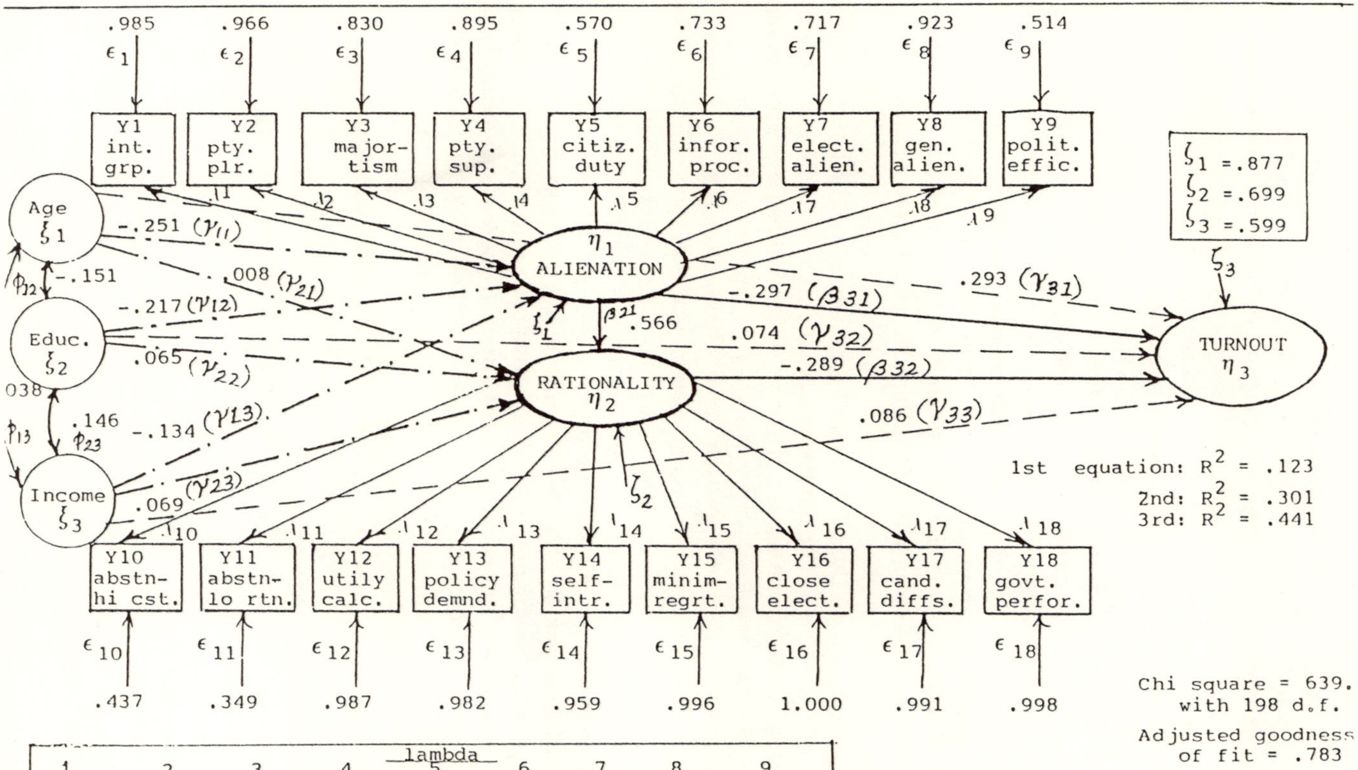

explicate our more general theoretical approaches in such a way that they become both more testable and mutually comparable. In the present inquiry we have made a beginning in defining what two major theoretical alternatives might be, as we develop our interpretative and empirical strategies for future inquiry.

One of these—the alienationist alternative—has so far been presented in mostly implicit and fragmentary fashion, at least as applied to the problem of turnout and nonvoting. Prior efforts have either been mostly indirect in establishing this variety of theory—as in the Campbell et al. or Kagay efforts cited above, or else they have taken only a narrow version of alienationism for their focus (e.g., Brody and Page 1973). What we have had, therefore, to guide relevant research efforts have been more deeds than words—as in the highly useful operationalizations of *The American Voter*. The present study aims to provoke more dialogue about, and more conscious definition of, what this theoretical alternative contains.

On the side of the rationalist alternative, we have had the opposite problem—namely, substantially more theoretical explication of relevant concepts, but fewer serious attempts to apply these concepts operationally to the study of voter turnout or abstention. Proponents of the rationalist/economic approach have operated mostly hypothetico-deductively—if often with great mathematical elegance—but have tended to ignore such basic questions as how often, among whom, and under what conditions such rational assumptions might have real world applications, especially in relation to the average person's decisions about whether or not to vote in particular elections. Opponents of such an approach often dismiss in various ways its applicability a priori—either because of the implausibility of its basic economic assumptions about human motivation and behavior, or because its critics cannot discern clearly that the theory is meant to be explanatory, rather than merely normative.

What I have tried to show is that rationalist concepts may have a significant area of explanatory application for these phenomena. Indeed, if we have more refined and more widely tested measures of rationalist orientations than the crude indexes introduced here, then rationalist theory might well prove to be the equal of any other theoretically guided set of operations that we have available, at least in this context. True Downsians and other rationalists will no doubt find the present effort to be rather superficial, so far as addressing empirically the many nuances of rationalist theory as it has developed over the past thirty years or as representing the points of view of various warring factions within the approach. To conduct this study I have chosen to go back to some original concepts of rationalist theory and, in operationalizing them, to see how well they stand up against the competition. The provisional conclusion that I reach on the basis of this study is that there may be more to this kind of theoretical perspective than at first meets the eye. Obviously, the truth of such a conclusion depends on going beyond the limited findings and measures of this one study—and the inherent limitations of design, place, time, and question wording associated with it.

One should bear in mind, amid such revived (if yet mild) optimism about the future of rationalist theory in voting behavior research, that the alienationist perspective probably has at least as much or more to recommend it as a theoretical focus for future work of this kind. Potential voters are likely to take electoral action in some part because of how they orient themselves to the perceived wider political reality that is embedded in the operative democratic system. As for rationalist orientations, there may be both positive and negative orientations associated with turnout that arise within this context. What we have seen for rationalist orientations is that some, such as perceived personal stake in politics or "self interest," lead one to participate, while others that are equally rational, such as a propensity to rational abstention, lead to the reverse. Closer reexamination of alienationist orientations in the future will need to make finer discriminations than were possible here among the negative and positive orientations of an alienation/support variety that lead more often to voter turnout. What I am suggesting is that part of the problem for future research in this area will be to look more closely at the subcomponents of this syndrome of turnout—relevant orientations. So far we have tended, in the voting area at least, to treat these matters as all of a piece. But as we attempt to accumulate knowledge in the future, both our conceptualizations and our measurements will need to become more differentiated and precise.

Despite the obvious limitations of the present analysis—such as trying in short space to identify, elucidate, operationalize, and empirically compare two broad theoretical perspectives—the results seem promising. One has the problem in comparing broad-gauged perspectives of knowing precisely what they are meant to cover, and of locating the most strategic aspects of each theory that are applicable to the phenomenon to be explained. Quite aside from the usual caveats of sample, timing, question wording, and the like, such theoretical ambiguities make the contribution of work such as the present difficult to assess. But the results of the present inquiry at least do not disconfirm that greater theoretical clarity has the potential of providing illumination of an area where the lights have been numerous but so far quite theoretically dim.

NOTES

I am indebted to Diana Owen for help in analyzing these data at the first stage and to Naeyoung Lee for assistance on this version of the data analysis.

Thanks are also due to the National Science Foundation for funding the data collection and to the Wisconsin Survey Research Laboratory for data collection. This is a revised version of a paper presented at the Annual Meeting of the Midwest Political Science Association, April 10–12, 1986, Chicago, Illinois.

1. Their discussion of political efficacy does contain references to self-esteem-like variables, but not in terms of any systematic theoretical account of the origins of political efficacy (see Campbell et al. 1960, 516–517, for example).

2. One can see some evidence of more group-focused approaches in some of the questions used in the 1980 and 1984 National Election Studies, but for the most part without the statement of any well-formulated theory standing behind them. Also see Miller et al. 1980; Conover 1984; Brady and Sniderman 1985; and Dennis 1987. For a more general discussion of the various theoretical approaches to the study of voting behavior, see Dennis 1991.

3. Even the most elegant and imaginative analyses of turnout that focus primarily on demographic antecedents—such as that of Wolfinger and Rosenstone (1980)—have this problem.

4. When one uses the questions indexed as rational abstention, a problem arises from the format of the lead-in question. Respondents could say that they voted all the time when asked the following: "Some recent studies have shown that very few Americans vote in every election for which they are eligible—if we include all primaries, referenda and local elections. Are you one of the very few who votes in every election, or are you in the vast majority who does not vote every single time?" About 35 percent said they always voted. To score this segment of the sample in terms of rational abstention is difficult given their unwillingness to admit that they may miss voting occasionally and thus could have reasons such as an expected cost of participating that is too high or a return that is too low. To try to crack this difficulty, I used another question about the cost of information to reclassify these recalcitrant (or extremely dutiful) respondents. This question was "How costly has it usually been for you to gather the information necessary to make reasonable choices in elections—especially to learn about the candidates and what they stood for? Has it taken very little of your own time, money and effort to find out what you needed to know; has it been fairly costly, but worth it; or has it been too costly in terms of your own time; money and effort?" To bring the scores of these respondents into line with the 2/3 scored on the rational abstention items directly, those who said it took little time were scored 1; those who said costly but worth it were scored 3; and those who said it had been too costly were scored 5. Of the 188 respondents who could be thus recorded, 144 received a 1, 37 had a 3, 3 had a 5, and 4 were DK/NA, or not scorable on each index item. Obviously, this is a round-about way of dealing with the propensity of significant numbers of respondents who are unwilling to admit to civic failure, even modestly. And it may not be satisfactory from every point of view. But it was the best that could be done, given how the sample responded to these items.

5. The age effect is not one due simply to the fact that younger adults have not had as many opportunities to vote in previous elections as those who are older. The relationship is virtually the same with the youngest adults treated

separately. In the data presented, those aged 26 and younger have scores weighted in terms of their number of opportunities to have voted.

REFERENCES

Abramson, Paul R. 1983. *Political Attitudes in America*. San Francisco: W. H. Freeman.
Baxter, Sandra, and Marjorie Lansing. 1983. *Women and Politics: The Visible Majority*. Ann Arbor: University of Michigan.
Brady, Henry E., and Paul M. Sniderman. 1985. "Attitude Attribution: A Group Basis for Political Reasoning." *American Political Science Review* 79:1061–1078.
Brody, Richard A. 1977. "Stability and Change in Party Identification: Presidential to Off-Years." Presented at the annual meeting of the American Political Science Association, Washington, D.C., Sept. 1–4.
Brody, Richard A. 1978. "The Puzzle of Political Participation in America." In *The New American Political System*, ed. Anthony King. Washington, D.C.: American Enterprise Institute. Pp. 287–324.
Brody, Richard A., and Benjamin I. Page. 1973. "Indifference, Alienation and Rational Decision: The Effects of Candidate Evaluations on Turnout and the Vote." *Public Choice* 15:1–17.
Campbell, Angus, Gerald Gurin, and Warren E. Miller. 1954. *The Voter Decides*. Evanston, Ill.: Row, Peterson.
Campbell, Angus, Philip E. Converse, Warren E. Miller, and Donald E. Stokes. 1960. *The American Voter*. New York: Wiley.
Carroll, Susan J. 1985. *Women and Candidates in American Politics*. Bloomington: Indiana University Press.
Citrin, Jack. 1974. "Comment: The Political Relevance of Trust in Government." *American Political Science Review* 68:973–988.
Conover, Pamela Johnston. 1984. "The Influence of Group Identifications on Political Perception and Evaluation." *Journal of Politics* 46:760–785.
Conway, M. Margaret. 1985. *Political Participation in America*. Washington, D.C.: Congressional Quarterly Press.
Dennis, Jack. 1970. "Support for the Institution of Elections by the Mass Public." *American Political Science Review* 64:819–835.
Dennis, Jack. 1981. "Public Support for Congress." *Political Behavior* 3:319–350.
Dennis, Jack. 1987. "Groups and Political Behavior: Legitimation, Deprivation and Competing Value." *Political Behavior* 9:323–373.
Dennis, Jack. 1988. "Political Independence in America, Part I: "On Being an Independent Partisan Supporter." *British Journal of Political Science* 18:77–109.
Dennis, Jack. 1991. "The Study of Electoral Behavior." In *Political Science: An Assessment*, ed. William J. Crotty. Vol. 3. Evanston, Ill.: Northwestern University Press.
Downs, Anthony. 1957. *An Economic Theory of Democracy*. New York: Harper and Row.
Easton, David, and Jack Dennis. 1967. "The Child's Acquisition of Regime Norms: Political Efficacy." *American Political Science Review* 61:25–38.

Easton, David, and Jack Dennis. 1969. *Children in the Political System*. New York: McGraw-Hill.
Ferejohn, John, and Morris Fiorina. 1974. "The Paradox of Not Voting: A Decision Theoretic Analysis." *American Political Science Review* 67:525–536.
Finifter, Ada. 1970. "Dimensions of Alienation." *American Political Science Review* 64:389–410.
Gamson, William A. 1968. *Power and Discontent*. Homewood, Ill.: Dorsey.
Hardin, Russell, and Brian Barry, eds. 1982. *Rational Man and Irrational Society? An Introduction and Source Book*. Beverly Hills, Calif.: Sage.
Hyman, Herbert H. 1960. "Reflections on Reference Groups." *Public Opinion Quarterly* 24:383–396.
Hyman, Herbert, and Eleanor Singer, eds. 1968. *Readings in Reference Group Theory and Research*. New York: Free Press.
Jennings, M. Kent, and Richard G. Niemi. 1974. *The Political Character of Adolescence*. Princeton, N.J.: Princeton University Press.
Kagay, Michael R. 1979. "What's Happening to Voter Turnout in American Presidential Elections?" *Vital Issues*, 34, no. 4.
Lane, Robert E. 1959. *Political Life*. Glencoe, Ill.: Free Press.
Lasswell, Harold D. 1930. *Psychopathology and Politics*. Chicago: University of Chicago Press.
Lasswell, Harold D. 1936. *Politics: Who Gets What, When, How*. New York: Whittlesey House.
Lasswell, Harold D. 1948. *Power and Personality*. New York: Norton.
Long, J. Scott. 1983. *Covariance Structure Models: An Introduction to LISREL*. Beverly Hills, Calif.: Sage.
Merriam, Charles E., and Harold F. Gosnell. 1924. *Non-Voting*. Chicago: University of Chicago Press.
Milbrath, Lester, and M. Goel. 1977. *Political Participation*. 2d ed. Chicago: Rand-McNally.
Miller, Arthur H. 1974. "Rejoinder to 'Comment' by Jack Citrin: Political Discontent or Ritualism?" *American Political Science Review* 68:989–1001.
Miller, Arthur H., Patricia Gurin, Gerald Gurin, and Oksana Malanchuck. 1980. "Group Consciousness and Political Participation." *American Journal of Political Science* 25:94–511.
Niemi, Richard G., and Herbert F. Weisberg. 1976. *Controversies in American Voting Behavior*. San Francisco: Freeman.
Riker, William H., and Peter C. Ordeshook. 1973. *An Introduction to Positive Political Theory*. Englewood Cliffs, N.J.: Prentice-Hall.
Sapiro, Virginia. 1983. *The Political Integration of Women*. Urbana: University of Illinois.
Sigelman, Lee, Philip W. Roeder, Malcolm E. Jewell, and Michael A. Baer. 1985. "Voting and Nonvoting: A Multi-Election Perspective." *American Journal of Political Science* 29:749–765.
Simon, Herbert A. 1985. "Human Nature in Politics: The Dialogue of Psychology with Political Science." *American Political Science Review* 79:293–304.
Southwell, Priscilla L. 1985. "Alienation and Nonvoting in the United States: A Refined Operationalization." *Western Political Quarterly* 38:663–674.

Verba, Sidney. 1961. *Small Groups and Political Behavior*. Princeton, N.J.: Princeton University Press.
Walton, Hanes. 1985. *Invisible Politics: Black Political Behavior*. New York: SUNY Press.
Wolfinger, Raymond E., and Steven J. Rosenstone. 1980. *Who Votes?* New Haven, Conn.: Yale University Press.

SARA JANE MOORE

JOHN HINCKLEY

JACK RUBY

OSCAR COLLAZO

3 Nonvoting in America: Attitudes in Context
John R. Petrocik and Daron Shaw

Viewed through the normative lens of citizenship, the voting rate of Americans is a cause of unease and even upset. Beyond its instrumental function of selecting governmental leadership, it is also a civic act which displays commitment to the political institutions and processes of the country. It indicates how strongly we feel about a central process of our democracy—the election of political leaders—and that so few perform it might betray a serious weakness in the political culture upon which government ultimately depends.[1]

Low turnout might also undermine the legitimacy of government. With turnout rates in presidential elections (contests in which voting is most popular) varying between 50 and 60 percent, and winners never receiving more than 60 percent of the turnout, presidents are selected by the votes of 25 to 30 percent of the citizenry. The winners should have been the "nonvoter candidate" who, with never less than 35 percent support, has won most elections in this century. One need not be Chicken Little to worry about the implications of turnout for democratic representation. Not only may the policy agenda of the majority remain unfulfilled, but the candidate of the majority may not be elected.

But low turnout is more than a moral question. Practical-minded politicians are concerned about a partisan bias in low turnout. Nonvoters are younger, less-educated, poorer, black, and otherwise marked by attributes associated with support for the Democratic party. It is conventional, therefore, to believe that low rates of participation favor the Republicans. For Democrats, low turnout might mean unwarranted Republican wins.

This chapter is concerned with nonvoting. More specifically, it is concerned with the attitudes and preferences of nonvoters compared to voters. The analysis rests upon data from the congressional elections of 1978 and 1986 and the presidential elections of 1980 and 1984. The 1980 election is used most extensively because of the wider range of attitude measures it included. These four surveys (and, for table 3.2, the 1964 national election study) were selected because each included an examination of official voter records, making it possible to ignore the respondent's report of his or her turnout in favor of more (though not completely) accurate official records. There is no reason to believe that the patterns identified in this paper are peculiar to these years or types of elections.

TURNOUT IN THE UNITED STATES

As would be true of any country with an increasing population, the number of Americans voting in presidential elections has increased almost continuously since the early 1800s (Petrocik 1981a, 1988). Wars caused downturns, and changes in the rules of eligibility have also retarded electoral growth (Burnham 1974; Rusk 1974). Over the long term, however, immigration, natural population growth, and liberalized election laws (the lowering of age and property requirements and women's suffrage) have produced an increase in the absolute number of voters in successive national elections.

By contrast, the turnout *rate* in national elections has fluctuated. It has surged during periods of party realignment (Eldersveld 1951; Degler 1964; Lubell 1952; Key 1955; Andersen 1979; Petrocik 1981a, 1988; Campbell 1985; Wanat 1979; Wanat and Burke 1982; Brown 1987) and as a result of massive, election-specific schemes to promote turnout (White 1961). It has declined when the franchise has been extended to groups whose political interest and sense of citizen duty are (at least initially) weak—women's suffrage in 1920 and the 18 year-old vote in 1972 (Abramson and Aldrich 1982).

More impressive than the fluctuation is the generally low and declining level of turnout in the United States (see table 3.1). Many factors depress American electoral turnout: the United States does not require voting; it doesn't have government initiated eligibility systems that register individual citizens prior to the election; we lack parties sufficiently linked to social groups for an election to become an occasion for voters to affirm their social group commitments as well as their partisanship. But even with these differences accounted for, American turnout falls below expectations.[2] Moreover, it is declining faster than turnout in other western democracies. During the last two decades, almost half of the eligible electorate abstained from presidential elections. In 1988, barely half of the potential electorate voted and, for the first time since the

Table 3.1
American Turnout in Perspective: The Record of Four Decades

	1950s	1960s	1970s	1980s
United States	63.0	63.3	56.5	55.0
Great Britain	80.5	76.5	76.0	73.0
Canada	73.3	77.0	73.0	72.0
Western Europe	83.7	85.3	85.1	83.1

Note: Table entries are the percent of the age-eligible electorate recorded as voting.

Second World War, there was an *absolute decline* in the total number voting (compared to 1984).[3]

Is nonvoting a problem? It's becoming more common. If there is a problem, it's getting larger. We believe that a problem exists to the extent that (1) voters have policy concerns different from those of nonvoters or (2) voters and nonvoters prefer different candidates. In assessing the "nonvoter problem," this chapter examines issues. It has three parts. The first part summarizes data on turnout rates, contrasting the United States with other countries and documenting demographic and contextual differences in electoral participation. The broad outlines of these data are familiar but the specifics are less clear. The purpose of this section is to provide some details about who votes and to establish a framework for the analysis which follows. The next part investigates the attitudes and perceptions of voters compared to nonvoters in order to formulate an explanation of why some vote and others do not. The last part formulates an understanding of the dynamics of turnout in American elections.

WHO VOTES?

Table 3.2 presents the voting rates of different education groups, religions, races, etc., at different points in time (1964 compared to the 1980s), and in different types of elections (high stimulus presidential contests—1980 and 1984, and less stimulating congressional races—1978 and 1986). Several contrasts deserve mention.

Social Class

Better-educated, high income "upscale" Americans are the core electorate, with turnout rates at or above 80 percent in presidential elections. Those with the least education and in the bottom third of the income distribution are the least likely to vote.[4] Upscale voters also seem to

Table 3.2
The Demography of Turnout

	Presidential		Congressional
	1964	1980/1984	1978/1986
Education			
Less than high school	61	50	34
High school degree	72	59	42
Some college	80	70	47
College graduate	82	84	63
Income			
Bottom third	61	57	40
Middle third	69	67	49
Top third	79	75	57
Married	69	67	47
Never married	65	50	33
Separated/Divorced	65	54	37
Age			
18 through 24	44	39	19
25 through 30	56	53	29
30 through 65	72	67	48
65 and above	68	68	58
Union household	66	65	46
Not a union household	69	61	42
Race			
White	70	65	46
Black	30	52	28
Latino	35	45	31
Religion			
Protestant	67	63	46
Catholic	76	67	48
Jewish	88	73	62
None	51	56	29
Church attendance			
Frequently	77	76	58
Infrequently/not at all	65	57	40
Region			
South	55	56	45
Not south	74	67	47

Note: Table entries are percentages who voted according to a check of official records.

resist better the forces that depress turnout. The overall turnout decline since the middle sixties (contrast columns one and two of table 3.2) seems to have been particularly strong among the less educated. Among those with a high school education or less, turnout declined approximately 18 percent; it dropped 13 percent among those with some college education; it didn't change at all (or may even have increased!) among college graduates.[5] Also, not surprising, the turnout of better educated voters declines less between on- and off-year elections. As a group, the turnout rate of those with no more than a high school education dropped about 30 percent between the more stimulating presidential years of 1980 and 1984 and the less interesting congressional elections of 1978 and 1986. The on-year/off-year pattern is less uniform than the change from the sixties to the eighties, but upscale voters seem more resistant to the forces that cause turnout to fluctuate.

Age and Marital Status

Age also strongly predicts turnout, because those under 30 years of age—and especially those under 24—have exceptionally low participation rates. The turnouts of the youngest ages have declined the most since the 1960s and they drop dramatically (about 50 percent) between stimulating presidential and less attractive congressional contests.

Age explains some, but not all, of the lower turnout rate of the unmarried, who are less likely to vote and whose turnout rates have declined more than the turnout of the married.

Race and Ethnicity

Blacks and Hispanics vote at a significantly lower rate than whites. In the 1980 and 1984 presidential elections black participation was 13 percentage points below white turnout, and it averaged 18 points less in the two congressional elections; Hispanic participation was even lower. The drop between high and low stimulus elections is also dramatically greater among blacks and Hispanics. White turnout was 29 percent less in the congressional elections compared to the presidential benchmark; black turnout was 46 percent less; Hispanic turnout declined more than 31 percent.

While black-white turnout differentials are substantial, the turnout rates of blacks have increased dramatically since the 1960s. In the sixties, white turnout exceeded black voting by more than 130 percent; in the eighties it was only about 25 percent greater. The improvement, as table 3.3 shows, reflects the tripling of southern black turnout between 1964 and 1984. Southern white turnout also bucked the national trend and increased slightly, while voting rates among nonsoutherners, black and white, declined.

Religion and Religiosity

Those who profess a religious preference are significantly more likely to vote than agnostics and atheists, Jews are more likely to vote than Christians, and, among Christians, Catholics seem to have slightly

Table 3.3
Black Turnout, 1964–1984

	Blacks 1964	Blacks 1984	Whites 1964	Whites 1984
South	18	49	55	57
Nonsouth	54	52	75	72
Total	30	50	70	67

Note: Table entries are the percentage voting.

higher turnout rates than Protestants. Further, those who are frequent church attenders are more likely to vote than those who rarely or never attend religious services.

The origins of these religious differences in turnout are as multifaceted as the groups involved. In part it reflects social class (and particularly educational) variation among the group; in part it reflects intergroup differences in civic norms. But whatever the specific source of the differences for any one of the groups, knowing a person's religious preference and the frequency of their religious practice provides a reliable predictor of electoral participation.

Summary: Who Votes

In general, the more closely an individual approximates the modal middle-class American, the more likely he or she is to be a voter. The most consistent voters are better educated, upper income, middle-aged (or at least over 30), Jewish, religiously observant, white, and outside the South. By contrast, the lowest turnout is recorded by lower income voters who have a high school education or less, are under 24 years of age, black, atheists or infrequent church attenders, or southerners. These differences shouldn't occasion much surprise. The American political culture treats voting as a civic obligation, and the modal social groups who are the most likely to conform to the society's social norms are also the most faithful to its political norms.

THE POLITICS OF TURNOUT

Nonvoters are younger, less-educated, poorer, black, and otherwise marked by attributes associated with support for the Democratic party. It should come as no surprise, therefore, that Democratic identifiers have

Table 3.4
Ideological Identification, Partisanship, and Turnout

	1980/1984	1978/1986
Party Identification		
Democrat	61	44
Independent	46	26
Republican	70	52
Ideological Identification		
Liberal	68	43
Moderate	61	43
Conservative	69	52

Note: Table entries are the percentage voting. Leaning identifiers are classified as partisan of the party toward which they lean.

lower rates of turnout than Republicans. The resulting ten percentage point turnout disadvantage has appeared in almost every national election of the past three decades and produced a voting population that is more Republican than the full electorate. This discrepancy persists in off-year congressional elections, when turnout declines. It does not, fortunately for the Democrats, increase: the fall-off in Democratic and Republican identifiers from presidential to congressional elections shows little or no bias. Each party can expect about 25 percent of its presidential electorate to abstain in congressional contests.

However, there is an ideological flavor to the off-year decline in turnout (table 3.4). Liberal turnout declines about 37 percent, while conservative turnout declines less. Whether the liberal/conservative difference turnout is rooted in ideological preferences or only a reflection of demographic factors with which ideological self-identification is associated is difficult to determine. It is also beside the point: Republicans and conservatives vote at higher rates than Democrats and liberals.

Policy Preferences

The partisan and ideological bias in turnout does not, surprisingly, extend to policy issues. Overall, voters and nonvoters are substantially similar in their attitudes on policy issues (compare the first and fourth columns in table 3.5). Nonvoters hold more liberal attitudes than voters on social welfare questions, but their attitudes on defense spending, women's issues, race relations, and on how the United States should deal with the Soviet Union are virtually indistinguishable. On the latter three issues, the opinions of the groups move left and right in concert. In 1980 and 1984 when voters were supportive of defense spending

Table 3.5
Policy Preferences of Voters and Nonvoters

	Voted			Nonvoter preferred:		
Issue:	All	Republican	Democrat	All	Republican	Democrat
Social Welfare	10	45	-42	-12	8	-33
Foreign/Defense	22	49	-13	21	42	3
Women Role	-53	-27	-65	-56	-45	-66
Race	46	69	22	50	69	35

Notes: Entries are percentage differences calculated by subtracting the liberal percentage from the conservative percentage. As a result, negative numbers indicate a percentage point excess of liberal responses, while positive numbers indicate the percentage point excess of conservative responses.

(more supportive in 1980 than in 1984), so too were the nonvoters; when voters were contradictory or moderate in their feelings about cooperating with the Soviet Union, so too were nonvoters; voters were generally quite liberal on women's issues, as were the nonvoters; and both voters and nonvoters were conservative on affirmative action and busing and were disinclined to believe in the need for faster changes in race relations.

The similarity of voters and nonvoters is not confounded by candidate preference. Reagan enthusiasts who voted had issue preferences that were very close to those who abstained (compare columns two and five); and Democratic voters matched the policy dispositions of nonvoters who preferred Carter in 1980 and Mondale in 1984 (columns three and six). There are some differences: GOP voters were a bit less representative of Reagan-preferring nonvoters, but the slippage was small. On social welfare matters, Reagan's voters were more conservative than Reagan supporters who stayed home on election day. Otherwise, the groups are both statistically and substantively identical. Reagan voters shared the policy preferences of nonvoting Reagan enthusiasts on women's issues, race matters, and foreign policy and defense questions. Were it not for the relative social welfare liberalness of Reagan nonvoters, there would be *no* policy differences between voters and nonvoters, of any candidate preference, in either year.

Nonpolicy Attitudes and Orientations

The similarity of voters and nonvoters does not uniformly extend to nonpolicy attitudes and orientations. As table 3.6 shows, voters, compared to nonvoters, are more interested in the campaign, care more about the outcome of the election, feel a stronger obligation to vote, and tend to be more efficacious. Further, there is a perceptible, albeit small, difference in the regard of voters and nonvoters for various governmental institutions (data not shown). Party differences on these items are clearly related to which party was in office—Republicans give a uniformly low rating to the national government in general, and the congress and presidency in particular in 1980, but where party effects can be neutralized the persisting voter-nonvoter difference seems to indicate that voters are more positive than nonvoters toward government in general and the branches of the federal government in particular. Also, nonvoters (whether they preferred Reagan or Carter) were slightly less likely than voters (whether for Reagan or Carter) to express confidence in the government's responsiveness to the public. About a quarter of voters and less than a fifth of nonvoters believed that the government pays attention to voters or that parties or elections contributed to assuring responsiveness to the citizens. Overall, however, there is con-

76   John R. Petrocik and Daron Shaw

Table 3.6
Nonpolicy Attitudes of Voters and Nonvoters, 1980

	Voted: Democrat	Voted: Republican	Nonvoter preferred: Democrat	Nonvoter preferred: Republican
Election interest:				
Not interested	22	14	40	39
Interested	44	39	19	19
Care about outcome of election	74	61	52	55
Strong sense of citizen duty	82	85	73	77
Government is wasteful or ineffective	65	75	65	72
Politicians honest:				
Many are crooked	36	50	43	58
Hardly any crooked	11	8	10	4
Government is responsive	24	26	17	16
Believes parties, elections, etc. not make government responsive	19	17	20	20
Efficacy:				
Has influence on government	58	64	40	38
Government not too complicated	22	31	15	24

Note: Table entries are percentages.

siderable similarity between voters and nonvoters on other orientations; and both groups, for example, expressed equally negative opinions about the honesty and intelligence of politicians and the wastefulness of government.

In all, it seems reasonable to conclude that there is no uniformly large difference between voters and nonvoters in their attitudes toward policy or towards government in general. This does not gainsay the very real differences between voters and nonvoters in their sense of civic duty and political efficacy. They are quite durable, and they are related to the vote. The point, rather, is that nonvoters are only slightly less efficacious and display only a slightly weaker obligation to participate in elections. On any given item, the attitudes of the voter are often only slightly different from the nonvoter. The slight difference may be consequential, but it is slight.

The Candidates and the Parties

One of the largest distinctions between voters and nonvoters is to be found in perceptions of "important differences" between the parties. In 1980, about 67 percent of the voters saw an important issue or policy difference between the the Democrats and Republicans, while some 29 percent did not. Among nonvoters, by contrast, the proportion who saw no difference (33 percent) were almost as numerous as the 39 percent who believed a difference existed. Asked in different ways, questions about party differences elicit varying estimates of how distinctive Americans believe their parties to be, but the overall result is invariant: voters are more likely than nonvoters to see differences—and large ones—between the parties or candidates.

It seems possible, therefore, that voters and nonvoters are distinguished not by their policy preferences nor their intrinsic orientation toward politics and government, but by their assessment of the policy choice inherent in the candidates. There is, after all, considerable research and a significant body of theory linking turnout as well as vote choice to perceptions of substantive differences between the parties and the candidates (the genesis of which is Anthony Downs' theory of competition, 1957). In general, the data match the theory. Whether the difference is measured as the proportion who perceive a small difference, the proportion who see a large difference, or (more compactly) the average absolute difference, voters are more inclined than nonvoters to perceive a substantively large issue choice between the candidates, between the parties, and between themselves and the candidates and parties.

Perhaps more to the point, voters, compared to nonvoters, not only see larger issue differences between candidates overall, but also see larger differences between their preferred candidate and his opponent. Consider table 3.7, which distinguishes voters and nonvoters by candidate preference. Reagan voters saw a 2.2 unit difference between the candidates in 1980 and a 2.3 unit difference in 1984. His nonvoting supporters saw less of a gap, 1.9 in 1980 and 2.0 in 1984. For their part, Carter and Mondale voters saw an issue distance that was .2 units greater than the issue distance perceived by their nonvoting supporters. (The data in the table are not broken down by year since the 1980 and 1984 differences were trivial.) Put a little differently, about 62 percent of those who voted in 1980 and 1984 saw the candidate for whom they voted as better representing their (the voters') preferences on the issues, and most of these voters (about two-thirds) saw a *substantial* difference (of more than one unit). About half of the nonvoters saw so large an issue choice between Reagan and his opponents in 1980 and 1984.

Table 3.7
Perceived Issue Differences Among Voters and Nonvoters by Candidate Preference, 1980 and 1984

	Voted: Democrat	Voted: Republican	Nonvoter preferred: Democrat	Nonvoter preferred: Republican
Perceived issue distance between:				
Candidates	2.2	2.2	2.0	1.9
Parties	2.2	2.1	1.8	1.7
Perceived issue distance between respondent and:				
Democratic				
Candidate	1.7	2.3	1.7	2.0
Party	1.7	2.1	1.8	2.0
Republican				
Candidate	2.3	1.6	2.0	1.7
Party	2.2	1.7	2.2	1.7

Note: Table entries are the average arithmetic differences on the standard seven-point NES indices across several questions. The calculations are based on questions dealing with social welfare, military spending, dealing with the Soviet Union, affirmative action for ethnic minorities, and the role of women. An example of how the table is read follows: The 2.2 in the upper left cell indicates that those who voted for Carter in 1980 or Mondale in 1984 placed Reagan, on average, over 2 positions away from their placement of Carter or Mondale on the issues.

Attitudes and Voting: A Summary

Perceived issue differences between candidates and parties and between respondents and the parties and candidates play a role in who votes. Some people see more at stake—they see larger policy consequences in the election—and they are more likely to vote. However, it's clear that the spatial theory (as it is understood in a Downsian sense) rests upon relatively small differences between voters and nonvoters. Although statistically significant, the differences between voters and nonvoters are not large. Many *nonvoters* see a *considerable* issue distance between the candidates and the parties; many *voters* see only a *little* difference, but turn out anyway. The largest correlation is around .20; most are substantially lower (see table 3.8).[6]

While attitude and issue difference between voters and nonvoters are modest, the differences have a large effect on turnout. A probit analysis predicting turnout as a function of the respondent's sense of duty, personal efficacy, strength of partisanship, interest in the election campaign, and perceived issue distances between the parties proved to be a re-

Table 3.8
Correlation of Perceived Issue Distances and Turnout

	1980	1984
Issue distance between:		
Candidates	.16	.20
Parties	.19	.20
Issue distance between respondent and:		
Democratic candidate	.08	.09
Democratic party	.11	.07
Republican candidate	.01	.01
Republican party	.03	.07
Preferred candidate	.16	.19

markably accurate model of turnout.[7] Over three-fifths (63 percent) conform to the pattern that is represented in the probit model: 40 percent were accurately predicted voters and 23 percent were accurately predicted nonvoters. Of the 37 percent who were mispredicted, most, 20 percent, were expected to vote but did not.

VOTING AND NONVOTING: ATTITUDES IN CONTEXT

In a recent essay on nonvoting, Frances Fox Piven and Richard Cloward blame the political culture, the party structure, and legal barriers for the political apathy and low participation rate of Americans. Nonvoting, they believe, is rooted in America's institutions, not in the intrinsic shortcomings of its voters. They claim that "the lack of motivation associated with the apathetic attitudes of nonvoters is not the cause of their marginalization from electoral politics, although it may be one of the outcomes" (1988, 119). From their perspective, an attitudinal analysis of voting misidentifies cause and effect. Without attempting to disprove their thesis (which, as formulated, is immune from empirical test), it is worth considering what might be the relative role of individual and systemic factors in turnout. There is considerable evidence that systemic variables such as the party system and the rules governing the vote regulate turnout (e.g., Verba, Nie, and Kim 1978; Powell 1986). Powell, in particular, elegantly demonstrated the turnout depressing qualities of legal systems which neither compel turnout nor automatically register voters and a coalitional party system which fails to arouse intense partisanship among voters.

Registration

Does it follow that institutional change will assure greater turnout among Americans, especially those who ignore elections under the current order? If registration were automatic or at least required less initiative from individuals, would there be more voting in the United States? On paper it would seem so. About 70 percent of those who fail to vote are not registered. A little casual arithmetic would lead one to believe that an automatic registration system might yield a turnout rate (at least in presidential elections) of about 80 or 85 percent.

The available, fragmentary evidence, while inconclusive, is substantial enough to at least leave one skeptical of an outcome approaching the preceding numbers. In the 1980 national election study, a small number of respondents (92) were interviewed in states with same-day registration laws. Their turnout rate was 62 percent, nine points above the rate of those living in states with more conventional registration systems. Various studies of turnout have produced a similar estimate of the effect of registration. The most careful survey data analysis of the issue projected an increase in the turnout rate of about 10 percentage points if laws governing registration and absentee balloting across the country were made as permissive as those of the most permissive state (Rosenstone and Wolfinger 1978). An equally well-done study of the efficacy of registration drives demonstrated that those who registered at their own initiative had higher election-day turnout than those put on the rolls through registration drives (Cain and McCue 1985). There is, almost certainly, an ever-declining payoff associated with rigorous registration efforts. More people will vote overall, but the turnout rate of the registered will decline since those put on the registration rolls only through the efforts of others have a weaker personal commitment to vote than those who registered on their own, and they are, consequently, harder to get to the polls on election day.

South Dakota and Minnesota offer a natural test of the likely effect of a more liberal eligibility system. While both states have permissive registration rules, their turnout rates are virtually identical to the 62 percent turnout observed in the 1980 election study. South Dakota, with no registration requirement, has a turnout rate of about 65 percent in presidential elections. Minnesota experienced no significant increase in turnout after establishing same day registration in 1978. On the contrary, both states have experienced turnout declines in the last 10 years. In Minnesota, turnout in the last three presidential elections has fallen below the levels of the 1960s; voter participation in presidential elections in South Dakota has declined about 5 percentage points between 1980 and 1988.[8] Same-day registration should increase turnout only a few percentage points.

Table 3.9
Party Competition and Turnout

		State is:	
		Competitive	Uncompetitive
Record shows respondent:	Attitudes predicted:		
Voted	Vote	43%	36%
Voted	No vote	16	17
Didn't vote	No vote	23	23
Didn't vote	Voter	18	24
	Total	100%	100%

Greater Competition

Would more competitive elections increase turnout? Candidates who foresee a close election typically put greater effort into voter identification and mobilization than candidates who expect a lopsided result. Mobilization begets counter-mobilization, the net effect of which is to raise the vote of both candidates, and turnout overall. Changes which decreased the security of incumbents and improved the prospects of challengers would, by this process of organization and counter-organization, also increase turnout. But, again, the change might be modest.

Consider table 3.9, which compares the turnout profile of competitive states with the turnout profile in noncompetitive states. The electorate is divided into four groups, with each group defined by whether the respondent voted and whether she or he was expected to vote (based on the attitude model described above). States with greater interparty competition had a higher turnout rate (about 59 percent as opposed to 53 percent), and the difference seems to reflect the turnout depressing effect of one-party dominance on voters who are predisposed to vote, but did not (24 percent as opposed to 18 percent).[9]

While an across the board voter contact effort—by both parties—designed to improve margins in their opponents' bastions should increase turnout rates, the net increase may be modest. The 22 percent of the electorate in competitive states who did not vote, even among those with attitudinal predispositions associated with voting, substantially exceeds the slightly higher average voting rate (6 percent) associated with living in a two-party competitive state. Clearly, more party competition is not going to drive turnout to Dutch or Italian levels.

The Political Culture

Is there a deficiency in the American political culture? Again, perhaps; but it is at least as reasonable to recognize that politics and government may not be more intrinsically important to citizens than many other civic "obligations." No one is surprised to discover less speeding when there is a police cruiser in the area. Similarly, we buy more fuel efficient cars when gasoline is expensive. Is voting any different? Just as some will heed the speed limit in fuel efficient cars because they have internalized beliefs about the propriety of doing so, some will vote because they believe they should and because they believe it matters for the way we are governed. Voting may conform to the same dynamics. Just as only the watchful gaze of the policeman keeps some of us within the speed limit (and we are exceeding the limit otherwise), only a great deal of public comment will stir some to vote. Some will vote in elections for the most trivial offices or with the shortest notice; others will abstain unless they are threatened with sanctions; most of us fall into the intermediate group. If the office, the candidates, or the issues catch our attention, and it is not too inconvenient or costly, we vote.

How large are these segments? A study of turnout in Kentucky by Sigelman et al (1985) provides a good estimate of the relative sizes of the chronic nonvoter group, the "never-miss-an-election" voters, and the "sometimes-to-usually" voters. Sigelman and his colleagues examined voting records to determine how often voters turned out for ten different general elections (local, state, congressional, and presidential) during a five-year period. They found that about 38 percent never voted, most because they were not registered (29 percent). Twenty-six percent voted in at least half of the elections; 45 percent voted at least once during the five years, but not more than six times; only 4 percent voted in nine or ten of the elections.

The preceding image of the electorate seems appropriate, however much it might offend the normative importance some attach to the vote. The vastly different turnout rates in school board, municipal, state, congressional, and presidential elections are clear evidence that turnout varies with the interest associated with the election. Presidents do important things, the press and political cognoscenti pay attention to them, and the agitation causes many of the marginally interested to be attentive and vote. By contrast, the typical school board election, that might be held in odd years, can go forward with the vast majority not caring and some not even being aware of it.

Is the American sense of obligation to participate in elections weaker than in other societies? Again the answer seems to be no, although definitive evidence is elusive. One of the better natural experiments on turnout occurred in the Netherlands. Holland's 90-plus percent turnout rates reflected many incentives to vote, one of which was a law requiring voters to present themselves at the polling place on election day. The law didn't require a person to vote; it only mandated their appearance at the polls. But, of course, after the effort of showing up, most followed through with a vote. In 1971 the mandatory provision was repealed. Turnout fell to about 71 percent in the next election.

Of course 71 percent is still about 15 points greater than turnout in the 1972 presidential election. Some of the remaining difference reflects the more liberal Dutch registration system and parties which evoked strong partisanship because of the close identity of the parties with keenly felt social group conflicts of the kind that the United States attempts to eliminate, for example, religious competition. Holding this constant, much, if not all, of the American turnout deficiency disappears.[10]

The Natural Level of Turnout: Attitudes, Laws, and Events

It seems reasonable to think of turnout as a product of: (1) individual motivations rooted in beliefs about civic duty and the would-be governors, (2) events which stimulate participation because of their interest value, and (3) institutions which encourage (or discourage) potential participants. The attitudinal motivation of some voters is so high that they vote in all elections. For others, the stimulation of a lot of media attention and controversy—when added to their intrinsic interest in voting—is just enough to send them to the polls. In any given election, therefore, the voting population comprises those who consistently vote and those who are more irregular in their voting habits but were sufficiently stimulated by the election at hand to join the regular voters. The nonvoters are similarly constituted: the chronic nonvoters are joined by the irregular participants who find nothing in the election at hand to stir them to troop to the polls. The differences between regular voters and consistent nonvoters are large, but in any given election the attitude differences between those who turn out and those who don't is muted (as tables 3.4 through 3.8 demonstrate) because in any given election the weaker motivations of the marginals—some of whom voted and some of whom didn't—draw voters and nonvoters toward the median. In short, the greater the election-specific stimulus, the higher the turnout since marginal voters will be stimulated by the event to a level of interest and concern that causes them to vote. Elections which receive little public comment and attention will depend more heavily upon individual motivations, producing what might be regarded as the "natural level of turnout," which is quite low. Systemic variables (laws and party system characteristics) will further increase or depress participation.

CONCLUSION

There is no doubt that the American legal order and party system do less to encourage turnout than those of comparable western countries. However, we do not believe that such systemic variables explain low turnout. It seems to us more reasonable to regard systemic differences as more of an effect than a cause, as manifestations of political norms which sanction relatively little regulation of individual behavior. In Belgium, for example, the political norms that permit the criminalization of nonvoting (thereby ensuring a very high turnout), also require parents to have national health service doctors (not one's private physician) perform an annual physical examination of all children between the ages of six and eighteen, to choose their infant's name from an approved list of names, to register their residence with the police, to register every telephone in the house, and periodically to renew a national identity card. In the United States, the ethos that allows Americans to live almost anywhere, in as large a residence as they can afford, to give their children any name that strikes their fancy, to keep one's place of residence a virtual secret, and to put a telephone on every wall of every room also resists institutions and practices which compel (however weakly) voting. In the United States, the decision to go to the polls is (with a very few exceptions) a wholly individual decision. However much we deplore nonvoting, we, as a nation, are unlikely to create the institutions which will compensate for the apparent weakness of the voting norm in mass publics.

Nonvoting: Should Anyone Care?

Finally, there is not a strong practical incentive to change. Normative considerations aside, it is not clear that the turnout rate has any consequence for election outcomes. Consider table 3.10, which presents the percentage reporting a vote for the winning candidate and the preferences of nonvoters. Of the ten presidential elections contested from 1952 through 1988, a majority of nonvoters disagreed with the choice of voters only twice, in 1952 and 1980.[11] Moreover, there is no consistent partisan bias to the preferences of nonvoters. While a greater turnout would have increased the winning margins of Democrats Kennedy, Carter, and (especially) Johnson, it would also have increased Eisenhower's majority in 1956 and Nixon's in 1972. In only two of the seven elections won by Republicans (1952 and 1980) did a majority of nonvoters seem to prefer the losing Democrat; in three (1968, 1984, and 1988) the Republican majority (plurality in 1968) among nonvoters was slightly smaller than the actual election; in the remaining two races (1956 and 1972) a 100

Table 3.10
Support for Winning Candidates

	Voters	Nonvoters	Difference*
1952	52	48	− 4
1956	57	71	+14
1960	50	51	+ 1
1964	61	73	+12
1968	44	41	− 3
1968**	57	56	− 1
1972	61	63	+ 2
1976	51	56	+ 5
1980	51	37	−14
1984	59	57	− 2
1988	52	51	− 1

* This is the arithmetic difference between the winner's share of the vote and the winner's support among nonvoters.

** The second 1968 figure includes the share of the vote won by Nixon and Wallace. The vote for these two might be regarded as the vote of the candidates favored by the short-term forces in the election.

Note: Table entries are percentages.

percent turnout would have increased the winning margins of Eisenhower and Nixon.

The success of the winning candidate, whether Republican or Democrat, among both voters and nonvoters ensures that nonvoting will not challenge the legitimacy of the winning candidate; in most cases a higher turnout even increases the (Democratic or Republican) winner's margin since nonvoters support the winner by a greater margin than the actual election outcome. In short, the political bias of turnout is not necessarily Democratic or Republican. The bias is in favor of the candidate who is doing well in the race.[12] The more unbalanced the contest, the greater the chance that high turnout will only increase the margin of the candidate who is certain to win. Low turnout is not a substantive challenge to election results, however much it may offend our civic sensibilities. Legal changes would increase turnout in most elections. However, barring changes that Americans are unlikely to make, turnout which depends heavily upon individual motivations to vote will probably fall short of normative expectations.

NOTES

The data used for this analysis were supplied through the Interuniversity Consortium for Social and Political Research. Neither the consortium nor the principal investigators are responsible for the analysis or the conclusions.

1. It should be pointed out that not everybody regards low turnout with concern. From this viewpoint, nonvoters might just be contented citizens. A low turnout rate may be symptomatic of political health: government may be producing enough satisfaction to allow nonvoters to concentrate on those things which are working less well—their occupation, income, or family relationships.

2. This conclusion is based on my reanalysis of the data used by Powell (1980) for his analysis of turnout in 30 western democracies. Also see his 1985 paper.

3. The turnout in 1984 was approximately 92.653 million voters. The estimated turnout for 1988 is about 91.595 million.

4. While both education and income predict turnout reasonably well, it is education which seems to be the causal factor. The values and outlook which are the proximate determinants of the vote (examined below) are dependent upon the socialization experiences that coincide with higher levels of education. The correlation with income largely reflects the higher income that accrues (albeit imperfectly) to the better educated.

5. There are several different methods of calculating change. The algorithm used here divides the percentage point change between the group's turnout in presidential and congressional elections by the turnout in presidential election. Specifically, let X = % voting 1980/1984 and Y = % voting 1978/1986. The change in turnout is then: $(X-Y)/X$.

6. The spatial model effectively predicts vote choice. The correlations between candidate choice and the issue differences average about .41 in 1980 and .37 in 1984.

7. The results of the probit analysis (with the standard error for the coefficient in parenthesis) are:

Duty	.189 (.035)
Party difference	.141 (.047)
Efficacy	.131 (.051)
Strength of partisanship	.215 (.059)
Campaign interest	.147 (.038)
Constant	−.722 (.047)

8. From the middle 1960s through the middle 1970s, turnout in Minnesota oscillated between 70 and 74 percent in presidential elections. After the establishment of same-day registration in 1978, turnout began to decline along with the drop in national voting rates. In 1980 turnout was 70 percent, it declined to 69 percent in 1984, and to about 66 percent in 1988. In South Dakota, turnout was 67 percent in 1980, 64 percent in 1984, and 62 percent in 1988. These rates are very similar to those of surrounding Great Plains states. It is difficult to see any unique registration-enhanced turnout. Results might be different in urban, industrial states such as Michigan, Illinois, New York, or California, but that remains to be demonstrated.

9. These "unexpected no-shows" are, as might be expected, disproportionately black, younger, southern (including southern whites), and residentially mobile.

10. These estimates are from a reanalysis of the Powell (1980) data.

11. However, the 1980 anomoly may be much smaller than it appears in table

3.10. There is considerable evidence of an election-eve shift toward Reagan. Because NES preelection interviewing is spread over a long period, with few interviews late in the campaign, this shift was not measured. The result is a substantial overestimate of the difference in the preferences of voters and nonvoters (see Petrocik 1990).

12. For a more detailed analysis of the responsiveness of peripheral voters (those who vote regularly or not at all) to the short-term forces in a campaign see Petrocik (1981b, 1987) and Denardo (1980).

REFERENCES

Abramson, Paul R., and John H. Aldrich. 1982. "The Decline of Electoral Participation in America." *American Political Science Review* 76 (September): 502–521.

Andersen, Kristi J. 1979. *The Creation of the Democratic Majority, 1928–1936*. Chicago: University of Chicago Press.

Brown, Courtney. 1987. "Mobilization and Party Competition within a Volatile Electorate." *American Sociological Review* 52 (February): 59–72.

Burnham, Walter Dean. 1974. "Theory and Voting Research: Some Reflections on Converse's 'Change in the American Electorate.'" *American Political Science Review* 68 (September): 1002–1023.

Cain, Bruce, and Ken McCue. 1985. "The Efficacy of Registration Drives." *Journal of Politics* 47 (November): 1221–1230.

Campbell, James E. 1985. "Sources of the New Deal Realignment: The Contributions of Conversion and Mobilization to Partisan Change." *Western Political Quarterly* 38 (September): 357–376.

Degler, Carl N. 1964. "American Political Parties and the Rise of the City: An Interpretation." *Journal of American History* (June): 41–59.

DeNardo, James. 1980. "Turnout and the Vote." *American Politcal Science Review* 74 (June): 406–420.

Downs, Anthony. 1957. *An Economic Theory of Democracy*. New York: Harper and Row.

Eldersveld, Samuel J. 1949. "The Influence of Metropolitan Party Pluralities in Presidential Elections since 1920." *American Political Science Review* 43 (December): 1189–1205.

Key, V.O. 1955. "A Theory of Critical Elections." *Journal of Politics* 17 (February): 3–18.

Lubell, Samuel. 1952. *The Future of American Politics*. New York: Harper and Row.

Petrocik, John R. 1981a. *Party Coalitions: Realignments and the Decline of the New Deal Party System*. Chicago: University of Chicago Press.

Petrocik, John R. 1981b. "Voter Turnout and Electoral Oscillation." *American Politics Quarterly* 9 (April): 161–180.

Petrocik, John R. 1987. "Voter Turnout and Electoral Preference: The Anomalous Reagan Elections." In *Elections in America*, ed. Kay Lehman Schlozman. Boston: Allen and Unwin.

Petrocik, John R. 1988. "Party System Structure and Electoral Change." Unpublished paper.

Petrocik, John R. 1990. "Estimating Turnout as a Guide to Predicting Elections."

Paper presented at the annual meeting of the American Political Science Association, San Francisco, August 30–September 2.

Piven, Frances Fox, and Richard Cloward. 1988. *Why Americans Don't Vote*. New York: Pantheon.

Powell, G. Bingham. 1980. "Voter Turnout in Thirty Democracies: Partisan, Legal, and Socio-economic Influences." In *Electoral Participation: A Comparative Analysis*, ed. Richard Rose. Beverly Hills, Calif.: Sage.

Powell, G. Bingham. 1986. "American Voters Turnout in Comparative Perspective." *American Political Science Review* 80 (March): 17–44.

Rosenstone, Steven J., and Raymond E. Wolfinger. 1978. "The Effect of Registration Laws on Voter Turnout." *American Political Science Review* 72 (March): 22–45.

Rusk, Jerrold G. 1974. "Comment: The American Electoral Universe: Speculation and Evidence." *American Political Science Review* 68 (September): 1028–1049.

Sigelman, Lee, Philip W. Roeder, Malcolm E. Jewell, and Michael A. Baer. 1985. "Voting and Nonvoting: A Multielection Perspective." *American Journal of Political Science* 29 (November): 749–765.

Verba, Sidney, Norman H. Nie, and Jae-on Kim. 1978. *Participation and Political Equality: A Seven-Nation Comparison*. London and New York: Cambridge University Press.

Wanat, John. 1979. "The Application of a Non-analytic Most Possible Estimation Technique: The Relative Impact of Mobilization and Conversion of Votes in the New Deal." *Political Methodology* 6 (May): 357–374.

Wanat, John, and Karen Burke. 1982. "Estimating the Degree of Mobilization and Conversion in the 1890s: An Inquiry into the Nature of Electoral Change." *American Political Science Review* 76 (June): 360–370.

White, Theodore H. 1961. *The Electing of the President, 1960*. New York: Atheneum House.

4 When Turnout Matters: Mobilization and Conversion as Determinants of Election Outcomes

Thomas E. Cavanagh

This chapter begins with a conundrum. In the United States, both turnout and party preference are related to social status. Yet studies at the individual level generally conclude that the class disparity in turnout has no significant effect on election outcomes (e.g., Wolfinger and Rosenstone 1980). To put it crudely, if one accepts the findings of these studies, turnout (at least in the United States) doesn't matter very much.

These counterintuitive findings are less puzzling, however, when juxtaposed with studies of voter turnout in the comparative tradition. Cross-national studies generally explain America's low level of voter participation as a product of our distinctive registration requirements, and the relatively weak relationship between social cleavages and political partisanship (e.g., Powell 1986). Analysis comprising an expanded universe of polities makes "American exceptionalism" an empirically measurable phenomenon. The degree to which socioeconomic factors determine partisanship may loom large in the American context when viewed in isolation, but it is far less impressive when compared to the dynamics prevailing in other advanced industrial democracies.

The argument of this chapter is that research on American voter turnout would benefit from a greater attention to modes of analysis more commonly found in studies of comparative politics. The structural factors highlighted by comparative research are explicitly political in nature, making their explanatory power intrinsically satisfying. They also vary across time and political units, making them suitable for comparative research. And their utility suggests the wisdom of approaching the problem of voter participation as part of a more general process of behavioral interaction between political elites and the social groups that comprise the mass electorate.

Viewing the American research findings in comparative perspective also reveals how little we really understand about the dynamics of voter turnout. Taken in its entirety, the extant body of research findings on voter participation is shot through with contradictions. Explanations of turnout that appear robust and persuasive in cross-sectional analyses generally fail to explain turnout variations across time. Explanations that appear to hold in the American case do not fare well when applied to other polities. We know even less about the determinants of turnout across subnational units such as states and cities. And generalizations that apply at the level of presidential elections (such as the assertion that virtually everyone who registers will turn out to vote) are demonstrably untrue at every other level of public office in the United States.

By examining the turnout rates of electorates in a variety of structural environments, we can also gain insight into the conditions under which a change in participation rates can effect a change in election outcomes. As we shall see, these conditions are quite restrictive. More interesting, perhaps, is the finding that they are far more likely to obtain in local than in national elections. In other words, research in comparative mode can help us to determine when turnout matters.

WHAT WE DON'T KNOW ABOUT VOTER TURNOUT

After several decades of quantitative research, it is striking to reflect upon how many things we still don't know about American voter turnout. Despite some impressive studies, the whole of this literature is decidedly less than the sum of its parts. The determinants of American voter participation during the contemporary era are of little utility in explaining turnout variation across time. The list of things that we don't understand about American voter turnout is daunting indeed:

1. *We don't know why education is the single strongest individual-level predictor of turnout.* Wolfinger and Rosenstone (1980) explain this finding on the basis of the cognitive sophistication that accompanies education and the ability it imparts to the individual to make sense of the political world and relate political choices to life circumstances. The relationship between education and turnout apparently assumed a much different form in the nineteenth century, however. One must rely on aggregate data, with all its pitfalls, for evidence on this score. But Kleppner (1982) finds that educational levels in most of the United States were *inversely* related to turnout rates in the late nineteenth century, as were most of the other socieconomic indicators.

The current positive association between turnout and social status apparently dates from the early years of the twentieth century. The levels of cognitive sophistication in the aggregate were, if anything, much *lower* in the nineteenth century than they are today; yet turnout levels were much *higher* in the last century. Even if one accepts the hypothesis about cognitive sophistication as valid for the present day, it is at best severely time-bound and cannot be taken as a universal constant in explaining levels of voter turnout.

If the least-educated and other lower-status groups had the highest turnout a century ago and the lowest turnout today, then the *decline* in the turnout of the disadvantaged must have been particularly steep relative to that of the rest of the electorate during the intervening decades. Interestingly, this time-series pattern has been observed in miniature during the contemporary participation slump, which has been particularly concentrated among the lower-income, blue-collar, and relatively uneducated sectors of the population since 1964 (Burnham 1982, chap. 5; Cavanagh 1981; Reiter 1979). Whatever stimuli in the political environment mobilized these voters in both the recent and more distant past, they are clearly less present today. In their absence, one is left with what Burnham sardonically terms "a kind of apolitical state of nature, in which formal schooling is the chief thing that matters" in determining the rate of participation (1982, 168).

The assumed political inclinations of the disadvantaged are the foundation upon which rests the seemingly reasonable assumption that increased turnout would aid the political left. The argument hinges on a demonstration that the "hole" in the American participation spectrum corresponds to the point in the partisan spectrum that would be filled by a social democratic party, if one existed (see Burnham 1974). As we shall see, however, a careful reading of both the American and crossnational literature casts doubt even on this proposition.

2. *We don't know why turnout in the North dropped so sharply after 1896.* Explaining the drop in the South after 1896 is easy enough: it reflects the imposition of literacy tests, poll taxes, the white primary, and other structural barriers designed to keep blacks and poor whites from voting (Key 1949; Kousser 1974). The North is a more difficult affair. Burnham (1982) and Kleppner (1982) have traced the decline to the evaporation of two-party competition in much of the country due to the regionally based party system that took shape in the 1896 election. Yet, as Piven and Cloward (1988, 64) note, the focus on party competition "fails to explain why the subsequent restoration of party competition—first in the North during the 1930s and then in the South in the 1960s—was not accompanied by a return to nineteenth century levels of turnout."

For their part, Piven and Cloward emphasize the barrier of registration as the key factor holding down turnout during the twentieth century. Kleppner (1982) has demonstrated that the imposition of registration requirements accelerated the turnout decline after the turn of the century, particularly in lower-status areas. Making registration easier would certainly boost turnout today. But even eliminating registration barriers altogether would not raise turnout to the 80 percent-plus levels prevailing in most of the western democracies.

Multivariate studies have found that election day registration or automatic registration would increase American turnout by 7 to 14 percentage points (Kelley, Ayres, and Bowen 1967; Kim, Petrocik, and Enokson 1975; Patterson and Caldeira 1983; Powell 1986; Wolfinger and Rosenstone 1980), or from the 50 percent level seen in 1988 to perhaps as high as 65 percent. Simple before-and-after comparisons of recent experiments in individual states suggest more modest effects. Minnesota and Wisconsin adopted election day registration in 1976; their turnout rates increased by less than 4 percentage points above their 1972 levels (Smolka 1977). Thus, neither the party competition nor the registration argument suffices to explain the low levels of turnout prevailing in the contemporary United States.

Analysts as disparate as Wolfinger and Rosenstone (1980) and Piven and Cloward (1988) have popularized the notion that virtually all registrants vote. But this assertion holds true only at the presidential level. While 86.2 percent of registrants reported voting in the 1988 election, nearly three out of ten reported staying home in the midterm election two years earlier. These figures are typical of the "surge and decline" parameters since 1974, a period marked by a remarkable degree of stability in registration rates (table 4.1).

Even in presidential years, it simply is not true that all registrants vote. Most of the variation in turnout by educational level is due to the variation in registration rates; but the turnout rate of *registrants* also varies directly with education. In the presidential election of 1988, 77.3 percent of the registrants with a grade school education reported voting, compared to 93.4 percent of the college graduates. In the preceding midterm election, this spread ranged from 64.7 percent of the registrants at the low end of the education scale to 80.3 percent at the high end (table 4.2).

If one looks beyond federal elections, the inadequacy of the registration argument becomes even more apparent. Turnout in state and local elections is notorious for being both low and variable. In an analysis of municipal election turnout in 170 cities, Karnig and Walter (1986) found that the registration rate explains only 8 percent of the variance in the turnout rate by city in 1975 and 1986. The secular decline in municipal turnout since the 1930s is due not to declining registration, but to the declining participation rate of registered adults (table 4.3).

In certain kinds of local elections, the turnout rate even among registered voters can be measured only with a micrometer. Consider, for

Table 4.1
Reported Voter Registration and Turnout, 1966–1988

Year	Percent of Adults Registered	Percent of Adults Voting	Percent of Registrants Voting
1966	70.3	55.4	78.8
1968	74.3	67.8	91.3
1970	68.1	54.6	80.2
1972	72.3	63.0	87.1
1974	62.2	44.7	71.9
1976	66.7	59.2	88.8
1978	62.6	45.9	73.3
1980	66.9	59.2	88.6
1982	64.1	48.5	75.6
1984	68.3	59.9	87.7
1986	64.3	46.0	71.6
1988	66.6	57.4	86.2

Source: U.S. Bureau of the Census (1987, tables A and B; 1989, tables A and C).

example, the turnout rates among registered voters in New York City's community school board elections, which have declined from 14 percent when the elections were first held in 1970 to 7.2 percent in the most recent canvass (figure 4.1; the data are reported in Buder 1989a, 1989b). When one pauses to consider that only about half of New York City's voting age population is even registered, one begins to appreciate how poorly registration alone can account for the lack of participation in elections below the presidential level. Clearly, the bulk of American nonvoting must be ascribed to other causes.

3. *We don't know why American voter turnout has been declining since 1960.* As Brody (1978) observed in his aptly named article on the "puzzle" of American voter participation, educational levels have increased dramatically in recent years, and registration barriers have been falling. These factors should have been sufficient to produce substantial *gains* in the level of turnout, all other things being equal. The intellectual challenge is thus to identify the things that are unequal. The extension

Table 4.2
Reported Voter Registration and Turnout by Education, 1986–1988

Years of Education	Percent of Adults Registered	Percent of Adults Voting	Percent of Registrants Voting
1988 Presidential Election			
0 to 8 years	47.5	36.7	77.3
9 to 11 years	52.8	41.3	78.2
12 years	64.6	54.7	84.7
13 to 15 years	73.5	64.5	87.8
16 years or more	83.1	77.6	93.4
1986 Congressional Election			
0 to 8 years	50.5	32.7	64.7
9 to 11 years	52.4	33.8	64.5
12 years	62.9	44.1	70.1
13 to 15 years	70.0	49.9	71.3
16 years or more	77.8	62.5	80.3

Source: U.S. Bureau of the Census (1987, table F; 1989, table B).

of the vote to 18-year-olds reduced aggregate turnout by about 2 percentage points. That leaves roughly 10 percentage points of the decline since 1964 unexplained (Cavanagh 1981, 58). The steady erosion of recent years must therefore be due to some peculiarly strong forces in the contemporary political environment which are acting as an undertow on the aggregate level of turnout.

Abramson and Aldrich (1982) claim that the contemporaneous declines in party identification and political efficacy explain most of the recent decline in participation. The problem with this finding is twofold. First, it vanishes when other variables are introduced into the analysis (such as education, which has the effect of boosting turnout during the period). The summary effects of the variables in a fully specified model largely cancel out, producing a prediction of stable rather than declining turnout during the post–1960 era (Cassel and Hill 1981; Cassel and Luskin 1988).

Table 4.3
Voter Participation in Municipal Elections, 1935–1986

Year	Percent of Adults Registered	Percent of Adults Voting	Percent of Registrants Voting
1935-37	64.7	40.5	62.6
1962	70.7	36.4	51.5
1975	69.2	31.2	45.1
1986	71.6	27.5	38.4

Source: Adapted from Karning and Walter (1986, table 2).

Figure 4.1
Turnout of Registered Voters: New York City School Board Elections

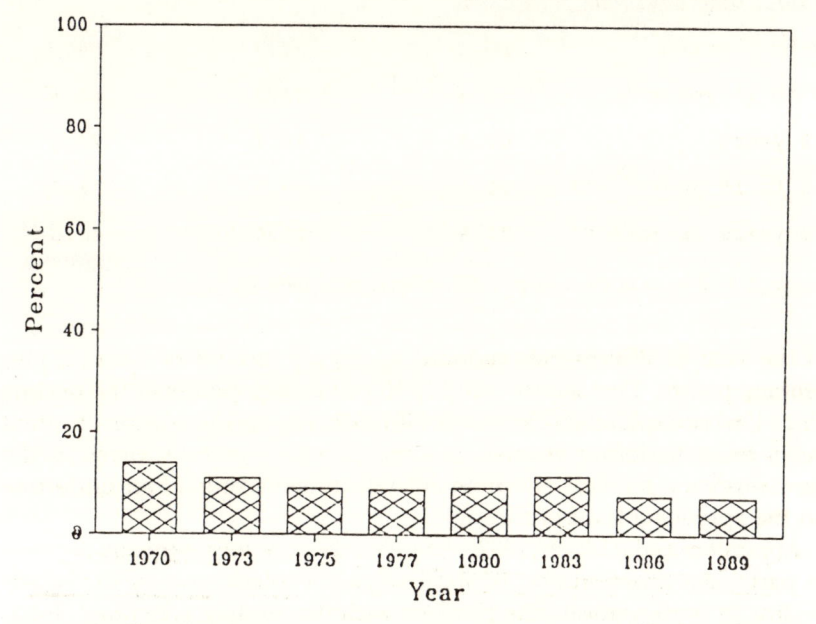

More fundamentally, the variables singled out for their causal significance don't really explain anything, except in the most literal statistical sense. They merely add another set of questions to the investigation: Why are people feeling less efficacious? And why are they less likely to identify with the two major political parties? To answer these questions, one must expand the scope of the inquiry well beyond the realm of individual-level attitudes and attributes.

Political attitudes are not exogenous variables in any meaningful sense. They constitute a *reaction* to political stimuli of a structural nature. In the immortal words of V.O. Key (1966, 2), "The voice of the people is but an echo." The standing decisions made by voters and potential voters are reactions to the cues emanating from political parties and their leaders. Partisanship and efficacy do not arise from within individuals any more than maggots arise through spontaneous generation from a piece of raw meat.

A truly behavioral approach to empirical political research must pay heed to political behaviors more meaningful than the simple recording of responses to attitudinal probing in a survey interview situation. In its insistent dwelling on the attributes of individuals, American electoral research has been looking through the wrong end of the telescope. The politically interesting and important question isn't what the voters feel, but why they feel that way; not how they respond, but what they are responding to; or, to put it yet another way, not who votes, but who mobilizes.

THE SOCIAL ROOTS OF ELECTORAL MOBILIZATION

To appreciate the relevance of environmental factors to nonvoting in the United States, it may be useful to think in terms of the hurdling event in a track meet. The higher the hurdles to be overcome, the more motivated an individual must be to surmount them. The barrier of registration presents a significant hurdle. But even if it were removed, it does not follow that turnout would increase dramatically in the absence of other environmental factors stimulating a desire to participate. The removal of the hurdle would matter little if the runner were to see nothing worth running toward at the end of the track.

The multivariate models indicate that registration is not the only thing keeping most of the unregistered away from the polls. A lack of desire to vote should not be taken as proof of apathy, but rather as an indication of inadequate stimuli in the political environment. Habitual nonvoters need to be persuaded that there is a party or candidate worth supporting—or, at the least, that the victory of one set of contenders could prove to be disagreeable or threatening.

The survey evidence from Western Europe indicates that a high aggregate turnout will engage the participation of lower-status voters (Burnham 1982, chap. 4; Powell 1986). But it does not necessarily follow that a European-style party of the democratic left would be the best means of mobilizing the disadvantaged in America. The European experience suggests that turnout is particularly high when two conditions are met:

- partisan cleavages correspond closely to the most salient social and cultural cleavages in the electorate
- organizational structures correspond closely to these cleavages and play an active role in mobilizing the electorate (Powell 1986)

The existence of class-based parties is simply a special case of these more general conditions. Indeed, in most of Europe, questions of religion and ethnic or linguistic culture are comparable in salience to socioeconomic differences in structuring the party systems of individual countries (Powell 1980; Rose 1974).

It is these social and cultural cleavages, and the rich organizational life they inspire, that assist in mobilizing many lower-status voters for political participation. Class interests also play a role because of the close links between trade unions and social democratic parties in many of these countries. But even those untouched by organized labor are generally reached by other important sources of political cues. The concordance between social and political organizations provides the crucial link between the citizen and the political system in the countries with high levels of voter participation.

Applying this insight to the United States leads in a somewhat different direction than the concentration upon the social status of American nonvoters might suggest. It was noted earlier that the participation rates of lower-status Americans were much higher in the nineteenth century than they are today. Analyses of the politics of that era consistently emphasize the importance of clashing ethnic and religious cultures as the basis for intense partisan loyalties, which in turn appear to have stimulated high rates of participation (Jensen 1971; Kleppner 1979). The sharply etched class cleavages of the New Deal/Fair Deal period were far less successful in mobilizing large numbers of voters. Ironically, then, a politics based on class is neither a necessary nor a sufficient condition for high turnout rates among lower-status Americans.

The most salient social cleavage for many contemporary Americans is probably race, rather than class per se. In recent years, religious beliefs over such issues as abortion, school prayer, gay rights, sex education, and the like have also risen to prominence on the political agenda. It is therefore not surprising that blacks and religious fundamentalists have been the most visible forces of political mobilization during the past decade.

The salience of race can be seen in the turnout of registered voters in the black-majority wards of Cleveland during the high point of black political influence in that city (figure 4.2; the data are reported in Nelson

Figure 4.2
Turnout of Registered Voters: Cleveland Mayoral Elections, Black Majority Wards

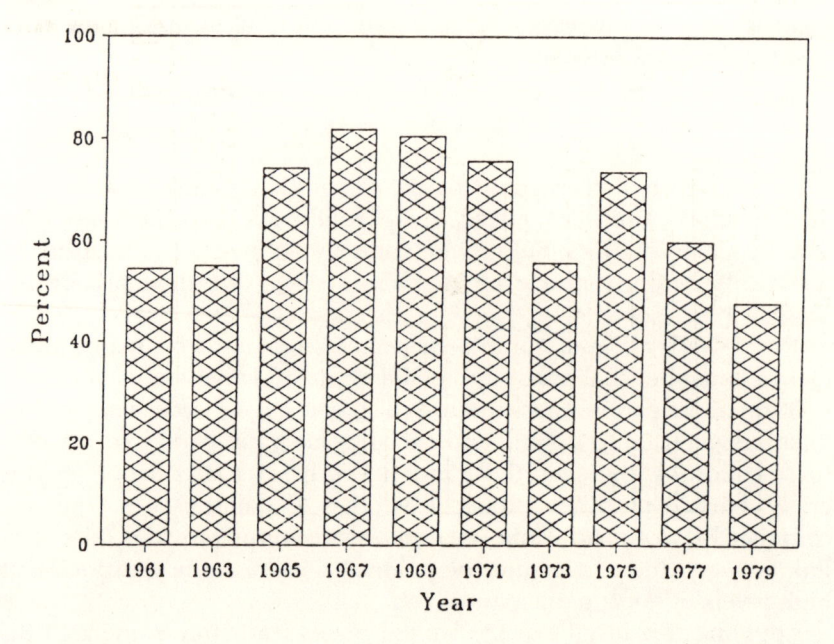

1982, table 8.1). Turnout in the black wards ranged from 73.5 to 81.7 percent of the registrants whenever a viable black mayoral candidate was on the ballot (from 1965 to 1971 and in 1975). In no other case did the turnout in black wards exceed 60 percent of the registrants. Roughly speaking, the presence of a black mayoral candidate perceived to have a chance of victory appears to have added 15 to 20 percentage points to black turnout during this period.

A similar picture can be gleaned from Chicago. In 1983, the year of Harold Washington's triumphant mayoral campaign, the long-standing turnout gap between the city's black- and white-majority wards completely vanished (figure 4.3; the data are reported in Preston 1984, table 1; see also Kleppner 1985, 149). In these two examples, we see particularly striking evidence of the responsiveness of turnout patterns to the appeal of the choices being offered at the ballot box when a campaign addresses the most salient aspects of the potential voter's social identity.

The consequences of demobilization are illustrated by the New York City school board elections noted above. Although approximately three-quarters of the students in the city schools are black or Hispanic, these minorities hold only 47.6 percent of the seats on the community school boards. The reason appears to be a dearth of minority candidates re-

Figure 4.3
Turnout of Registered Voters: Chicago Mayoral Primaries

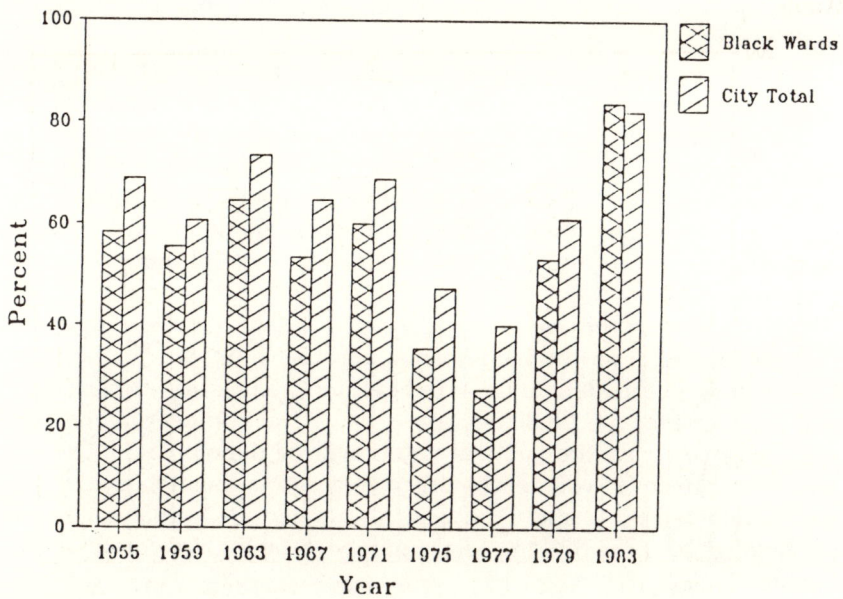

cruited by labor unions, religious groups, and political clubs, which are the major agents of mobilization in these low-visibility elections. The absence of minority candidates, in turn, results in minority turnout levels even lower than those prevailing in the city as a whole (Buder 1989a, 1989b).

There is a growing literature on the importance of mobilization efforts as determinants of turnout in subpresidential elections. Direct indicators of mobilization activity, such as campaign spending, have been shown to increase voter participation. In addition, such variables as a narrow electoral margin and the existence of simultaneous Senate races, which one would expect to generate mobilization activity, have also been shown to predict higher turnout (Cox and Munger 1989; Patterson and Caldeira 1983). Clearly, mobilization matters in stimulating turnout. But under what conditions does turnout matter in changing election outcomes?

WHY TURNOUT DOESN'T MATTER (USUALLY)

The seemingly paradoxical finding that turnout doesn't matter can be ascribed to a number of factors. At the most rudimentary level, the finding can be seen as a simple proof of the law of large numbers. The preferences of the habitual nonvoters who are newly mobilized at a given point in time must be distinctively different from those of the habitual voters for even a sizeable turnout increment to affect the distribution of the total vote.

This can be seen by stripping the problem down to its most basic elements through the use of a heuristic model. Let us partition the voters at a given election into two groups: *habitual voters*, who also voted in the previous election; and *mobilized voters*, who did not vote in the previous election. We shall assume that all of the people who voted in the previous election have voted again; that is, there are no cases of previous voters failing to vote again due to abstention or mortality between elections.

Voters can vote for one of two parties. We shall call the winners of the previous election the Incumbents, and the losers we shall call the Challengers. Let us denote the votes cast for the Incumbent party by I, and votes cast for the Challenger party by C. The number of votes each party receives from the habitual voters will be denoted by I_h and C_h, while the number of votes each party receives from the mobilized voters will be denoted by I_m and C_m. The total number of habitual voters will be denoted by T_h, while the total number of mobilized voters will be denoted by T_m.

Let us assume for the time being that once a voter chooses a party, that voter remains faithful to that party forevermore. In other words, election results depend exclusively on each party's success in mobilizing its supporters to go to the polls. We shall relax this assumption later in the discussion; but for now, we are examining a world in which conversion from one party to another is not a factor, so mobilization is all that matters.

By definition, the Incumbent party leads among the habitual voters. Thus, the Challenger party can only win if its plurality among the mobilized voters exceeds the Incumbent party's plurality among the habitual voters. In other words, the addition of new voters can reverse the previous outcome if and only if:

$$(C_m - I_m) > (I_h - C_h)$$

This is a tall order, because the total number of newly mobilized voters $(C_m + I_m)$ will ordinarily be a good deal smaller than the total number of habitual voters $(C_h + I_h)$. That is, the number of newly mobilized voters is probably much less than the total size of the electorate in the previous election, or $T_m < T_h$.

If we compare the *percentage* distributions of party adherents among the pools of habitual voters and mobilized voters, we can better appreciate the restrictiveness of the conditions for a reversal to occur. Generally speaking, the Challengers must receive a higher percentage of the votes of the mobilized voters than the Incumbents receive among the habitual voters. This is true except in the unlikely case that $T_m > T_h$, that is, the number of newly mobilized voters actually exceeds the number of habitual voters, in which case the turnout in the current election is at least double the level of turnout at the previous election. The smaller the ratio of newly mobilized voters (T_m) to habitual voters (T_h), the larger the plurality the Challengers must attain among the population of mobilized voters to overcome the Incumbent lead among the population of habitual voters. In other words, a reversal is possible if and only if:

$$\frac{C_m - I_m}{T_m} \times \frac{T_m}{T_h} > \frac{I_h - C_h}{T_h}$$

Some hypothetical cases can be devised to illustrate the implications of this formula. Let us use as a starting point the turnout from the 1988 presidential election: 50 percent of the voting age population. If turnout in 1992 were to rise from 50 to 60 percent—an enormous increase in such a short period of time—then the population of mobilized voters would represent 10 percent of the voting age population. In this case, the group of newly mobilized voters would be only one-fifth as large as the group of habitual voters. Thus, in order for the Challengers to win, their plurality expressed as a percentage of the mobilized voters would have to be over five times as high as the plurality enjoyed by the Incumbents among the habitual voters. Now suppose that the Incumbents carried the habitual voters by 54 to 46 percent, or 8 percentage points—roughly the size of the Bush margin over Dukakis in 1988. Then the Challengers would have to carry the newly mobilized voters by a plurality of more than 40 percentage points—that is, by a margin exceeding 70 to 30 percent—in order to win the election.

As this example demonstrates, given even a mediocre level of turnout, mobilization alone can effect a reversal of outcomes only with a heroic rate of success in attracting the support of the available pool of nonvoters, unless the balance of forces among the habitual voters is extremely close. If we assign some fairly routine values to the variables in the model, then the possibility of a reversal based solely on turnout becomes vanishingly small rather quickly. For example, if turnout increases from 50 to 55 percent, and the Incumbent plurality among the habitual voters is a comfortable but not overwhelming 55 to 45 percent, then the Challengers must carry 100 percent of the newly mobilized voters merely to produce a tie!

THE IMPORTANCE OF CONVERSION

The model presented above helps to clarify why real-world politicians generally place more emphasis on the conversion of previous voters

Table 4.4
Presidential Votes Cast by Mobilized and Habitual Voters, 1936–1984

	Mobilized Voters			Habitual Voters		
	Dem.	Rep.	Total	Dem.	Rep.	Total
1936	59%	41%	19.1%	60%	40%	80.9%
1940	56	44	15.6	51	49	84.4
1944	57	43	13.6	51	49	86.4
1948	64	36	16.0	55	45	84.0
1952	46	54	17.4	41	59	82.6
1956	50	50	13.0	39	61	87.0
1960	58	42	15.5	48	52	84.5
1964	75	25	10.6	66	34	89.4
1968	42	58	12.4	46	54	87.6
1972	55	45	11.7	32	68	88.3
1976	68	32	14.6	47	53	85.4
1980	49	51	17.0	41	59	83.0
1984	32	68	11.5	39	61	88.5

Source: 1936 Gallup survey data reported in Campbell (1985); 1940–1948 Gallup postelection survey data reported in Key (1966, table 2.4); 1952–1980 SRC/CPS data and 1984 General Social Survey data reported in Marquette and Hinckley (1988, table 1).

than on the mobilization of new voters. A shift in the size of the plurality among habitual voters will ordinarily dwarf any plausible benefit from mobilization as a determinant of the election outcome. This formal logic, rather than the empirical distribution of opinion, explains the seemingly perverse finding that turnout fluctuations have so little apparent effect on election outcomes. Of course, at times an election is close enough that the plurality among mobilized voters can reverse the outcome that would be produced if the electorate consisted only of habitual voters. But even in this seemingly clear-cut instance, a close examination usually reveals that conversion, rather than mobilization, is the more important factor in producing the election result.

This point can be demonstrated through an empirical analysis of contemporary presidential elections. Table 4.4 compares the preferences of mobilized and habitual voters from 1936 to 1984. (Because we are interested in the effects of mobilization on the margin separating the two

Table 4.5
Voting Behavior in Consecutive Presidential Elections, as Percentage of Voting Age Population, 1952–1984

	1952	1956	1960	1964	1968	1972	1976	1980	1984
Abstention									
NV to NV	19.8	18.4	15.2	13.3	17.1	19.4	20.0	21.1	19.3
Withdrawal									
Dem. to NV	4.3	2.8	1.9	5.5	7.5	5.0	3.7	8.1	5.7
Rep. to NV	1.8	6.3	5.1	3.1	2.9	5.4	6.5	5.4	3.5
Mobilization									
NV to Dem.	6.0	4.7	7.0	6.2	3.8	5.0	7.0	5.4	2.7
NV to Rep.	6.9	4.7	5.0	2.1	5.2	4.1	3.2	5.7	5.6
Conversion									
Rep. to Dem.	1.1	5.2	9.8	7.0	1.0	4.1	10.3	3.4	2.7
Dem. to Rep.	10.9	4.0	2.4	5.5	14.6	7.7	2.7	8.9	8.4
Retention									
Dem. to Dem.	23.8	19.3	21.5	39.2	28.4	16.4	17.7	19.0	22.0
Rep. to Rep.	25.4	34.6	32.0	18.2	19.5	33.0	28.9	23.1	30.2

Source: Adapted from Marquette and Hinckley (1988, table 1).

major parties, votes for third-party candidates have been ignored.) A quick glance at the two columns of figures reveals only two cases where one can argue that mobilization may have reversed the outcome: the closely fought elections of 1960 and 1976. The inherent noise in the survey data makes even these cases problematic, of course, because the apparent reversals are well within the margin of sampling error. But even if we take these numbers at face value, a more detailed analysis reveals that the effects of conversion must be given the bulk of the credit for determining the outcomes of even these two elections.

In table 4.5, the entire voting age population has been partitioned into categories according to the self-reported voting behavior of survey respondents in two consecutive elections. (Once again, to keep the focus on the competition between the two major parties, all respondents reporting third-party voting have been deleted in each year.) The flows from one category to another can be conceptualized in terms of five basic processes: *abstention*, or nonvoting in two consecutive elections; *withdrawal*, or a shift from voting for a major party to nonvoting in the next election; *mobilization*, or a shift from nonvoting to voting for one of the major parties; *conversion*, or a shift from supporting one major party to supporting the other party; and *retention*, or supporting the same party in two consecutive elections.

Looking at the 1960 and 1976 elections, it becomes clear that conversion effects exceeded mobilization effects as determinants of the outcomes. Among the newly mobilized voters in 1960, the Democrats edged the Republicans by 7.0 to 5.0 percent, for a plurality of 2.0 percent of the voting age population. However, a more important factor was the population of converted voters. Democratic conversions exceeded Republican conversions by 9.8 to 2.4 percent, for a plurality of 7.4 percent of the voting age population. Thus, the Democratic plurality contributed by conversion was over three times the size of the Democratic plurality contributed by mobilization. The 1976 election was characterized by similar dynamics: the Democratic plurality due to conversion was 7.6 percent of the voting age population, exactly twice the Democratic plurality due to mobilization (3.8 percent).

As a general matter, then, there is more net change in the electorate due to conversion than to mobilization. Or, looked at another way, mobilization of previous nonvoters is unlikely to reverse an election outcome unless a strong partisan tide is simultaneously producing a strong conversion effect among habitual voters. Because the pool of habitual voters is usually so much larger than the pool of newly mobilized voters, a short-term political stimulus acting equally on the two populations will tend to produce larger pluralities due to conversion than due to mobilization.

Specifying a model to capture these effects depends upon assumptions concerning the partisan preferences of habitual voters in the *absence* of short-term stimuli (see also Petrocik 1987, for one interesting approach to the problem). From the standpoint of devising political strategy, the smaller the prospective increase in aggregate turnout—or, more precisely, the smaller the ratio of the expected turnout increase (T_m) to the previous turnout level (T_h)—the more cost-effective it is for political strategists to concentrate their efforts upon increasing their share of the habitual voters, as opposed to mobilizing previous nonvoters. The existence of entry barriers, such as the registration requirement for previous nonvoters, makes the cost-benefit ratio of mobilization especially unattractive to American political elites.

The only major exception to this generalization occurs at low levels of turnout (such as 25 percent or below). In this case, the pool of non-voters is so large that even a relatively small turnout increase in absolute terms produces a pool of mobilized voters that begins to approach the pool of habitual voters in size. As we noted above, local elections in the United States are often noted for a rather low level of turnout. It therefore follows that incumbents running for office at the local level (as opposed to candidates for statewide and national office) would be the most threatened by mobilization efforts, because their core constituencies among established voters are often relatively small in absolute terms.

Considering the even lower turnouts often seen in local primaries, mobilization efforts by insurgent factions within the incumbent's party might well be more threatening to local incumbents than mobilization by the opposition. This is especially true where the incumbent's party overwhelmingly dominates the local electorate, and victory in the primary is tantamount to election. In this rather perverse case, local party leaders might perceive personal incentives to discourage mobilization efforts in their constituencies, even though such efforts might benefit their party by improving its showing in statewide or national elections.

Let us imagine that the Incumbent party's habitual voters (I_h) are divided into two factions: the Barnacles (B_h) and the Youngbloods (Y_h). To keep the example simple, we shall assume that all habitual voters participate in the Incumbent party's primary as well as in the general election. Now let us imagine a district in which a Barnacle currently holding office is running for renomination against a Youngblood in the Incumbent party primary. If the Incumbent party is sufficiently dominant over the Challenger party, then the only meaningful contest will occur in the Incumbent party primary. Indeed, among the district's habitual voters, let us suppose that the Barnacle office-holder faces more opposition from supporters of the Youngblood faction in the primary than from supporters of the Challenger party in the general, or, more precisely, that $B_h > Y_h > C_h$.

In this situation, a Barnacle office-holder is not likely to worry very much about the Challenger party, as long as the Incumbent party's voters are united in November, because it is obvious that $(B_h + Y_h) > C_h$. However, the Barnacles may have good reason to feel threatened if the Youngbloods undertake a registration drive. If the Youngblood faction succeeds in mobilizing more new voters (Y_m) than the Barnacle faction (B_m), then the Youngblood candidate can beat the Barnacle in the primary if and only if:

$$\frac{Y_m - B_m}{I_m} \times \frac{I_m}{I_h} > \frac{B_h - Y_h}{I_h}$$

The lower the prevailing level of turnout—that is, the smaller the size of I_h—then the more likely it becomes that a registration drive could result in a successful insurgent candidacy in the Incumbent party's primary. And because there is no meaningful competition in the general election, the prevailing level of turnout is likely to be very low indeed.

Given this potential, the Barnacles have strong incentives to prevent the Youngbloods from registering, even if *all* of the newly mobilized Youngbloods were to vote for the Incumbent party in the general election. A Youngblood registration drive would swell the Incumbents' local plurality in November, that is,

$$(I_h + Y_m) - C_h > (I_h - C_h),$$

but this only helps the Incumbent party's position in terms of state or national politics. In terms of local politics, it is essentially irrelevant, because $I_h > C_h$ in any event. From the Barnacles' point of view, therefore, mobilization is undesirable, because a registration drive provides tangible benefits to state and national leaders of the Incumbent party, while offering nothing to local office-holders but the opportunity to lose control of local politics to their factional rivals.

Precisely these dynamics were observed by Piven and Cloward (1985) in the course of their work for the Human/SERVE registration campaign in 1984. In general, they found that the only officials responsive to their desire to register social welfare recipients were Democratic governors (like Cuomo of New York and Celeste of Ohio) who were elected in 1982 partly through the efforts of get-out-the-vote campaigns by minority groups and labor unions. In addition to strenuous opposition from the Reagan administration and Republican office-holders generally, many Democratic officials at the local level were openly hostile to their efforts, the prospective benefit to the national Democratic campaign notwithstanding. Politicians (including black incumbents) not supporting Jesse Jackson were especially suspicious of mobilization efforts, given the high level of Jackson support among the newly mobilized black voters (see Cavanagh 1985, 13–14).

THE TARGETING OF MOBILIZATION EFFORTS

In sum, a change in the level of turnout will not produce a change of election outcome unless three conditions are met:

- the election is closely fought to begin with, due to a close partisan balance or a strong conversion trend
- a large turnout increase can be expected, relative to the size of the habitual electorate
- a group of habitual nonvoters with distinctive partisan preferences can be readily mobilized

In the contemporary American context, there is only one set of political circumstances that routinely fits this description: the mobilization of black voters in areas of heavy black population concentration.

This phenomenon has been most clearly visible in big-city mayoral campaigns between black and white candidates. Because the vote often polarizes along racial lines, a city where blacks and whites are roughly equal in population will often produce a closely fought campaign. In this case, the racial composition of the habitual voters (derived from a racial breakdown of the total vote cast in the previous mayoral election) can often be used as a rough stand-in for the "expected" vote in the absence of mobilization effects. Of course, whites will frequently counter-mobilize to oppose a black candidate, but if most of the new voters are black, then a black mayor can potentially result from the campaign. The archetypal example of a situation when turnout matters is the Chicago mayoral election of 1983:

> During Harold Washington's mayoral campaign, Chicago met all of the conditions that can alter the composition of a local electorate: the black population makes up 40 percent of the local electorate; 99 percent of blacks cast their ballots for Washington; and black voter turnout increased by a remarkable 30 percentage points. In addition, blacks and whites were severely polarized during the campaign. (Cavanagh 1987, 139)

The Chicago example highlights the importance of looking at distinctive subpopulations, a point often lost in discussions of the effects of turnout variations. For example, Wolfinger and Rosenstone (1980, chap. 6) compare the political preferences of voters and the total adult population, and conclude that 100 percent turnout would bring about no discernible change in election outcomes. But we never observe 100 percent turnout in the empirical world. To apply this finding to actual conditions, one must assume that a purely random subset of nonvoters is being mobilized in a given election. Yet this does not seem intuitively reasonable, either.

The nonvoters being contacted to vote in a given election are likely to be a nonrandom, purposively selected subpopulation which is expected to lend disproportionate support to the political forces undertaking the mobilization. The high support of blacks for the Democratic party has made them an especially prominent target of mobilization efforts in recent years, but both parties have promising pools to draw upon. Careful screening can winnow nonvoters from almost any group in favor of almost any point of view, no matter how unpromising the aggregate distribution of opinion.

For example, in 1984 the Republican National Committee undertook a comprehensive registration effort in Colorado. Consultants matched the addresses of 2.2 million drivers' licenses against those of 1.2 million registered voters, to produce a list of 800,000 unregistered drivers. They pared this list down to 120,000 names by eliminating all those who lived in heavily Democratic areas, and phone numbers were located for 60,000 of these names. Phone bank contacts with these 60,000 people enabled the Republicans to compile a final list of 20,000 nonvoters who favored Republican candidates but had not yet registered. Each person on this target list then received a letter from the state chairman with instructions on how to register (Salmore and Salmore 1985, 188). In short, given sufficient resources, virtually any randomly selected population of nonvoters can be winnowed to yield a population of potential voters with political characteristics making them suitable for mobilization efforts.

The purposive aspects of mobilization further enrich the discussion of the seeming lack of connection between turnout and electoral outcomes. For the mobilization of one group can be offset by the countermobilization of another, producing an increase in aggregate turnout but no significant net benefit for either side. In 1984, the success of registration drives targeted at minorities and lower-income people was countered by Republican drives among Christian fundamentalists, retirees, suburbanites, and upscale Latinos (Piven and Cloward 1988, chap. 6). The mobilization of new voters is rather like the mobilization of troops in World War I: once one side begins to call up the reserves, the other side dares not let its soldiers stay at home (see Tuchman 1962). Political strategists, like their military counterparts, are rarely afforded the luxury of competing in an environment free from the risk of escalation.

There are additional subtleties working to erode the relationship between turnout fluctuations and election outcomes. As DeNardo (1980) has demonstrated with an ingenious model, turnout gains will be drawn (more or less by definition) from a "peripheral" political population whose partisanship will be more weakly ingrained than that of the core electorate. In the American case, even though the nonvoter pool is disproportionately comprised of lower-status people, their tendency to vote Democratic is less reliable than that of the lower-status individuals who vote consistently. Thus, mobilization drives in a heavily Democratic constituency can activate so many political independents that the Democratic share of the local electorate may actually drop. In the extreme case, DeNardo's degenerate "world without a core," election outcomes are completely unaffected by turnout fluctuations because the partisan attachments of both voters and nonvoters are so weakly developed as to produce essentially random changes in voting behavior from election to election.

CONCLUSION

The analysis presented above offers some sobering and, I hope, useful guidelines for how to tackle the problem of increasing turnout among the disadvantaged in the United States. By all means, registration should be made as easy as possible—through election day registration, mail-in registration, sign-ups at public facilities like libraries and public assistance offices, or whatever format seems most applicable in a given local environment. But even universal registration, assuming such a thing were politically possible, should not be regarded as a panacea. In the absence of other changes in the political environment, there is no reason to suppose that the complete removal of registration barriers would have any consistent effect on election outcomes, other than to increase the volatility of the results from one election to the next. To the extent that the Republicans are disadvantaged by the prevailing party balance in subpresidential voting, they should have little to fear from attempts to stimulate turnout in the aggregate.

The surest route to empowerment of the disadvantaged is not through registration per se, but through organizations that link habitual nonvoters to the political world. If parties and candidates fail to reach many potential voters, then relying on community organizations may prove more effective. Target groups need to be identified and associated with organizational infrastructures: schools for reaching the young; senior citizen centers for the elderly; churches and civil rights groups for blacks; labor unions for blue-collar workers; tenant associations, environmental groups, farm organizations, and so on (for some examples drawn from case studies, see Cavanagh 1987; Kimball 1972; and Nelson and Meranto 1977).

Both scholars and activists would do well to heed another implication of this analysis: we need to expand our focus beyond presidential elections if we are to understand the dynamics of voter turnout. Turnout matters far more in local elections, where participation levels tend to be very low, and politically distinctive subpopulations are likely to loom larger in the electoral equation than is generally the case in national elections. Scholars can best enrich our understanding of the influences of the political environment on turnout by studying a variety of such environments. Comparative state- and city-level research designs, employing both qualitative and quantitative techniques—a sort of home-grown analog to the multicountry research designs common in comparative politics—are the most promising route to comprehending the full range of variation in American turnout patterns.

But even more important, activists may have more success in enhancing participation by channeling it toward local concerns. The response of local office-holders to constituent input is often far more visible and immediate than the response to attempts to change the course of events in Washington. The link between participation and policy-making is ultimately the most important reason for studying political activity, as well as for undertaking it. By shifting the focus closer to home, we may come closer to a true understanding of the forces that condition the level of voter participation in America.

REFERENCES

Abramson, Paul R., and John H. Aldrich. 1982. "The Decline of Electoral Participation in America." *American Political Science Review* 76:502–521.

Ashenfelter, Orley, and Stanley Kelley, Jr. 1975. "Determinants of Participation in Presidential Elections." *Journal of Law and Economics* 18:695–731.

Brody, Richard A. 1978. "The Puzzle of Political Participation in America." In *The New American Political System*, ed. Anthony King. Washington, D.C.: American Enterprise Institute.

Buder, Leonard. 1989a. "Local Boards Often Fail to Reflect Schools." *New York Times*, February 16.

Buder, Leonard. 1989b. "School Boards: More Women, Fewer Incumbents." *New York Times*, June 11.

Burnham, Walter Dean. 1974. "The United States: The Politics of Heterogeneity." In *Electoral Behavior*, ed. Richard Rose. New York: Free Press.

Burnham, Walter Dean. 1982. *The Current Crisis in American Politics*. New York: Oxford University Press.

Campbell, James E. 1985. "Sources of the New Deal Realignment: The Contributions of Conversion and Mobilization to Partisan Change." *Western Political Quarterly* 38:357–376.

Cassel, Carol A., and David B. Hill. 1981. "Explanations of Turnout Decline: A Multivariate Test." *American Politics Quarterly* 9:181–195.

Cassel, Carol A., and Robert C. Luskin. 1988. "Simple Explanations of Turnout Decline." *American Political Science Review* 82:1321–1330.

Cavanagh, Thomas E. 1981. "Changes in American Voter Turnout, 1964–1976." *Political Science Quarterly* 96:53–66.

Cavanagh, Thomas E. 1985. *Inside Black America*. Washington, D.C.: Joint Center for Political Studies.

Cavanagh, Thomas E., ed. 1987. *Strategies for Mobilizing Black Voters*. Washington, D.C.: Joint Center for Political Studies.

Cox, Gary W., and Michael C. Munger. 1989. "Closeness, Expenditures, and Turnout in the 1982 U.S. House Elections." *American Political Science Review* 83:217–231.

DeNardo, James. 1980. "Turnout and the Vote: The Joke's on the Democrats." *American Political Science Review* 74:406–420.

Jensen, Richard J. 1971. *The Winning of the Midwest*. Chicago: University of Chicago Press.

Karnig, Albert K., and B. Oliver Walter. 1986. "Municipal Voter Turnout: A Longtitudinal View." Presented at the annual meeting of the American Political Science Association, Washington, D.C.

Kelley, Stanley, Jr., Richard E. Ayres, and William G. Bowen. 1967. "Registration and Voting: Putting First Things First." *American Political Science Review* 61:359–379.

Key, V. O., Jr. 1949. *Southern Politics*. New York: Alfred A. Knopf.

Key, V. O., Jr. 1966. *The Responsible Electorate*. Cambridge, Mass.: Belknap Press.

Kim, Jae-On, John R. Petrocik, and Stephen N. Enokson. 1975. "Voter Turnout Among the American States: Systemic and Individual Components." *American Political Science Review* 69:107–131.

Kimball, Penn. 1972. *The Disconnected*. New York: Columbia University Press.

Kleppner, Paul. 1979. *The Third Electoral System, 1853–1892*. Chapel Hill, N.C.: University of North Carolina Press.

Kleppner, Paul. 1982. *Who Voted?* New York: Praeger.

Kleppner, Paul. 1985. *Chicago Divided*. DeKalb, Ill.: Northern Illinois University Press.

Kousser, J. Morgan. 1974. *The Shaping of Southern Politics*. New Haven, Conn.: Yale University Press.

Marquette, Jesse F., and Katherine A. Hinckley. 1988. "Voter Turnout and Candidate Choice: A Merged Theory." *Political Behavior* 10:52–76.

Nelson, William E., Jr. 1982. "Cleveland: The Rise and Fall of the New Black Politics." In *The New Black Politics*, eds. Michael B. Preston, Lenneal J. Henderson, Jr., and Paul Puryear. New York: Longman.

Nelson, William E., Jr., and Philip J. Meranto. 1977. *Electing Black Mayors*. Columbus, Ohio: Ohio State University Press.

Patterson, Samuel C., and Gregory A. Caldeira. 1983. "Getting Out the Vote: Participation in Gubernatorial Elections." *American Political Science Review* 77:675–689.

Petrocik, John R. 1987. "Voter Turnout and Electoral Preference: The Anomalous Reagan Elections." In *Elections in America*, ed. Kay Lehman Schlozman. Boston: Allen and Unwin.

Piven, Frances Fox, and Richard A. Cloward. 1985. "Prospects for Voter Registration Reform: A Report on the Experiences of the Human SERVE Campaign." *PS* 18:582–593.

Piven, Frances Fox, and Richard A. Cloward. 1988. *Why Americans Don't Vote*. New York: Pantheon Books.

Powell, G. Bingham. 1980. "Voting Turnout in Thirty Democracies: Partisan, Legal, and Socio-Economic Influences." In *Electoral Participation*, ed. Richard Rose. Beverly Hills, Calif.: Sage.

Powell, G. Bingham. 1986. "American Voter Turnout in Comparative Perspective." *American Political Science Review* 79:17–43.

Preston, Michael B. 1984. "The Resurgence of Black Voting in Chicago: 1955–1983." In *The Making of the Mayor: Chicago, 1983*, eds. Melvin G. Holli and Paul M. Green. Grand Rapids, Mich.: William B. Eerdmans.

Reiter, Howard L. 1979. "Why is Turnout Down?" *Public Opinion Quarterly* 43:297–311.

Rose, Richard. 1974. "Comparability in Electoral Studies." In *Electoral Behavior*, ed. Richard Rose. New York: Free Press.

Salmore, Stephen A., and Barbara G. Salmore. 1985. *Candidates, Parties, and Campaigns*. Washington, D.C.: Congressional Quarterly Press.

Smolka, Richard G. 1977. *Election Day Registration*. Washington, D.C.: American Enterprise Institute.

Tuchman, Barbara W. 1962. *The Guns of August*. New York: Macmillan.

U.S. Bureau of the Census. 1987. Voting and Registration in the Election of November 1986. *Current Population Reports*. Ser. P–20, no. 414. Washington, D.C.: U.S. Government Printing Office.

U.S. Bureau of the Census. 1989. Voting and Registration in the Election of November 1988 (Advance Report). *Current Population Reports*. Ser. P–20, no. 435. Washington, D.C.: U.S. Government Printing Office.

Wolfinger, Raymond E., and Steven J. Rosenstone. 1980. *Who Votes?* New Haven, Conn.: Yale University Press.

5 Legal-Institutional Factors and Voting Participation: The Impact of Women's Suffrage on Voter Turnout
Jerrold G. Rusk and John J. Stucker

The historical impact which the adoption and alteration of suffrage laws have had on electoral patterns in the United States is a topic which has received far less attention than it deserves. It is true that a number of scholars have, in recent years, investigated the electoral consequences of legal factors; however, most of this work has been focused on contemporary electoral processes, and very few analysts have explored these relationships in a historical framework.[1]

The general disregard students of electoral phenomena have shown for the impact of legal reforms on their subject matter, particularly from a historical perspective, is unfortunate on several grounds. First, these legal artifacts have, for the most part, served as the main devices for defining who is allowed to participate in the balloting process and the circumstances under which that participation may take place. In that sense they have established the systemic parameters within which the much-analyzed (individual level) social-psychological antecedents of voting behavior function. Accordingly, we believe they should receive the attention they deserve as independent predictors of electoral patterns.

With respect to the study of historical suffrage patterns, the lack of concern for institutional factors becomes particularly ironic. The size and shape of the American electorate has been a matter of interest to political analysts for a number of years, and much of this work has focused on the dramatic changes in the level of participation between the nineteenth and twentieth centuries.[2] Few of the explanations offered for this phenomenon, however, have considered a possible role for electoral laws even though this was a period of intense legislative activity regarding

114   Jerrold G. Rusk and John J. Stucker

Table 5.1
A Typology of Election Laws

Substantive Qualifications	Procedural Qualifications	Balloting Process
religion	registration system	ballot form
property ownership	poll tax	ballot type (machine
tax payer	literacy test	vs. paper ballots)
race		absentee balloting
citizenship		release time
residency		assistance to voters
Indian suffrage		(for illiterates,
sex		the unsophisticated,
age		the blind, etc.)
criminals, insane		procedures for chal-
paupers		lenging voters

suffrage regulations.[3] Finally, the manner in which these statutory changes were adopted provides an excellent opportunity for the application of the time series analysis design which has been too infrequently employed in electoral research.[4]

The objective of this chapter is to suggest a set of research strategies which the authors believe will be useful in filling some of the gaps mentioned above. First, we discuss the type of election laws we will investigate and describe a formal model which accounts for the effects these laws have on individual citizens. Next, we take up the question of how historical electoral participation has been measured in the past and then discuss some alternative approaches to measuring this concept. Then, we present an aggregate level generalization of the formal model in order to explain how these legal changes impact on electoral patterns. Finally, we present an outline of our analytic framework and the results of our various analyses.

THE EFFECTS OF LEGAL ARTIFACTS ON VOTING BEHAVIOR

In order to determine the manner in which suffrage laws affect electoral patterns, we must necessarily begin by defining the election laws and the electoral patterns with which we are concerned. We will take up election laws in this section. In another work on this subject the authors have developed a typology of election laws which differentiates between voter qualifications and laws which regulate the balloting process itself, and then subdivides voter qualifications into substantive and procedural criteria (see table 5.1).[5] In this paper we will be concerned with substantive voter qualifications; these are the provisions of the law which define the personal attributes a person must possess in order to be admitted to the polling booth. Some examples of substantive qualifications which have appeared on the statute books over time include criteria based on sex, religion, property ownership, residency, age, citizenship, and race.[6] In general, the history of substantive voter qualifications in this country has been marked by the gradual elimination of restrictive provisions until today the only substantive requirements which remain are that a person be an 18-year-old citizen who has lived at his or her current residence for a relatively short period of time (one to two months).

As successive changes in voting laws were adopted, expanding the pool of eligible electors, what effect did this have on the individuals involved? William McPhee has proposed a formal model, based on learning theory, which he uses to explain the development of stable partisan voting patterns.[7] If we substitute a few terms, it should be possible to use this same model to explain how it is that an individual learns whether or not to participate in the electoral process at all (regardless of which partisan group he or she learns to support). Simply put, McPhee's model states that each citizen embarks on a political life with a prior probability that he or she will participate as a voter and that this probability increases throughout that individual's life cycle each time he or she exercises the franchise (and conversely decreases each time he or she abstains). The value of the initial prior probability is a function of both the general societal norms regarding who should vote and the specific role models which have been provided by the individual's parents.

In considering how this model should operate when the franchise is extended to a new group in the population, we will use as an example the adoption of women's suffrage. When females were inducted into the electorate, they should all, regardless of age, have possessed the same prior probability since this would have been the first opportunity for all of them to vote; and this probability should have been low, owing to the lack of appropriate role models (specifically mothers, sisters, aunts, etc. who had voted), as well as to the long-standing norms against women participating in politics. After women's suffrage was implemented, the older cohorts of women who were socialized in the era before women's suffrage became a popular issue should have retained low probabilities and, in fact, did participate at very modest levels throughout their lives. Succeeding cohorts, however, should have entered the electorate with surprisingly higher prior probabilities of voting as role models became more numerous and social mores shifted in favor of women participating in politics.

The question remains, however, what effect will all these individual level changes have at the system level, that is, what will be the level of electoral participation before, during, and after a change such as the enfranchisement of women? For this answer, we must turn to a consid-

Figure 5.1
Presidential Turnout Estimates

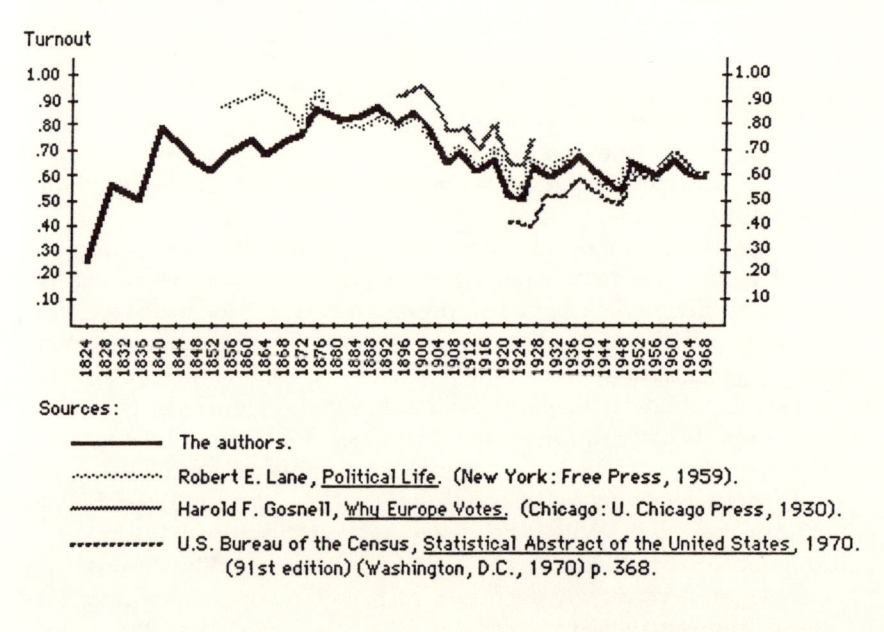

Sources:
──────── The authors.
············ Robert E. Lane, Political Life. (New York: Free Press, 1959).
──────── Harold F. Gosnell, Why Europe Votes. (Chicago: U. Chicago Press, 1930).
─ ─ ─ ─ ─ U.S. Bureau of the Census, Statistical Abstract of the United States, 1970. (91st edition) (Washington, D.C., 1970) p. 368.

eration of the manner in which we measure the concept of electoral participation.

MEASURING ELECTORAL PARTICIPATION

The question of electoral participation levels in the United States has been a matter of lively interest to students of American politics for many decades now, and the most studied aspect of this phenomenon has been the secular change in participation rates which has been traced through the late nineteenth and early twentieth centuries. According to these studies, the level of participation was remarkably high and stable throughout most of the nineteenth century; however, in the last decade of that century a decline set in which continued into the early decades of the twentieth century and which has resulted in an overall lower level of voter participation in this century. Figure 5.1 contains several series of turnout estimates generated by various authors which have been used to demonstrate the phenomenon described in the previous sentence. It is interesting to note that the method used by all of these authors to trace this empirical phenomenon has been the traditional measure of voter turnout:

$$T = \frac{\text{number of votes cast}}{\text{number of legally eligible electors}}$$

Based on Donald Campbell's multitrait, multimethod matrix approach to research design,[8] the question must be asked—is turnout the only appropriate and meaningful measure of the concept of electoral participation? Walter Dean Burnham has given a partial answer to this question by suggesting four additional measures of electoral behavior, two of which speak directly to the concept of the level of participation, while the other two deal with the tangential issue of the quality of that participation.[9] Adam Przeworski and John Sprague have subsequently offered several additional operationalizations of participation.[10] Of the measures proposed by Przeworski and Sprague, the most interesting for our purposes is the one termed mobilization, and it is defined as:

$$M = \frac{\text{number of votes cast}}{\text{number of adults}}$$

The reason we find this particular measure so interesting is twofold. In the first instance, there is virtually no census data available which permits one to accurately separate out aliens as opposed to citizens in the adult male population prior to the census of 1870. Accordingly, it is not possible to extract alien male adults from the denominator of the turnout index prior to 1870 while after 1870 it is possible to make this adjustment. Given this shift in the composition of the turnout index, it appears to be a somewhat risky proposition to utilize a turnout series which spans the 1870 time point.

An even more important reason for considering the mobilization index, however, relates to the question posed earlier: how do legal changes affect aggregate electoral patterns? The answer to this question ultimately depends on how one has measured participation. Since turnout and mobilization each measure a different aspect of the concept, electoral participation, the simultaneous use of these two measures makes it possible to observe the differential effects which changes in suffrage laws can have on this phenomenon.

A FORMAL SYSTEM MODEL

In their analysis of voting patterns, Stanley Kelley and his associates employed Anthony Downs's "opportunity cost" model to explain the differences in aggregate voting behavior which are brought about by the differential application of procedural voter qualifications, specifically

118 Jerrold G. Rusk and John J. Stucker

Table 5.2
Hypothetical Data on Voting and Eligibility for Five Elections Before and Five Elections After the Adoption of Women's Suffrage

		Men Only Eligible to Vote					Women and Men Eligible to Vote				
		E_{-5}	E_{-4}	E_{-3}	E_{-2}	E_{-1}	E_{+1}	E_{+2}	E_{+3}	E_{+4}	E_{+5}
Votes Cast	Males	80	80	80	80	80	80	80	80	80	80
	Females	-	-	-	-	-	20	25	35	45	60
	Both Sexes	80	80	80	80	80	100	105	115	125	140
Number of Persons Eligible		100	100	100	100	100	200	200	200	200	200
Number of Adults		200	200	200	200	200	200	200	200	200	200

(Adoption of Woman Suffrage between E_{-1} and E_{+1}.)

voter registration systems.[11] A similar generalization of the McPhee model will help us to explain the effects which changes in substantive voter qualifications have on aggregate electoral patterns.

According to McPhee's model, we would expect that a group of newly enfranchised individuals will not exercise the franchise with the same degree of intensity as those members of the citizenry who are experienced electors. Now let us assume a political system which is completely stable. In this political system there are 100 adult males and 100 adult females. As the hypothetical data in table 5.2 indicate, during the five elections before (E_{-5} to E_{-1}) and the five elections after (E_{+1} to E_{+5}) the adoption of women's suffrage, 80 of the 100 men voted in each election. When the women became enfranchised, however, only 20 of them voted in the first election in which they were eligible. According to McPhee's model, though, with each successive election more and more women should show up at the polls so that by the fifth election after women's suffrage, we would expect, for example, 60 out of the 100 women to be participating.

Looking at the turnout trendlines by sex (see figure 5.2), we see the differential turnout rates for each group. When these rates are combined into a single trendline for the entire electorate (see figure 5.3), we note that turnout drops precipitously after the enfranchisement of women but then gradually begins to move up again. This results from the fact that during the transition from E_{-1} to E_{+1}, the denominator of the turn-

Figure 5.2
Turnout Trendlines by Sex

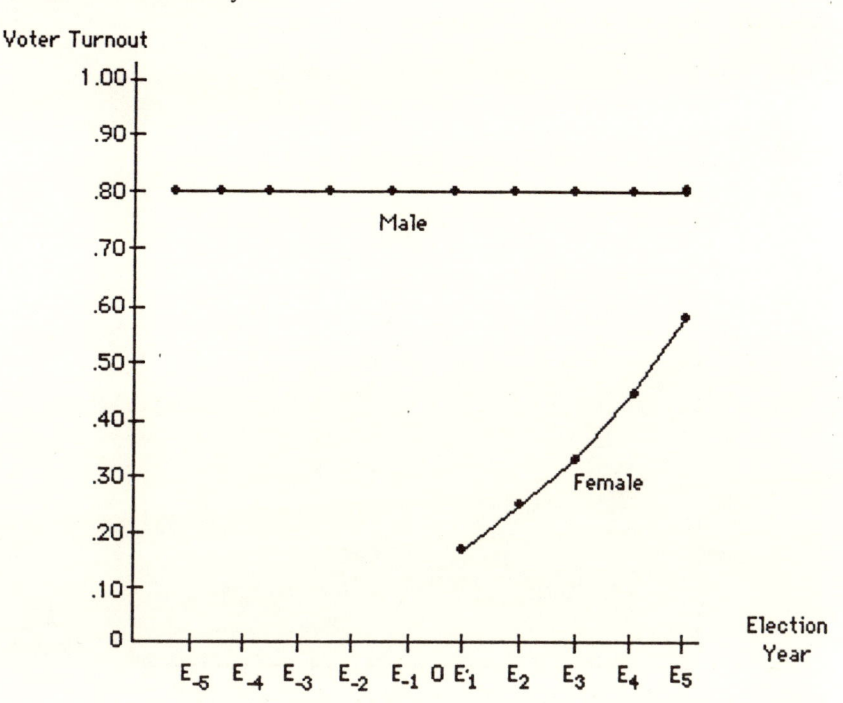

out index has doubled, while the numerator has not grown by nearly the same amount. Turnout measures the proportion of those eligible by law to vote who actually do vote, and it is simply the case that a smaller proportion of the eligibles are participating after women are added to the numerator and the denominator of this index. In the years following the enfranchisement of women, however, the turnout rate slowly rises as women gradually increase their rate of participation.

In the case of the mobilization index, we would expect a reversal of the patterns shown by the turnout index after women are enfranchised. Since mobilization measures participation as the ratio of the total number of votes cast over the total number of adults in society, the denominator of the mobilization index remains constant through both the before and after time periods of women suffrage enactment (i.e., at 200 adults). As the hypothetical data in figure 5.4 show, when only men are allowed to vote and only 80 of those actually show up at the polls, the mobilization rate is 40 percent, but when women are inducted into the electorate, the mobilization rate increases because even though only a handful of women might participate, any increment in the total number of voters, no matter how small, will push the mobilization index upward.

Figure 5.3
Overall Turnout Trendline for Periods Before and After Women's Suffrage Adoption

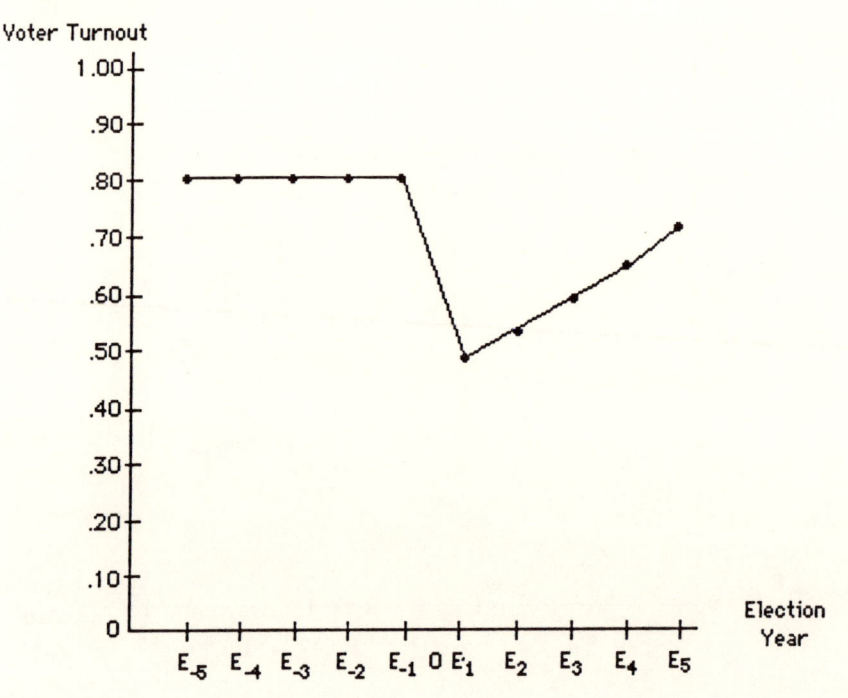

In subsequent election years, the mobilization index continues to rise as more and more women participate in the election process.

Of course, we are dealing with a hypothetical election system in this example, and we do not expect data from the real world to exhibit such clearcut patterns. But the essential point remains. Extensions of the franchise should inevitably show a decline in participation when this concept is measured with a turnout index. If, on the other hand, one employs the mobilization index, the data will normally reveal that the vigor and intensity of democratic participation have been enhanced whenever a new group has been inducted into the electorate.

FRAMEWORK FOR ANALYSIS

The analysis reported in this chapter is concerned with the effects of the enfranchisement of women into the American electorate, a process which occurred in the decades surrounding the turn of this century. In exploring the effects of women's suffrage on voter participation, we will measure the dependent variable three different ways: (1) the turnout index for presidential elections,

Figure 5.4
Mobilization Trendline for Periods Before and After Women's Suffrage Adoption

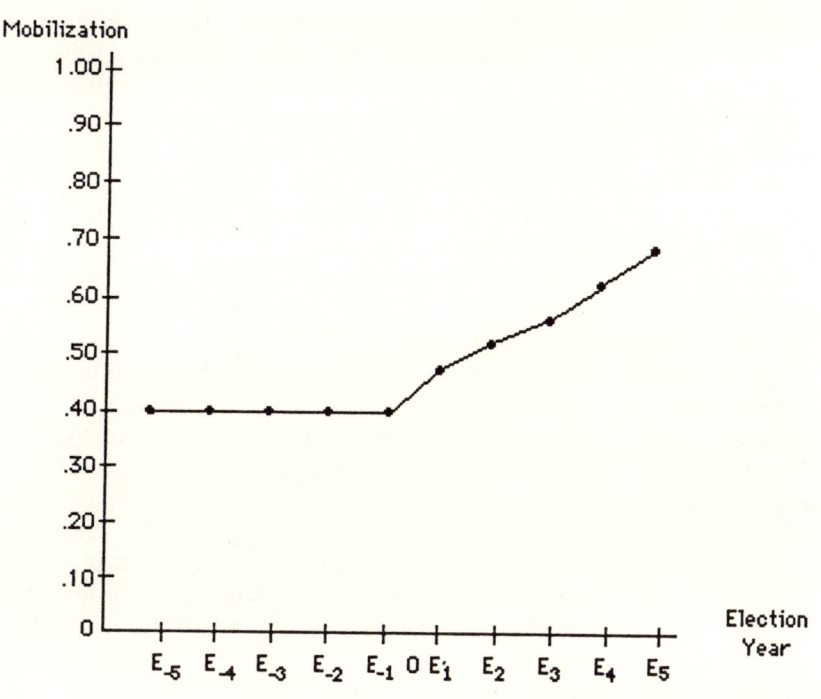

[Graph: Mobilization (y-axis, 0 to 1.00) vs. Election Year (x-axis, E_{-5} to E_5). Line is flat at .40 from E_{-5} through E_{-1}, then rises through 0, E_1, E_2, E_3, E_4, E_5 reaching approximately .68.]

$$T_p = \frac{\text{total votes cast for president}}{\text{total persons eligible to vote for president}}$$

(2) the mobilization index for presidential elections,

$$M_p = \frac{\text{total votes cast for president}}{\text{total adults}}$$

and (3) the turnout index for congressional voting in off-year elections,

$$T_c = \frac{\text{total votes cast for congressional candidates}}{\text{total persons eligible to vote for congressional candidates}}$$

The basic framework for our analysis has been adopted from Donald Campbell's model for quasi-experimental design.[12] Campbell has suggested that some of those elements of the experimental approach to data collection which aid in establishing causal linkages between variables can be approximated by the field analyst in a quasi-experimental design. One aspect of this approach deals with the question of the temporal sequencing of the factors under investigation. If changes in suffrage laws cause changes in voting patterns, then we must have a way of demonstrating that the laws changed before the electoral pattern did.

Since we have available a series of repeated measurements of our dependent variable, both before and after the change in the independent variable, we can adopt Campbell's concept of the interrupted time series to show the level of voter participation for a given period of time before the suffrage law is changed and then the level of participation which results after the legal change has occurred. If the level of participation shifts substantially between the "before" and "after" periods, then we can be reasonably confident that the legal change did, in fact, temporally precede the behavioral change.

A second aspect of the quasi-experimental design involves the concept of randomization. In the experimental design, the researcher randomizes the selection of subjects so as to control for extraneous variables which might confound (and thereby obscure) the expected relationship between independent and dependent variables. In the quasi-experimental design, Campbell suggests a randomization of the treatment effect (i.e., the occurrence of the independent variable), if possible, in order to accomplish the same goal.

The historical analysis of suffrage law changes offers a unique opportunity to employ this randomization of treatment effects procedure. The Constitution delegates to the states the responsibility for regulating the franchise. As a consequence of this diffusion of authority, equivalent changes in suffrage laws usually occur in different states at different points in time. We have incorporated this variance in changes in the independent variable across time and use it in our data matrix in order to achieve at least a modest degree of control over those short-term factors which might influence the level of participation in a given election in a particular state or region of the country.

In constructing our analysis data frame, we begin with a data matrix in which the presidential turnout value is recorded for each presidential election year in which the state was a member of the Union from 1824 to 1968 (see table 5.3).[13] We then extract for each state a series of twenty data points beginning with the turnout value of the tenth presidential election before women were granted the vote and continuing up to the tenth election after the legal change occurred. These data series are inserted into what we call a quasi-experimental time frame (see table 5.4). The resulting data matrix contains twenty variables, defined as E_{-10}, E_{-9}, E_{-8} and so on up to E_{+9}, and E_{+10}, for forty-eight cases (states).[14] This same procedure is then applied to the other two measures of the dependent variable, the M_p and the T_c indices. It can, of course, also be employed to investigate the effects of changes in other substantive voter qualifications.

Legal-Institutional Factors 123

Table 5.3
Example of Real Time Data Frame

	Presidential Turnout by Election Year						
State	1824	1828	1832		1960	1964	1968
State₁							
State₂							
State₃							
⋮	⋮	⋮			⋮	⋮	⋮
State₄₉							
State₅₀							

THE EFFECTS OF WOMEN'S SUFFRAGE: PAIRED COMPARISONS

Our initial approach to the data consists of some basic before/after comparisons which lend themselves to visual inspection in order to observe the effects of women's suffrage. We begin this discussion with reference to the results contained in table 5.5. These values are mean difference scores for all the states derived by subtracting the average of the two elections immediately preceding the adoption of women's suffrage from the average of the two elections after the legal change and then obtaining the mean of these difference scores across all the states. A minus sign indicates that the value of the participation index declined from the period before to the period after the enfranchisement of women, while a plus sign denotes an increase in the index between the two time periods.

We have compared pairs of elections rather than individual elections in order to average out the short-term effects which might be operative in a single election. At first glance it would appear that this type of control function should have been accomplished by the randomization process described earlier. In the case of women's suffrage, however, we felt it wise to bolster the effects of this procedure somewhat. Since approximately two-thirds of the states did not admit women into their electorates until the passage of the Nineteenth Amendment in 1920, for the majority of the cases we are working with the quasi-experimental (Q-E) time frame is identical to the real time matrix from which it was drawn. Accordingly, the effects of the randomization process in the quasi-experimental design are attenuated in the case of women's suffrage.

We have limited our averaging technique to two election years in

Table 5.4
Quasi-Experimental Time Frame

	Change in Suffrage Laws		
	Elections Before Change		Elections After Change
	E_{-10} E_{-9} E_{-8} E_{-7} E_{-6} E_{-5} E_{-4} E_{-3} E_{-2} E_{-1}		E_{+1} E_{+2} E_{+3} E_{+4} E_{+5} E_{+6} E_{+7} E_{+8} E_{+9} E_{+10}
$State_1$			
$State_2$			
$State_3$			
$State_{40}$			
$State_{50}$			

Table 5.5
Mean Difference Scores

Presidential Turnout	-.097
Presidential Mobilization	.171
Off-Year Congressional Turnout	-.104

NOTES:

1. Between two elections before and two elections after adoption of woman suffrage, for three indices of voter participation, averaged across states.

2. $$\frac{(\bar{E}_{+1,+2}) - (\bar{E}_{-1,-2})}{N}$$

accordance with the logic expressed by Donald Campbell in his article, "Reforms as Experiments."[15] In discussing techniques for studying the impact of legal changes on aggregate data patterns, Campbell says: "It is only abrupt and decisive changes that we have any chance of evaluating. A gradually introduced reform will be indistinguishable from the background of secular change, from the net effect of the innumerable change agents continually impinging."[16]

While our emphasis is undoubtedly on the two-election-year paired comparison technique, as shown in table 5.5, we also looked at the results of our averaging technique for three, four, and five elections. As Campbell predicted, it becomes difficult, if not impossible, to observe the effects of women's suffrage on voting in this way since these effects become mixed in with other system effects which are constantly operating and impinging on voter participation.

Considering the results of our two-election-year paired comparison technique in table 5.5, we note that all three of our participation indices behave in the expected manner. Both the presidential and congressional turnout measures declined in value after women joined the electorate, while the mobilization index increased in value. Even more notable, however, is the relative size of the changes in the various indices. Both of the turnout ratios show a decline of approximately 10 percentage points which clearly suggests that the democratic ideal was weakened in practice with the advent of women's suffrage. In contrast, however, the M_p index has increased substantially more than the decline recorded by the two turnout measures. This should lead political scientists to a more positive evaluation about the state of participatory democracy after this particular change in the suffrage laws. We can now see very clearly the importance of Przeworski and Sprague's discussion of the various meanings of voter participation and the necessity for careful measurement and investigation of this phenomenon in all its various dimensions, both historically and with respect to contemporary political events.[17]

Having considered a comparison of the before/after election pairs for each of the three indices, we will now move these paired-comparisons backward and forward across the Q-E time frame in order to observe the mean difference scores for all possible combinations of contiguous sets of two elections. For example, moving backward from the midpoint of the Q-E time frame (table 5.4) involves the comparison of

$$(\overline{E}_{-1,+1}) - (\overline{E}_{-2,-3})$$

and

$$(\overline{E}_{-1,-2}) - (\overline{E}_{-3,-4})$$

and so on up to

$$(\overline{E}_{-7,-8}) - (\overline{E}_{-9,-10}).$$

Similarly, moving forward from the midpoint includes

$$(\overline{E}_{+2,+3}) - (\overline{E}_{-1,+1})$$

and

$$(\overline{E}_{+3,+4}) - (\overline{E}_{+1,+2})$$

and so on up to

$$(\overline{E}_{+9,+10}) - (\overline{E}_{+7,+8}).$$

Our purpose in extending these paired-comparisons across the entire range of the Q-E time frame is to determine if the difference observed across the midpoint of the time frame (i.e., the point at which the suffrage law was changed) is greater than all the other paired-comparison differences which can be derived from the data. If the change in an index pursuant to the adoption of women's suffrage is, in fact, simply a part of a secular trend in that index (see figure 5.5), then the midpoint difference score will not be substantially larger than the other difference scores. If, however, the change in the index is related to, and the result of, the change in the suffrage law (see figure 5.6), the midpoint difference will be the largest, or at least among the largest, of all the difference scores computed.[18]

Figure 5.5
General Secular Decline in Participation Index

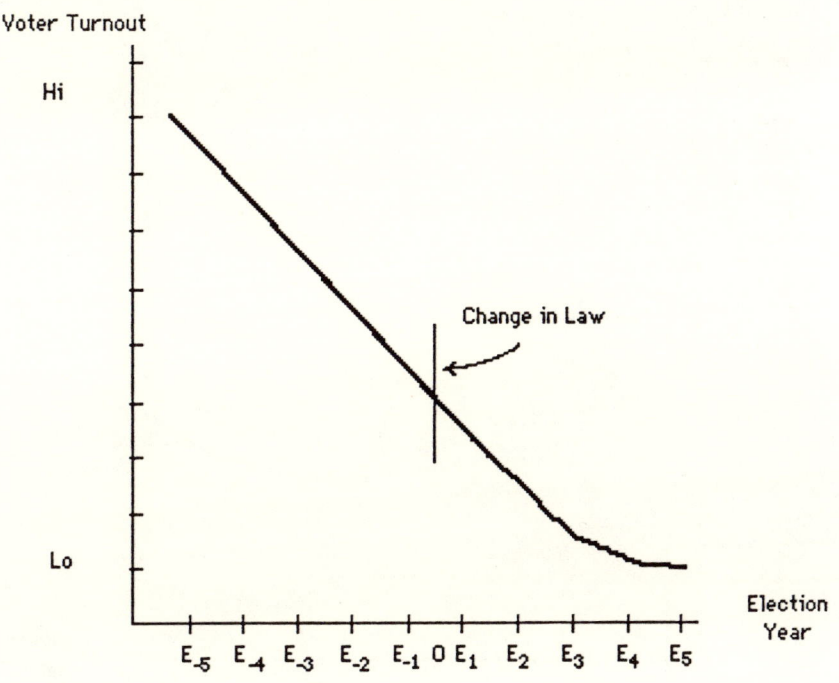

Voter Turnout

[Figure: Downward-sloping curve from Hi to Lo across election years E_{-5} through E_5, with a "Change in Law" marker at the midpoint (0).]

The results of these moving paired-comparisons are given in table 5.6. Several aspects of this table merit comment. Beginning with the T_p measure, it will be noted that while the midpoint difference is not the largest value in the series (it misses first place by .001 points), it clearly stands above most of the other values in the series both before and after women's suffrage reform.

Secondly, in addition to the decline in T_p which is directly associated with the advent of female voting, the reader will also observe two other trends which appear in the data. The first of these is the decline which occurs early in the series and which corresponds to the declining levels of participation in the 1890s and the 1900s to which Burnham and others have referred.[19] The second pattern, which makes its appearance shortly after the change in women's suffrage, is the rise in T_p associated with the Al Smith–New Deal period. Considering the strength of these two trends, which encompass the midpoint period, the reader can now appreciate the validity of Campbell's warning that system effects will inevitably drown out the impact of legal changes and, therefore, make necessary the use of special analysis techniques such as our two-election-year averaging technique for paired-comparisons.

Figure 5.6
General System Stability: Decline in Participation Index Due to Change in Suffrage Law

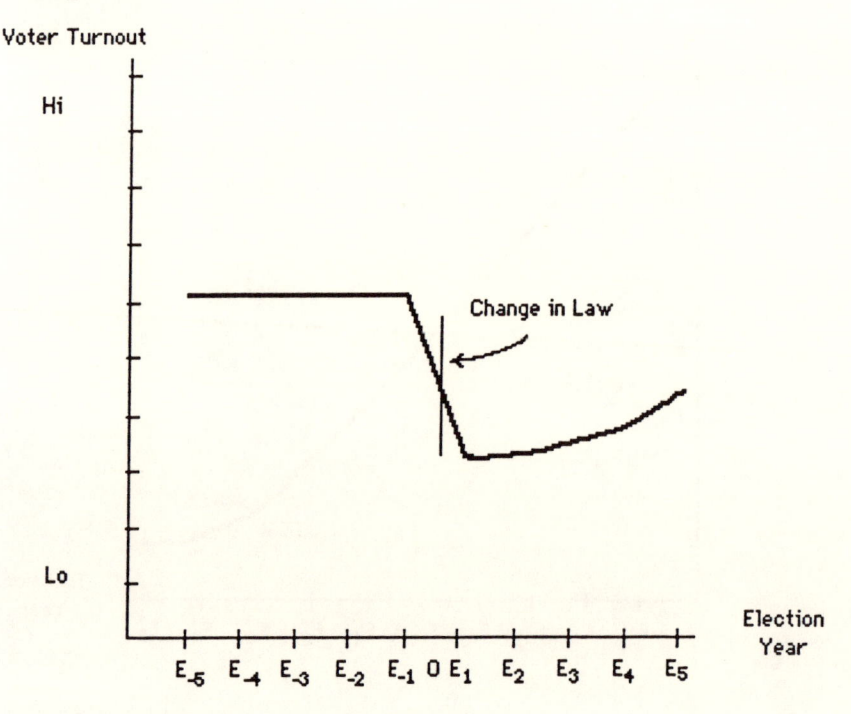

Voter Turnout

Hi

Change in Law

Lo

E_{-5} E_{-4} E_{-3} E_{-2} E_{-1} 0 E_1 E_2 E_3 E_4 E_5 Election Year

With respect to the M_p measure, one can also see the effects of the decline in participation around the turn of the century. What is more notable about this empirical series, however, is the dramatically abrupt manner in which that trend was halted as a result of the enfranchisement of women. The midpoint change of the M_p series is the largest difference score of the crucial midpoints in our three time series. It is, also, by far the largest difference score of all the paired-comparisons in our three time series.

Finally, the patterns exhibited by the T_c index substantially mirror those which we have discussed in the case of the T_p measure. The only significant difference is that this measure shows itself to be susceptible to the surge and decline effects of off-year elections. This phenomenon is most evident in the difference score immediately preceding the midpoint which reflects the very low level of participation in the 1918 congressional election and in the values toward the end of the series which are evidence of the low turnout in the off-year elections during the late Depression and World War II period.

Table 5.6
Average Difference Scores Between Pairs of Elections

		Presidential Turnout	Presidential Mobilization	Off-Year Congressional Turnout
$E_{-7,-8}$	$-E_{-9,-10}$	-.020	-.009	.009
$E_{-6,-7}$	$-E_{-8,-9}$	-.032	-.015	-.019
$E_{-5,-6}$	$-E_{-7,-8}$	-.032	-.015	-.089
$E_{-4,-5}$	$-E_{-6,-7}$	-.073	-.038	-.090
$E_{-3,-4}$	$-E_{-5,-6}$	-.098	-.052	-.051
$E_{-2,-3}$	$-E_{-4,-5}$	-.061	-.033	-.017
$E_{-1,-2}$	$-E_{-3,-4}$	-.026	-.015	-.043
$E_{-1,+1}$	$-E_{-2,-3}$	-.048	.086	-.100
$E_{+1,+2}$	$-E_{-1,-2}$	-.097	.171	-.104
$E_{+2,+3}$	$-E_{+1,-1}$	-.040	.101	-.047
$E_{+3,+4}$	$-E_{+1,+2}$	.046	.055	.042
$E_{+4,+5}$	$-E_{+2,+3}$	.047	.055	.070
$E_{+5,+6}$	$-E_{+3,+4}$	.038	.045	-.014
$E_{+6,+7}$	$-E_{+4,+5}$	.002	.010	-.069
$E_{+7,+8}$	$-E_{+5,+6}$	-.056	-.044	-.005
$E_{+8,+9}$	$-E_{+6,+7}$	-.004	.008	.046
$E_{+9,+10}$	$-E_{+7,+8}$	.075	.085	.037

NOTES:

1. For three indices of voter participation, averaged across all states.

THE EFFECTS OF WOMEN'S SUFFRAGE: REGRESSION ON TIME

We now take up a second analytic approach to the data, as a complement to, rather than as a substitute for, the paired-comparison technique we have just discussed. The paired-comparison results are useful in that they give us an image of the effects of women's suffrage on voter participation in comparison with the effects of other system factors which were operative over a large period in the history of our republic. Now, however, we must employ a technique which will help us to answer the question: were the effects of women's suffrage all that significant? Here we do not mean "significance" in an inferential sense, since we

Table 5.7
Results of Regression-on-Time Analysis for Three Indices of Voter Participation

	$\overline{Y}_{E+1}$	$\tilde{Y}_{E+1}$	$\overline{Y}_{E+1} - \tilde{Y}_{E+1}$	s.e. E_{-10}, E_{-1}
T_p	.564	.517	.047	.195
M_p	.269	.465	.196	.096
T_c	.440	.390	.050	.202

NOTES:

1. Based on data from all the states.

are dealing with population data, but "significance" with regard to whether the change in a given index due to women's suffrage was larger than the change which we would have expected on the basis of the past behavior of the index.

Our methodology in this phase of the analysis involves simple linear regression of each of the three participation indices on time.[20] We have generated three regression equations for the United States as a whole by regressing state values of each of the indices on time measured from E_{-10} to E_{-1}. These equations were then used to generate an estimate of the three different Y values for the time point E_{+1} ($\hat{Y}_{E+1}$). The absolute difference between the $\hat{Y}_{E+1}$ and the average of the state values on each of the three indices for the time point E_{+1} is then calculated

$$|\hat{Y}_{E+1} - \tilde{Y}_{E+1}|$$

This value is compared with the standard error of the estimate from the equations generated (s.e.$_{E-10,E-1}$). If

$$|\hat{Y}_{E+1} - \tilde{Y}_{E+1}| > (s.e._{E-10,E-1}),$$

then we may conclude that the shift in the electoral index after the incorporation of women into the electorate was larger than what we would have expected given a continuation of status quo politics.

The results of these regression analyses are given in table 5.7. When we consider this nationwide data, the results appear quite contradictory. In the case of turnout, both in presidential elections and in off-year congressional races, the changes in the indices are decidedly less than the shifts we might have expected based upon the trends established in the previous ten elections. With respect to M_p, however, the situation is reversed, since the increase in mobilization is substantially outside the limits of expectation based on previous experience.

At this point we shall venture only a limited commentary on these results, pending a more thorough investigation of the data. One reason, and possibly the major reason, for the unimpressive findings with respect to turnout is the fact that both of these indices came into E_{+1} with downward sloping regression lines for the period E_{-10} to E_{-1}, and thus we are caught in the bind to which Campbell referred, whereby the impact of women's suffrage is masked by long-term system effects. On the other hand, the wholly pleasing results from the M_p index not only reinforce the idea that the enfranchisement of women reversed a declining participation pattern, as measured by the M_p factor, but they also lend further support to the notion that we must revise the conventional wisdom about the halting effects of women's suffrage on the vitality of democratic practices in the early twentieth century in the United States.

THE EFFECTS OF WOMEN'S SUFFRAGE: REGIONAL DIFFERENCES

We stated in this chapter that our basic goal was to scratch the surface with respect to the analysis of the relationship between electoral laws and electoral patterns. This much we have accomplished in our presentation of results for the nation as a whole. Before concluding, however, we would like to probe beyond this somewhat by repeating the analyses reported above for different regions of the country. While region is not the only control variable which could be used, we feel it is entirely appropriate since one would expect the effects of women's suffrage, particularly as these relate to other systemic trends noted earlier, to vary from region to region across the nation.

For the following analysis, the states were divided into five separate regions: Northeast, Midwest, Plains, South, and West.[21] The two basic analyses outlined above, the moving paired-comparisons and the regression on time, were then applied to the states in each of these regions. The results of the moving paired-comparisons for each of our three participation indices are given in tables 5.8, 5.9, and 5.10. Considering the T_p index, we note that the Northeast, Midwest, and Plains regions each experienced only a modest decline in turnout during the late nineteenth century. However, when they reach the midpoint comparison, each of these regions shows a sharp decline in T_p. In the South, the most dramatic decline occurs during the 1880s and 1890s; however, there is also a notable decline which takes place at the time women are enfranchised. Finally, the West offers the most curious results, since there is virtually no impact recorded at the midpoint.

With respect to the M_p index by region, shown in table 5.9, the Northeast, Midwest, and Plains once again tend to follow the national pattern beginning with a very modest decline in the 1890–1900 period and then

Table 5.8
Average Difference Scores Between Pairs of Elections

		Northeast	Midwest	Plains	South	West
$E_{-7,-8}$	$-E_{-9,-10}$	-.017	.007	.054	-.061	-.067
$E_{-6,-7}$	$-E_{-8,-9}$	-.011	.004	.014	-.096	-.029
$E_{-5,-6}$	$-E_{-7,-8}$	-.026	.044	.014	-.124	.035
$E_{-4,-5}$	$-E_{-6,-7}$	-.041	-.016	-.014	-.197	-.007
$E_{-3,-4}$	$-E_{-5,-6}$	-.040	-.081	-.086	-.174	-.101
$E_{-2,-3}$	$-E_{-4,-5}$	-.028	-.078	-.070	-.056	-.105
$E_{-1,-2}$	$-E_{-3,-4}$	-.015	-.069	-.033	.000	-.037
$E_{-1,+1}$	$-E_{-2,-3}$	-.065	-.084	-.053	-.017	-.024
$E_{+1,+2}$	$-E_{-1,-2}$	-.134	-.135	-.105	-.091	-.013
$E_{+2,+3}$	$-E_{+1,-1}$	-.008	-.069	-.033	-.065	-.035
$E_{+3,+4}$	$-E_{+1,+2}$	.120	.052	.069	.032	-.033
$E_{+4,+5}$	$-E_{+2,+3}$	.074	.063	.065	.035	.006
$E_{+5,+6}$	$-E_{+3,+4}$	.045	.041	.055	.014	.041
$E_{+6,+7}$	$-E_{+4,+5}$	-.013	-.005	-.017	.003	.034
$E_{+7,+8}$	$-E_{+5,+6}$	-.098	-.090	-.115	-.008	.001
$E_{+8,+9}$	$-E_{+6,+7}$	-.022	-.051	-.027	.066	-.008
$E_{+9,+10}$	$-E_{+7,+8}$	.073	.055	.086	.121	.035

NOTES:

1. For presidential turnout, averaged across states within regions.

exhibiting a very substantial upswing with the advent of women's suffrage. The South, on the other hand, runs against the national pattern. The dominant characteristic of this region's time series is the notable declines which are recorded in the early paired-comparisons, and the fact that these declines are not compensated for by a large increase at the midpoint. Finally, in the West, we note that, unlike the situation with the T_p index, the M_p series shows a striking similarity to the national trend as well as the trendlines of the three non-southern regions.

Finally, we report the T_c values by region in table 5.10. For the most part this table conforms to the patterns which were noted in table 5.8 (the T_p index) for each region with two exceptions. In the case of the Northeast, very few effects of the "System of 1896" are to be observed in this region's T_c series. Secondly, in the four nonwestern regions, the effects of the low-stimulus election of 1918 are once again visible (as they were on the national chart). Despite the empirical proximity of this

Table 5.9
Average Difference Scores Between Pairs of Elections

		Northeast	Midwest	Plains	South	West
$E_{-7,-8}$	$-E_{-9,-10}$	-.008	.003	.026	-.026	-.041
$E_{-6,-7}$	$-E_{-8,-9}$	-.005	.002	.006	-.045	-.015
$E_{-5,-6}$	$-E_{-7,-8}$	-.010	.021	.004	-.061	.017
$E_{-4,-5}$	$-E_{-6,-7}$	-.021	-.008	-.017	-.097	-.004
$E_{-3,-4}$	$-E_{-5,-6}$	-.027	-.042	-.047	-.086	-.053
$E_{-2,-3}$	$-E_{-4,-5}$	-.020	-.045	-.035	-.028	-.055
$E_{-1,-2}$	$-E_{-3,-4}$	-.008	-.040	-.015	.000	-.025
$E_{-1,+1}$	$-E_{-2,-3}$	.094	.105	.110	.044	.092
$E_{+1,+2}$	$-E_{-1,-2}$	.186	.226	.221	.050	.213
$E_{+2,+3}$	$-E_{+1,-1}$	.159	.122	.143	.012	.086
$E_{+3,+4}$	$-E_{+1,+2}$	.121	.062	.080	.033	-.015
$E_{+4,+5}$	$-E_{+2,+3}$	.086	.072	.073	.036	.021
$E_{+5,+6}$	$-E_{+3,+4}$	.061	.050	.059	.014	.049
$E_{+6,+7}$	$-E_{+4,+5}$	.009	.005	-.013	.003	.039
$E_{+7,+8}$	$-E_{+5,+6}$	.066	-.076	-.105	-.009	.010
$E_{+8,+9}$	$-E_{+6,+7}$	.007	-.037	-.018	.066	.006
$E_{+9,+10}$	$-E_{+7,+8}$	.092	.064	.092	.123	.049

NOTES:

1. For presidential mobilization, averaged across states within regions.

decline to the midpoint comparison, however, the effects of women's suffrage are still evident in these regions and appear to be substantial.

The results of the regression analysis by region are reported in table 5.11. Space considerations will allow us to make only a few brief comments on this table. With respect to the two turnout indices, it is interesting to note that for the South and the West the s.e.$_{E-10, E-1}$ is far in excess of the $\hat{Y}_{E+1} - \hat{Y}_{E+1}$ difference score, whereas for the other three regions (with the slight exception of the Plains T_c index) the reverse is true, showing the strong impact of women's suffrage in these three regions. When we observe the M_p indices, however, we note that the infusion of women voters shows a large increase in participation across all five regions.

Probably the most notable aspect of this table, however, lies not in the results themselves, but rather in the correspondence which these results show with those derived from the paired-comparisons technique

Table 5.10
Average Difference Scores Between Pairs of Elections

		Northeast	Midwest	Plains	South	West
$E_{-7,-8}$	$-E_{-9,-10}$	-.029	.036	.071	-.041	-.046
$E_{-6,-7}$	$-E_{-8,-9}$	-.000	-.014	.013	-.065	-.020
$E_{-5,-6}$	$-E_{-7,-8}$	-.043	-.073	-.085	-.176	.020
$E_{-4,-5}$	$-E_{-6,-7}$	-.009	-.113	-.096	-.168	-.057
$E_{-3,-4}$	$-E_{-5,-6}$	.012	-.093	-.052	-.074	-.092
$E_{-2,-3}$	$-E_{-4,-5}$	.002	-.014	-.004	-.005	-.109
$E_{-1,-2}$	$-E_{-3,-4}$	-.058	-.026	-.040	-.030	-.060
$E_{-1,+1}$	$-E_{-2,-3}$	-.157	-.138	-.111	-.063	-.002
$E_{+1,+2}$	$-E_{-1,-2}$	-.151	-.174	-.105	-.064	-.031
$E_{+2,+3}$	$-E_{+1,-1}$	-.034	-.058	-.053	-.027	-.077
$E_{+3,+4}$	$-E_{+1,+2}$	.092	.082	.057	.028	-.031
$E_{+4,+5}$	$-E_{+2,+3}$	.134	.113	.110	.017	.004
$E_{+5,+6}$	$-E_{+3,+4}$	-.007	-.014	-.021	-.033	.005
$E_{+6,+7}$	$-E_{+4,+5}$	-.130	-.097	-.120	-.032	.010
$E_{+7,+8}$	$-E_{+5,+6}$	-.024	.016	-.052	.027	-.011
$E_{+8,+9}$	$-E_{+6,+7}$	.072	.065	.049	.073	-.022
$E_{+9,+10}$	$-E_{+7,+8}$	.043	.012	.034	.050	.040

NOTES:

1. For off-year congressional turnout, averaged across states, within regions.

applied to the regions. According to Campbell's multitrait, multimethod matrix approach to research design,[22] such a tidy state of empirical affairs would suggest that we are on to something solid when we assert that the incorporation of women into the electorate will, all things being equal (which they obviously are not in all regions of the country), lead to a decline in turnout and an increase in the rate of mobilization.

CONCLUSIONS

We do not feel it is necessary to reemphasize that the analysis reported in this chapter was meant to be suggestive rather than definitive. With respect to women's suffrage, more work must be done to determine why this variable shows so little impact in certain regions of the country, particularly in the West. In researching this point it may be helpful to

Table 5.11
Regression-on-Time Analysis for Three Indices of Voter Participation, Within Regions

	$\hat{Y}_{E_{+1}}$	$\bar{Y}_{E_{+1}}$	$\left\| \hat{Y}_{E_{+1}} - \bar{Y}_{E_{+1}} \right\|$	s.e.$_{E_{-10}, E_{-1}}$
Presidential Turnout				
Northeast	.676	.561	.115	.107
Midwest	.784	.650	.134	.073
Plains	.723	.610	.113	.084
South	.169	.221	.052	.167
West	.587	.615	.028	.085
Presidential Mobilization				
Northeast	.278	.473	.195	.056
Midwest	.373	.598	.225	.044
Plains	.356	.575	.218	.045
South	.089	.216	.126	.083
West	.318	.541	.223	.057
Congressional Turnout				
Northeast	.585	.441	.144	.116
Midwest	.563	.418	.145	.104
Plains	.550	.483	.066	.084
South	.068	.109	.042	.174
West	.497	.534	.037	.089

use additional measures of the dependent variable, voter participation. In conjunction with region as a control variable, it would be interesting to control for other factors, such as urban-rural residency or percentage foreign-born. It should be noted, however, that these controls would require the use of county-level data which is considerably more difficult to work with when it comes to building our various participation indices.

Beyond the question of women's suffrage, we are currently working on the application of the conceptual and analytic models described in this chapter to changes which have occurred in other substantive voter qualifications over the past 200 years. In addition, we eventually hope to apply the Downsian model to several of the procedural voter qualifications which were first implemented in the nineteenth century.

Finally, we plan to improve our analytic approach to the data by adopting more sophisticated techniques for time series analysis. It is our hope and expectation that these future efforts will help to decipher some of the often discussed but seldom explained patterns of behavior which characterized the American electorate during previous periods in our nation's history.

NOTES

1. Several examples of work dealing with the relationship between suffrage laws and electoral patterns are: Donald Matthews and James Prothro, *Negroes and the New Southern Politics* (New York: Harcourt Brace and World, 1966); Stanley Kelley, Jr. et al., "Registration and Voting: Putting First Things First," *American Political Science Review* 61 (June 1967): 359–379; Jack L. Walker, "Ballot Forms and Voter Fatigue: An Analysis of the Office Bloc and Party Column Ballots," *Midwest Journal of Political Science* 10 (November 1966): 448–463; Austin Ranney, "Turnout and Representation in Presidential Primary Elections," *American Political Science Review* 66 (March, 1972): 21–37; Jae-On Kim, John Petrocik, and Stephen Enokson, "Voter Turnout Among the States," *American Political Science Review* 69 (March 1975): 107–123; Raymond Wolfinger and Steven Rosenstone, *Who Votes?* (New Haven: Yale University Press, 1980); and, for a comparative perspective, Douglas W. Rae, *The Political Consequences of Electoral Laws* (New Haven: Yale University Press, 1967). For one of the many books dealing with historical vote patterns and their explanation, see Joel Silbey, Allan Bogue, and William Flanigan, eds., *The History of American Electoral Behavior* (Princeton: Princeton University Press, 1978). Work by the authors on the effects of election laws includes the following: Jerrold G. Rusk, "The Effects of the Australian Ballot Reform on Split Ticket Voting: 1876–1908," *American Political Science Review* 64 (December 1970): 1220–1238; Jerrold G. Rusk and John J. Stucker, "The Effect of the Southern System of Election Laws on Voting Participation: A Reply to V. O. Key," in Joel Silbey et al., eds., *The History of American Electoral Behavior* (Princeton: Princeton University Press, 1978): 198–250; and Jerrold G. Rusk and John J. Stucker, "Measuring Patterns of Electoral Participation in the United States," *Micropolitics* 3 (Spring 1984): 465–498.

2. As we can see, concern with what E. E. Schattschneider called the "System of 1896" goes back to the early part of this century: Arthur M. Schlesinger and Erik M. Erikson, "The Vanishing Voter," *The New Republic* 40 (October 15, 1924): 162–167; Harold F. Gosnell, *Why Europe Votes* (Chicago: University of Chicago Press, 1930); Edward M. Sait, *Political Institutions: A Preface* (New York: Appleton, Century and Croft, 1938); E. E. Schattschneider, *The Semi-Sovereign People* (New York: Holt, Rinehart and Winston, 1960); and W. Dean Burnham, *Critical Elections and the Mainsprings of American Politics* (New York: Norton, 1970).

3. Among the few authors who have speculated on these possibilities are Burnham, *Critical Elections*; Philip E. Converse, "Change in the American Electorate," in Angus Campbell and Philip E. Converse, eds., *The Human Meaning of Social Change* (New York: Russell Sage, 1972); and Jerrold G. Rusk, "The American Electoral Universe: Speculation and Evidence," *American Political Science Review* 68 (September 1974): 1028–1049.

4. A few authors have used time series data in their analyses of electoral phenomena. Burnham, *Critical Elections*; Philip E. Converse, "Survey Research and the Decoding of Patterns in Ecological Data," in Mattei Dogan and Stein Rokkan, eds., *Quantitative Ecological Analysis in the Social Sciences* (Cambridge: MIT Press, 1969); and Donald E. Stokes, "A Variance Components Model of Political Effects," in Joseph L. Bernd, ed., *Mathematical Applications in Political Science* (Dallas: Southern Methodist University, 1965).

5. Jerrold G. Rusk and John J. Stucker, "Legal-Institutional Factors in American Voting" (Ann Arbor: Unpublished Manuscript, 1972).

6. Two different treatments of the history of suffrage laws are Robert E. Lane, *Political Life* (New York: Free Press, 1959) and Chilton Williamson, *American Suffrage: From Property to Democracy, 1760–1860* (Princeton: Princeton University Press, 1960).

7. William A. McPhee and R. A. Smith, "A Model for Analyzing Voting Systems," in William A. McPhee and William Glaser, eds., *Public Opinion and Congressional Elections* (New York: Free Press, 1962), 123–154.

8. Donald T. Campbell and Donald W. Fiske, "Convergent and Discriminant Validation by Multitrait-Multimethod Matrix," *Psychological Bulletin* 56 (March 1959): 81–105.

9. Walter Dean Burnham, "The Changing Shape of the American Political Universe," *American Political Science Review* 59 (March 1965): 7–28.

10. Adam Przeworski and John Sprague, "Concepts in Search of Explicit Formulation: A Study in Measurement," *Midwest Journal of Political Science* 15 (May 1971): 183–218.

11. Kelley et al., "Registration and Voting."

12. Donald T. Campbell and Julian C. Stanley, *Experimental and Quasi-Experimental Designs for Research* (Chicago: Rand McNally Co., 1966).

13. The indices used in this analysis were constructed from raw census and election data supplied by the Historical Archives of the Inter-University Consortium for Political and Social Research. We wish to acknowledge Eric Austin, Michael Traugott, and Janet Vavra, staff members of the Archive, whose patient assistance made it possible for us to utilize the large quantities of data required to build these measures.

14. Alaska and Hawaii were not included in the analysis.

15. Donald T. Campbell, "Reforms as Experiments," *American Psychologist* 24 (1969): 409–429.

16. Ibid., 416.

17. Przeworski and Sprague, "Concepts in Search of Explicit Formulation."

18. As was the case with the two-election-year averaging technique, we are employing a procedure which would not really be necessary if Campbell's randomization procedure was fully operative for the time frame in which women's

suffrage was enacted but, as noted earlier, this assumption does not fit the historical record.

19. Again, we speak about the Q-E time data as though it were a real time matrix since the two are equivalent for so many of the states. When we perform our regional analysis later, the correspondence of the two data frames will be particularly close for all the regions except the West, which contains most of the states which adopted women's suffrage prior to 1920.

20. The rationale for this technique comes from Donald Campbell, and the methodology used here is a variation of the single Mood test where we have left out the element of significance testing for population effects.

21. The states included in each of these regional categories are as follows: (1) *Northeast*—Connecticut, Maine, Massachusetts, New Hampshire, Rhode Island, Vermont, Delaware, New Jersey, New York, Pennsylvania, and Maryland; (2) *Midwest*—Illinois, Indiana, Michigan, Ohio, Wisconsin, Kentucky, and West Virginia; (3) *Plains*—Iowa, Kansas, Minnesota, Missouri, Nebraska, North Dakota, South Dakota, and Oklahoma; (4)*South*—Alabama, Arkansas, Florida, Georgia, Louisiana, Mississippi, North Carolina, South Carolina, Texas, Tennessee, and Virginia; (5) *West*—Arizona, Colorado, Idaho, Montana, Nevada, New Mexico, Utah, Wyoming, California, Oregon, and Washington.

22. Campbell and Fiske, "Multitrait-Multimethod Matrix."

6 Political Participation and Discrimination: A Comparative Analysis of Asians, Blacks, and Latinos

Carole Jean Uhlaner

The formation and persistence of the Democratic New Deal coalition earlier in this century has fostered expectations among many politicians and political observers that something like that coalition might arise in the latter part of this century. Just as the children of European immigrants had joined with Northern blacks to elect a generation of Democratic office-holders (Anderson 1979), so too would the children of the new immigrants—Latino and Asian-American—take their natural political place, with blacks, in the party traditionally chosen by ethnic minorities. Concurrently, the Republican Party has been wooing these voters, especially Latinos and Asian-Americans. Whether or not the interests of various minority groups find representation under the aegis of the same political party hinges upon, among other factors, whether these groups share policy concerns. Then, their individual and collective ability to make an impact upon the political system depends upon their success in political mobilization of group members.

Shared perceptions of prejudice and experiences of discrimination may provide the common ground for a coalition of minorities, and such a coalition is more likely to the extent that members of each minority group have reasonably favorable perceptions of each other. Perhaps most important, prejudicial treatment can lead to political mobilization, both through reinforcement of an ethnic identity and by providing an individual with reasons to take political action. This chapter investigates perceptions of prejudice and discrimination by blacks, Mexican-Americans, and Asian-Americans, and the impact of these perceptions upon political participation by members of these groups.

Were minority groups to come together politically, it would be plausible that this would be in response to shared experiences of discrimination based upon race or ethnicity and shared perceptions of prejudice and of inequities in the opportunity structure of American society. In many respects, there are substantial differences between the experiences of blacks, Mexican-Americans, and Asian-Americans, which could serve to politically divide them from each other. These differences include objective economic standing, place of residence, educational attainment, and cultural traditions. Nevertheless, common perceptions of disadvantage can provide the foundation for formation of a coalition. Personally experienced discrimination might well be a particularly potent basis. The personal experience of discrimination is relevant political information which is effortlessly acquired in the routine of daily life. In addition to personal experience, individuals also develop opinions about the general attitude of others toward their group and of their group's access to opportunity. Taken together, these opinions contribute to a perception of the presence or absence of prejudice and discrimination toward oneself based on race or ethnicity.

Of course, perceived disadvantage does not automatically generate political alliances. Although such perceptions might make some members of a particular minority group more sympathetic toward other minority groups, others might become more antagonistic in response. For blacks the issue is especially poignant: are newly arrived Latinos fellow victims of discrimination, or just the latest wave of immigrants who serve to retard black progress as they scramble up the economic ladder?

Whether or not a coalition forms, however, perceived discrimination does reinforce—or develop—a sense of ethnic identity. Keefe and Padilla (1987, 192) conclude in their study of Chicanos that "perceived discrimination is a major contributory force in the maintenance of ethnic loyalty across our four generations of respondents."

Ethnic or racial identity can, in turn, lead to increased activity; Olsen (1970) and Verba and Nie (1972) concluded that black consciousness accounted for black participation rates above the levels predictable from income and education. In a series of books and articles, Gurin and her collaboraters argue that the key to identity leading to activity is the linking of ethnic identity with a political consciousness of the external structures producing the group's circumstances (Gurin and Epps 1975; Miller, Gurin, Gurin, and Malanchuk 1981; Gurin, Miller, and Gurin 1980; Gurin, Hatchett, and Jackson 1989). They distinguish between group identification and group consciousness, and argue that both are components of group solidarity. The former refers to feeling similar to others, that is, identity with the group. The latter refers to political beliefs arising from the identity, including, although not limited to, the sense that the group's condition is illegitimately inferior to that of others in society. They argue that high degrees of group solidarity increase political activity. Similarly, I have argued that group identity often leads to participation (Uhlaner 1989a, 1989b). Perceptions of prejudice and discrimination are components of a sense that one's group is treated unfairly. They are thus expected to correspond to higher levels of political activity, as they reinforce a sense of ethnic identity and also indicate that the perceiver relates the situation of his or her group to external social structures.

Extrapolating from the literature which links the incidence of discrimination to increased protest by disadvantaged groups, Salamon and Van Evera (1973) also suggest that discrimination might increase other participation, in particular, voter turnout. They conclude it does not and argue instead that fear reduces turnout. However, their analysis of aggregate data from Mississippi had to rely upon measures of income and education inequality instead of perceived discrimination. Henig and Gale (1987) find black suburbanites in Washington, D.C. were *less* likely to be politically active (over a range of items) as they perceived race relations in their neighborhood to be less friendly. Thus, according to these authors' results, perceived prejudice could depress levels of activity. Given the limitations on these prior analyses, it is worth testing whether prejudice and discrimination have a positive, negative, or null effect on electoral and other forms of participation.

An alternative view of the motivations for activity focuses upon the interests shared by members of a group. Persons who perceive that they are treated prejudicially have some common interests to defend, but there are other sources of interests. Whether or not an individual perceives discrimination, he or she may believe that the group has shared interests, which can be pursued through political action. In this case, ethnic identity can lead to action without necessarily any perception of inequality or unfairness. In addition, identities other than ethnic ones are politically salient for some individuals and can lead to alternative or additional sets of interests motivating action. Henig and Gale do find that "dissatisfaction with neighborhood conditions" was "one of the strongest and most consistent predictors of political involvement" (1987, 410). Scholars of racism have argued about the relative weight of "symbolic racism" versus "self-interest" (or group interest) as components of majority-group members' opposition to policies to aid minority groups (Sniderman and Tetlock 1986; Sears and Kinder 1985; Sears et. al. 1980; Bobo 1983). The problem examined here can loosely be considered the converse one, namely, the relative role of perceived prejudice and discrimination and of perceived interests in motivating minority group activity. Just as with the racism problem, it is likely to be difficult to claim that the operationalized measures clearly separate the one from the other. In any event, both sources are expected to contribute to activity. Minority group members' perceptions of the opportunities available to their group and to other minorities and of their interests thus may be crucial to understanding present and future coalition and mobilization patterns.

The increased Latino and Asian-American populations are not evenly spread across the United States. [Instead, they are concentrated in certain areas, especially in such large, politically competitive states as Texas, Florida, Illinois, and California; political consequences felt in these states will have ramifications across the country, and the patterns observed may foreshadow behavior elsewhere.] Because the demographic changes have arguably been the most dramatic in California, it is a good site for the study of minorities. California is also one of the few sites where all three groups discussed above are present in sufficient numbers to make comparative analysis feasible. From a methodological perspective, a simple national frame for the study of minority behavior is infeasible, as the resulting sample will contain a handful of Latinos and even fewer Asian-Americans. By selecting a California population frame, it is possible to locate minority respondents and a comparable sample of non-Hispanic whites in a political context where the issues of minority participation are, increasingly, politically salient.

The data on which the analyses below are based are drawn from a statewide survey of Californians undertaken in late 1984. The study yielded completed interviews with 574 Latinos, 308 Asian-Americans, 335 blacks, and 317 non-Hispanic whites. Details on the sampling design are reported in the Appendix. The Latino sample includes 61 individuals of national origin other than Mexican. They are excluded from the analyses which follow, leaving us with 513 Mexican-American respondents.[1] For ease of exposition, non-Hispanic whites are referred to in the text which follows as "whites."

In order to assess the importance of perceived prejudice and discrimination and of group-interests in producing political activity, I will need to control for other variables which affect the amount of participation. First, however, I examine the perceptions of Californians with regard to prejudice and discrimination and the existence of group interests.

PERCEPTIONS OF PREJUDICE

Many survey researchers believe that blacks and members of other minority groups are frequently reluctant to discuss matters of race and ethnicity with white interviewers, even over the telephone. They also suspect that in opinion surveys whites are reticent about expressing racist views which are no longer socially acceptable. Although many of the interviewers were Asian-American or Latino (bilingual interviewers were employed to conduct interviews in Spanish), matching the race/ethnicity of respondents with the race/ethnicity of interviewers was not

Table 6.1
Perceptions That Racial/Ethnic Groups Receive Fewer Opportunities Than They Deserve

Race/Ethnicity of Respondent	White	Black	Mexican	Asian
Fewer Opportunities Than Deserved Received By:				
Blacks	20	42	20	19
Latinos	13	21	24	14
Asians	4	4	4	9

Table 6.2
Perceptions That Racial/Ethnic Groups Receive More Opportunities Than They Deserve

Race/Ethnicity of Respondent	White	Black	Mexican	Asian
More Opportunities Than Deserved Received By:				
Whites	6	25	15	15
Blacks	5	0	3	4
Latinos	4	2	2	2
Asians	1	8	7	2

feasible. Had it been done, it is possible that more minority group members would have reported perceiving prejudice or that their group did not receive the opportunities that they deserved.

Respondents were asked about their perception of the opportunity structure in the United States, using the following parallel batteries of questions:

> Do you think there are any groups of people in the United States today who get *fewer* opportunities than they deserve?... Any other groups?
> Do you think there are any groups of people in the United States today who get *more* opportunities than they deserve?... Any other groups?

To mitigate any reluctance by respondents to express perceptions of discrimination, the interviewers solicited up to four responses to each question. Tables 6.1 and 6.2 display the responses of whites, blacks,

Mexican-Americans, and Asian-Americans to the questions regarding discrimination and group opportunities. Note that the entries in each cell of tables 6.1 and 6.2 are not mutually exclusive. The same respondent, for example, could state that blacks, Latinos, and Asian- Americans are disadvantaged, and all three responses would be registered.

Several things are readily apparent from these figures. First, it is clear from table 6.1 that blacks are far more likely than Mexican-Americans to perceive that people of their race/ethnicity are disadvantaged; 42 percent of black respondents stated that blacks received fewer opportunities than deserved, while only 24 percent of the Mexican-Americans said that Latinos were deprived of deserved opportunity. Although they were given up to four chances to say so, only 9 percent of the Asian-Americans in our sample reported that being Asian-American limited their opportunities. Reports that whites lacked opportunities were virtually nonexistent, and for that reason are not reported.

Reports that whites were unfairly advantaged, however, were fairly widespread, as indicated in table 6.2. Consistent with the pattern in table 6.1, blacks were more likely than members of other racial/ethnic groups to report the belief that whites received more opportunities than they deserved; one out of four blacks said so, compared to 15 percent each of the Asian-Americans and Mexican-Americans, and only 6 percent of the whites. Besides whites, no other group was perceived to be unfairly advantaged by more than a small number of respondents, regardless of their race/ethnicity. There is a glimmer of black and Mexican-American resentment of Asian-Americans, in that 8 percent of the blacks and 7 percent of the Mexican-Americans reported that Asian-Americans were unfairly advantaged. This is tempered, however, by figures in Table 6.1 which indicate that 4 percent of the blacks and Mexican-Americans believed that Asian-Americans were unfairly disadvantaged. There is also an interesting asymmetry across the board between tables 6.1 and 6.2, in that respondents, whatever their race/ethnicity, were considerably more likely to perceive a particular group or groups as unfairly disadvantaged than to assert that some group received more opportunities than they deserved. The prospects for coalition across racial and ethnic lines seem enhanced by this apparent greater sympathy for the underdog than resentment against the privileged.

Although there were substantial differences in the perceived situation of members *of* different racial/ethnic groups, there was substantial agreement by respondents *from* different groups as to the structure of opportunities in American society. As indicated earlier, when asked which groups in the country today received fewer opportunities than they deserved, blacks referred to blacks more frequently than to any other group. But so did whites and Asian-Americans; 20 percent and 19 percent, respectively, of respondents in these categories reported that blacks

Table 6.3
The Effect of Race/Ethnicity and Education on Perceptions of Group Opportunities

Race/Ethnicity of Respondent	White		Black		Mexican		Asian	
	\multicolumn{8}{c}{Attended College}
	Yes	No	Yes	No	Yes	No	Yes	No
Opportunities Received by Particular Groups:								
Blacks Fewer	26	12	45	38	23	19	18	19
Latinos Fewer	17	7	24	19	21	25	15	8
Whites More	8	2	31	18	17	14	15	15

did not receive the opportunities they deserved. For Asian-Americans this figure was far higher than the number who mentioned Asian-Americans. Blacks, similarly, were almost as likely to report that Latinos were disadvantaged (21 percent said so) as were Mexican-Americans (24 percent). Finally, only a handful of respondents, regardless of whether they were white or not, reported that any minority group received more opportunities than warranted, or stated that whites received too few opportunities. These attitudes are consistent with continued support for efforts to assist minority populations.

A respondent's level of education may well affect his or her perception of the opportunities faced by different groups. For whites, greater education often corresponds to exposure to a broader spectrum of social reality. For members of minority groups, education may lead to greater opportunity, yet also place individuals in situations where they are blocked by more subtle barriers. Thus, as reported in table 6.3, perceptions of opportunity structure controlling for respondent's educational attainment are examined. A dichotomous measure for education is used; in one category are respondents who have a high school diploma or who dropped out before finishing high school, while the other contains everyone who reported attending college, whether they earned a degree or not. Whites who attended college were considerably more likely than those who had not to perceive that blacks and Latinos received fewer opportunities than they deserved and that whites received more. Blacks who had attended college were also much more inclined to believe that whites were advantaged, but their perceptions of blacks' and Latinos' opportunities were only marginally different. Among Mexican-Americans and Asian-Americans, however, level of education had little impact

Table 6.4
Degree of Prejudice Directed Toward One's Racial/Ethnic Group

Race/Ethnicity of Respondent	Black	Mexican	Asian
American's Degree of Prejudice:			
Most Are Prejudiced	17	10	5
Some Are Prejudiced	63	54	52
Most Are Not Prejudiced	21	36	42

upon the perceptions of these minorities regarding groups' opportunities in the country today, with one exception. Better-educated Asian-Americans were more likely to perceive Latinos as disadvantaged, paralleling the effect of education on whites' perceptions.

Another way to measure respondents' perception of their group's position in American society is to ask what they believe to be other Americans' attitude toward someone of their race or ethnicity. Such perceptions were tapped with the following question:

> As you mentioned previously, you are [Black, Mexican-American, Asian-American] (respondent's race/ethnicity inserted automatically by the computer). Do you think most Americans are prejudiced against . . . only some Americans are prejudiced, or that most Americans are not prejudiced?

White respondents were not asked the question about Americans' degree of prejudice. Responses to this question broken down by race/ethnicity are reported in table 6.4.

Compared to Mexican-Americans and Asian-Americans, blacks perceive Americans in general to be considerably more prejudiced. Asian-Americans perceived Americans in general to be less prejudiced than did Mexican-Americans. Asian-Americans, in fact, were twice as likely as blacks (42 percent compared to 21 percent) to report a belief that most Americans were not prejudiced against them.

However, differences between the groups diminish when asked to think of future race/ethnic relations. Respondents were asked:

> Do you think that over the next 10 years or so Americans will become more prejudiced against . . . (respondent's race/ethnicity inserted automatically by the computer), less prejudiced, or do you think that their attitudes probably won't change much?

Table 6.5
Future Amount of Prejudice Directed Toward One's Racial/Ethnic Group

Race/Ethnicity of Respondent	Black	Mexican	Asian
American's Degree of Prejudice in 10 Years:			
More	8	9	11
Won't Change Much	48	46	48
Less	44	45	41

Again, this question was not posed to white respondents. The responses, by ethnicity, are reported in table 6.5. Despite the fact that, as shown by the previous tables, blacks perceive more prejudice in contemporary American life than do members of the other two groups, there is little difference across groups in their perceptions of the future. Members of all groups display optimism, with very few respondents anticipating more prejudice in the future, and close to half in each group expecting to see less.

Consider now respondents' responses to direct questions about their personal experiences of discrimination. These perceptions were elicited from the following questions:

> Have you, yourself, personally experienced discrimination because you are . . . ? (The respondent's race/ethnicity was inserted automatically at this point by the computer).
>
> (If "yes" to the previous question) Thinking of the most serious discrimination you have experienced . . . was it in getting a job, or getting into school, in getting a house or apartment, in a social situation, or in some other respect?

As in the case of the questions pertaining to perceptions of Americans' attitude toward the respondent's group, these questions were not posed to white respondents. The breakdowns of responses to these questions by respondents' race/ethnicity are reported in table 6.6.

As these figures indicate, the degree and nature of personally experienced discrimination reported in the survey varied dramatically across groups. Not only were blacks more likely to report personally experienced discrimination (62 percent), the discrimination they cited was largely economic in nature—over half reported that the discrimination involved a job. Although Asian-Americans perceived Americans in general as less prejudiced than did Mexican-Americans, they were more likely to report having personally experienced discrimination (46 percent

Table 6.6
Personally Experienced Discrimination Reported by Blacks, Mexican-Americans, and Asian-Americans

Race/Ethnicity of Respondent	Black	Mexican	Asian
Respondent Personally Experienced Prejudice:	62	36	46
As Percentage of Those Who Said Yes, Most Serious Discrimination Personally Experienced:			
Social Situation	26	40	55
Job	52	32	23
Education	7	13	7
Housing	7	12	6

to 36 percent). In contrast to blacks, over half of the Asian-Americans who reported being personally discriminated against referred to social situations—presumably snubs, misguided attempts at ethnic humor, or insults—but not something which was obviously economically injurious. Only a quarter reported discrimination involving a job. Mexican-Americans fell between these extremes, with a third reporting job discrimination and 40 percent reporting discrimination in a social situation. Mexican-Americans were more likely than those in either of the other groups to report serious discriminatory experiences involving education or housing, although even for them these reports involved substantially fewer respondents than the job and social situation categories.

In both their perceptions of opportunity structures and in their personal experiences, then, blacks are more likely than either Mexican-Americans or Asian-Americans to believe that their race/ethnicity has hindered them, especially with respect to their pursuit of material well-being. From the analyses undertaken so far, it is clear that minority group status is far more salient to blacks than to either Asian-Americans or Mexican-Americans. Blacks are far more likely than members of the other minority groups to feel that as a group they do not get the opportunities they deserve, that whites get more opportunities than they deserve, that blacks have personally experienced discrimination, and that many Americans are prejudiced against them. For the most part, they seem to be sympathetic to the lot of other minority groups. Latinos and Asian-Americans, in contrast, appear to be no more likely than whites to perceive that blacks are unfairly disadvantaged. It would appear that blacks are as likely to receive sympathy for their circumstances from whites as from members of other minority groups.

Another factor which may affect a person's experience of prejudice and discrimination is being native born versus being an immigrant. The experiences of white ethnic immigrants attests to the virulence of nativist sentiments at times in the United States. Even in relatively tolerant periods, immigrants, and possibly the children of immigrants, face somewhat different circumstances than those whose families have been resident in the United States longer. Thus Tables 6.7 and 6.8 report the relationship between how long a respondent's family has been in the United States and the respondent's experience of discrimination and perception of prejudice. As virtually all of the black respondents had parents born in the United States, and whites were not asked about prejudice, the investigation is limited to the Asian-Americans and Mexican-Americans.

Mexican-American and Asian-American perceptions of prejudice and discrimination did vary as a function of how long their families had been in the United States. The pattern, however, was an uneven one. As shown in table 6.7, for both groups reports of personally experienced discrimination *increased* from the immigrant to the second generation (those who were born in the United States, but whose parents were not) and then declined for third and later generations (those whose parents were born in the United States). The first part of the pattern is consistent with data reported by Portes and Bach (1985) that Cuban and Mexican immigrants to the United States perceive more discrimination after three years in the country than when they first arrive.

Examination of the lower part of the table gives some insight as to why there was no simple monotonic pattern, as the situations in which discrimination is perceived vary from generation to generation. For both the Mexican-Americans and Asian-Americans, the incidence of job-related discrimination decreases with the number of generations their family has been in the country, although the dramatic drop occurs between the immigrant and second-generation respondents. On the other hand, for respondents from both groups, discrimination in social situations increases from the immigrant to the second-generation. Third generation Asia-Americans report still more social discrimination. The groups also differ with regard to the remaining two spheres. Whatever the generation, Mexican-Americans are almost equally likely to point to education as a problem area, while for Asian-Americans mention of this as an area where discrimination occurs drops after the immigrant generation. On the other hand, problems with housing are greater for second-generation Asian-Americans than for immigrants or those in the

Table 6.7
Personally Experienced Discrimination Among First Generation, Second Generation, and Third Generation or More Mexican-Americans and Asian-Americans

Race/Ethnicity of Respondent	Mexican			Asian		
	\multicolumn{6}{c}{Generations in the U.S.}					
	First	Second	Third+	First	Second	Third+
Respondent Personally Experienced Prejudice:	32	44	35	41	61	44
As Percentage of Those Who Said Yes, Most Serious Discrimination Personally Experienced:						
Social Situation	27	48	43	46	60	75
Job	45	21	28	33	11	6
Education	13	11	15	10	3	6
Housing	13	13	9	3	11	6

third-generation, while for third-generation Mexican-Americans housing problems diminish. Overall, Asian-American experiences of discrimination were likely to be in the social sphere, and increasingly so with time in the country; fully three-quarters of those third generation Asian-Americans who experienced discrimination did so in a social situation. On the other hand, for the immigrant generation in both groups, jobs and education frequently presented the occasion for bias.

The responses of Mexican-Americans and Asian-Americans also differ with regard to their perception of the attitudes of most Americans toward their ethnic group. As indicated in table 6.8, Mexican-Americans' perceptions of how prejudiced most Americans tended to be against them were unrelated to the generation of their family's arrival. Among Asian-Americans, however, perceptions of prejudice dropped sharply between second-generation respondents and those whose parents had been born in the United States. Under 40 percent of the latter group felt most or some Americans were prejudiced, while 61 percent said most were not. In the first and second generations, by contrast, about 60 percent felt some or most Americans were prejudiced, while 40 percent felt most were not. The perceptions of the immigrant and second-generation

Table 6.8
Degree of Prejudice Perceived by First Generation, Second Generation, and Third Generation or More Mexican-Americans and Asian-Americans

Race/Ethnicity of Respondent	Mexican			Asian		
	\multicolumn{6}{c}{Generations in the U.S.}				
	First	Second	Third+	First	Second	Third+
Americans' Degree of Prejudice:						
Most Are Prejudiced	8	13	9	5	5	3
Some Are Prejudiced	53	51	56	54	56	36
Most Are Not Prejudiced	39	36	35	41	39	61

Asian-Americans are thus close to those of the Mexican-Americans, while third-generation Asian-Americans perceive substantially less prejudice than do these others.

Finally, we turn to the question of whether or not the respondents perceive that they have interests specific to their racial/ethnic identity. These interests could provide another motivation for action, instead of or in addition to those provided by perceptions of discrimination and prejudice. The following questions assess whether or not respondents believed that they had interests related to their race/ethnicity and, if so, which interests were most salient:

> Do you think there are problems today of special concern to... Americans? (respondent's race/ethnicity inserted automatically.) White respondents were asked, "Do you think there are problems today of special concern to people of your racial or national background?"
>
> Thinking of those problems which are of special concern to... Americans, what would you say is the most important? (respondent's race/ethnicity inserted automatically). White respondents were asked, "Thinking of those problems which are of special concern to people of your racial or national background, what would you say is the most important?

As indicated by the figures in table 6.9, blacks were considerably more likely than either whites or members of other minority groups to name a particular problem of special concern to them as members of a racial/ethnic/national group. Sixty-five percent of the blacks in the survey said there was a problem of special concern, while only 24 percent of the

Table 6.9
Problems of Special Concern to One's Racial/Ethnic Group

Race/Ethnicity of Respondent	White	Black	Mexican	Asian
Problem Reported:				
None	76	35	54	63
Unemployment	1	31	10	4
Education	0	3	9	2
Crime, Gangs, Drugs	1	4	3	3
Race Relations/ Discrimination	7	12	10	8
Loss of Ethnic Heritage/ Ethnic Issues	1	0	0	7

white respondents did so. It is also clear that unemployment stood out in blacks' minds as especially troublesome for the black community. Over three out of ten blacks cited this problem, compared to 10 percent of the Mexican-Americans and only a handful of whites and Asian-Americans. Mexican-American respondents stood out in their relatively high propensity to refer to education. Recall that they were also more likely to cite education as an arena in which they personally experienced discrimination. Blacks were more likely than respondents from other groups to refer to race relations, but not by a large margin. Asian-Americans stand out in their concern with loss of ethnic heritage, or such ethnically specific problems as the Philippines or World War II reparations. The primary message of this table, however, is that parallel to blacks' greater perception of themselves as affected by prejudice, they also see themselves as more adversely affected by unemployment and other problems than do other Americans.

Perceptions of group interests and experiences of discrimination are not necessarily independent, as the findings about education for Mexican-Americans hint. Individuals who have experienced discrimination may differ from those who have not in their perceptions of the existence and nature of group interests. Conversely, those who have a keen sense of group interests may be more ready to perceive discrimination. In table 6.10, respondents' characterizations of the most important problem facing their group are tabulated by race/ethnicity and by whether or not they report a personal experience of discrimination. Since whites were not asked about discrimination, they are excluded from the table.

Individuals who report personal experience of discrimination differ

Table 6.10
Personally Experienced Discrimination and Problems of Special Concern to Respondent's Racial/Ethnic Group

Race/Ethnicity of Respondent	Black		Mexican		Asian	
	Yes	No	Yes	No	Yes	No
Percentage Reporting Group-Specific Problem:						
None	30	44	38	62	51	73
Unemployment	36	25	8	10	3	3
Education	4	2	17	5	2	1
Crime, Gangs, Drugs	4	6	–	4	5	1
Race Relations/ Discrimination	14	7	17	7	12	5
Loss of Ethnic Heritage/ Ethnic Issues	36	25	8	10	3	3

from those who do not. First, such individuals, regardless of whether they were black, Mexican-American, or Asian-American, were much more likely to report a problem which they viewed to be of special concern to their group. The salience of race relations and discrimination is higher—by a factor of two—among those who have had such experiences themselves than for others in each group. For each minority group, the incidence of mentions of one additional issue area differs substantially between those who have experienced discrimination and those who have not. For blacks, the issue is unemployment, where the number reporting this as a problem jumps from a quarter of those not reporting discrimination to over one-third of those who do report it. For Mexican-Americans, education is the arena of marked difference; 17 percent of those who reported having personally experienced discrimination referred to education as a major group problem, as opposed to 5 percent among those who did not. Although the absolute numbers are small, the issue of more concern to Asian-Americans who have experienced discrimination is crime.

A similar pattern appears in table 6.11, although the effects are smaller. Minority respondents who reported personal experiences of discrimination were more likely to have joined an organization intended to address some type of serious problem, and there were some differences in the frequency of types of problems. These data came from replies to the following pair of questions:

Table 6.11
Personally Experienced Discrimination and Organizational Participation

Race/Ethnicity of Respondent	Black		Mexican		Asian	
	_____Personally Experienced Discrimination_____					
	Yes	No	Yes	No	Yes	No
Percent Who Joined an Organization To Work on Problem	44	28	29	14	29	18
As Percent of Those Who Joined, Problem Addressed by Organization:						
Crime	37	41	26	32	25	27
Education	4	9	20	5	6	4
Ethnic	5	3	10	10	6	4
Pollution	6	6	6	5	11	31
Poverty / Welfare	4	6	6	7	14	4

Have you ever joined or worked in an organization to do something about a problem in your community, or a state or national level problem?

(If "yes" to the previous question) The last time you did this, what was the particular problem you were concerned about?

There were no dramatic differences between those who have and have not experienced discrimination among blacks in the problem the organization addressed. In both groups, crime was the single most frequently mentioned problem. However, there are substantial differences among the Mexican-Americans and the Asian-Americans. The former are vastly more likely, if they have worked in a group, to have worked in one involved with education if they experienced discrimination. Among Asian-Americans, experience of discrimination goes along with increased involvement in issues of poverty and welfare and decreased attention to pollution issues.

Thus, a hefty proportion of these minority populations perceive inequalities in the opportunities available to members of different groups and some degree of discrimination. There is little indication of intergroup conflict on this dimension, and some indication of intergroup sympathy. These factors suggest the possibility of coalition formation. However, the groups vary in the nature of their experience of discrimination, decreasing the likelihood of finding a unifying ground. Substantial numbers in each group also identify issues of special concern to them in terms of their racial or ethnic identity. Thus, perceived interests may also serve as a basis for political organization. Although blacks are most likely to perceive discrimination and identify group-specific interests, and Asian-Americans the least likely, these components of group solidarity appear available in each of the three groups.

ANALYSIS OF PARTICIPATION

Does either of these components of ethnic consciousness—perceived discrimination or perceived group interests—contribute to participation in political life? The data contain six measures of electoral participation and three measures of nonelectoral participation. As table 6.12 indicates, the extent of participation varies both across activities and across ethnic groups. Because a substantial portion of the Mexican-Americans and Asian-Americans are not citizens, voting and registration figures percentaged on the entire sample understate the amount of participation. Nonetheless, even citizens in these groups are less active than blacks or whites.[2] Because few respondents displayed posters, worked on campaigns, or attended rallies, and no satisfactory scale could be constructed from these three items, they were excluded from subsequent analyses. Subsequent analysis is also restricted to citizens.

In order to assess the impact of the perception of prejudice and discrimination and of group interests upon activity, the other variables which affect the amount of participation must be controlled. Notable among these are measures of class, such as education and measures of financial status. In addition, young people are well-known to be less active than older persons, while the very old again drop off in activity. Men have traditionally been more active than women in politics; although that difference is disappearing, it may persist for some activities. In addition to these standard demographic variables, two additional factors address specific characteristics of the immigrant portion of the sample. Individuals who do not speak English have reduced access to majority political life, whatever their level of education or other characteristics.[3] Also, persons who have spent a substantial portion of their life abroad, before immigrating to the United States, may be less involved in political life than those who had lived here longer. A detailed discussion of these variables, and of their distribution for the respondents in the sample, can be found in Uhlaner, Cain, and Kiewiet 1989.

The socioeconomic and demographic variables discussed above serve mainly as controls for examining the effect of two other sets of variables, capturing discrimination and group interests, as discussed in the first part of the chapter. First, two variables capture perceived interests, one

Table 6.12
Participation in Political Activities by Ethnic Group

	Non-Hispanic Whites	Blacks	Mexican-Americans	Asian-Americans
Voted in 1984				
All	76*	80	45	48
Citizens	80	81	60	69
Registered				
All	82	87	55	55
Citizens	87	88	72	77
Contributed money				
All	20	17	12	18
Citizens	-	-	14	24
Non-citizens	-	-	7	6
Displayed poster/sticker				
All	8	10	11	6
Citizens	-	-	11	4
Non-citizens	-	-	10	6
Worked on campaigns				
All	6	5	3	3
Citizens	-	-	4	4
Non-citizens	-	-	1	2
Attended political rally				
All	15	16	10	8
Citizens	-	-	12	11
Non-citizens	-	-	4	4
Contacted officials				
All	47	37	26	26
Citizens	-	-	29	31
Non-citizens	-	-	19	20
Contacted Media				
All	22	20	18	25
Citizens	-	-	20	25
Non-citizens	-	-	13	23
Worked with group to solve community problem				
All	33	38	20	24
Citizens	-	-	24	32
Non-citizens	-	-	12	11
Number of respondents				
All	317	335	513	308
Citizens	300	313	356	199
Non-citizens	14	4	137	84

*Entries are percent of total in cell who said they did activity.

ethnically based, the other not. I introduced a dummy variable, coded "one" for those individuals who believe that there are problems of special concern to their race/ethnic group and coded "zero" for those who see no such problem. Of course, individuals may not find their racial or ethnic group particularly salient when it comes to politics, or may find some other group salient as well. Thus respondents were also asked if there was any other group they felt especially part of, and whether they identified any problems specific to that group. Another dummy variable picks up these nonethnic identifications. Secondly, I introduced measures of perceived prejudice and discrimination for blacks, Mexican-Americans, and Asian-Americans. These consist of three variables which indicate, respectively, if the respondent personally experienced discrimination, perceives his or her own group as receiving fewer opportunities than deserved, or perceives most or some Americans as prejudiced. Each of the three variables is coded "one" for respondents who report the experience or perception and "zero" for the other respondents. Since all three of these variables address some aspect of a respondent's belief that he or she is treated unfairly because of race or ethnicity, I constructed a new variable that combines them. The new scale simply adds the three variables together; as a result, its values range from zero to three. In the interests of parsimony I refer below to the combined scale as "perceived discrimination" (despite the fact that the third element of the scale assesses perceptions of prejudice). Thus, to summarize, I have one set of items that refers to ethnic and other interests and another set that involves prejudice and discrimination toward the respondent's racial or ethnic group.

Finally, I introduced the strength of the respondent's partisanship into some of the estimations. This raises a few qualms because partisanship itself is a function of some of the variables discussed above. (See Cain, Kiewiet, and Uhlaner 1991.) However, partisanship has consistently been found to have a significant impact upon levels of participation, especially for electoral activities (see Conway 1985), so excluding it may distort some of the findings. I thus ran each estimation both with and without strength of partisanship as an independent variable.

Because the dependent variables are dichotomous, the models were estimated with probit analysis. Table 6.13 reports the coefficients and associated t-statistics for the estimates involving the three electoral activities, while table 6.14 reports the same information for the three nonelectoral activities. The top portion (A) of each table reports the estimates for a model that excluded strength of partisanship and included the combined measure of discrimination. The second portion (B) reports the results when strength of partisanship was added to the model. Because the coefficients and t-statistics of the variables, other than the constant, remain virtually identical, only information for the new constant and

Table 6.13
Probit Estimations of Citizens' Electoral Participation

	Voted in 1984		Registered		Contributed $	
Independent Variables:	coeff.*	t#	coeff.	t	coeff.	t
A.						
Constant	-1.18	-6.18	-0.66	-3.25	-2.38	-10.9
Mexican-American	-0.25	-1.82	-0.20	-1.33	-0.15	-0.99
Black	-0.04	-0.26	-.012	-.072	-0.27	-1.71
Asian-American	-0.55	-3.75	-0.59	-3.75	-0.16	-1.06
Age	.038	10.00	.030	7.41	.020	5.33
65 or older	-0.62	-3.12	-0.35	-1.59	-0.27	-1.56
Some College	0.65	7.01	0.68	6.80	0.45	4.57
Homeowner	0.36	4.22	0.33	3.58	0.38	3.89
Head unemployed	-0.19	-1.69	-0.12	-0.99	-.093	-0.67
Single mother	-0.20	-1.41	-.018	-0.12	-0.33	-2.03
Male	-.063	-0.69	-.082	-0.84	0.29	3.01
Pct. life not US	-.001	-0.50	-.001	-0.40	.0040	1.29
Non-English lang.	-0.26	-2.20	-0.22	-1.75	-0.14	-1.00
Ethnic problem	.077	0.84	0.15	1.55	0.12	1.19
Non-ethnic id.	0.12	0.85	0.37	2.15	0.27	2.08
Perceive prej.	0.12	2.29	0.12	2.25	0.10	1.86
Log likelihood at Convergence:	-598.02		-504.44		-524.16	
B. With strength of partisanship in the model:						
Constant	-1.79	-8.47	-1.29	-5.76	-2.56	-10.9
Party strength	0.26	7.87	0.28	8.13	.078	2.12
Log likelihood at Convergence:	-566.33		-470.57		-521.87	
C. With Perceived Prejudice broken down into components:						
Constant	-1.18	-6.16	-0.67	-3.29	-2.37	-10.9
Personal exp.	0.12	1.21	.048	0.43	0.17	1.49
Prej. toward grp.	0.17	1.59	0.11	0.97	0.11	0.95
Fewer opp.	.039	0.33	0.26	1.97	.0075	.059
Log likelihood at Convergence:	-597.72		-503.71		-523.75	
D. With strength of partisanship and Perceived Prejudice components:						
Constant	-1.80	-8.46	-1.29	-5.75	-2.55	-10.8
Personal exp.	0.13	1.21	.051	0.45	0.16	1.41
Prej. toward grp.	0.15	1.39	.092	0.80	0.11	0.90
Fewer opp.	-.030	-0.24	0.19	1.42	-.005	-.044
Party strength	0.26	7.91	0.28	8.08	.078	2.13
Log likelihood at Convergence:	-565.68		-470.26		-521.43	
N:	1233		1232		1225	

*Probit coefficients
#t-statistics. Critical value of t for p < .05 = 1.96.

Table 6.14
Probit Estimations of Citizens' Nonelectoral Participation

	Work in Group		Contact Media		Contact Official	
Independent Variables:	coeff.*	t#	coeff.	t	coeff.	t
A.						
Constant	-1.44	-7.90	-0.99	-5.31	-0.98	-5.69
Mexican-American	-0.29	-2.20	-0.14	-1.02	-0.46	-3.62
Black	-0.21	-1.51	-0.40	-2.63	-0.61	-4.47
Asian-American	-0.27	-1.90	.011	.080	-.066	-4.79
Age	.008	2.54	-.003	-0.81	.014	4.34
65 or older	-0.30	-1.85	.017	.097	-0.25	-1.64
Some College	0.56	6.56	0.39	4.30	0.43	5.21
Homeowner	0.15	1.81	-.041	-0.48	0.20	2.51
Head unemployed	-.004	-.031	-0.11	-0.93	-0.17	-1.46
Single mother	.036	0.27	.097	0.72	.061	0.50
Male	0.27	3.10	.087	0.97	-.0005	-.006
Pct. life not US	-.004	-1.25	-.004	-1.18	-.0012	-0.44
Non-English lang.	-0.29	-2.31	-0.11	-0.88	-0.35	-2.90
Ethnic problem	0.31	3.57	0.20	2.18	.085	1.02
Non-ethnic id.	0.37	3.09	0.21	1.69	0.21	1.79
Perceive prej.	0.14	2.81	0.13	2.56	0.16	3.37
Log likelihood at Convergence:		-682		-616.32		-740.82
B. With strength of partisanship in the model:						
Constant	-1.44	-7.33	-0.97	-4.85	-1.20	-6.43
Party strength	-.003	-.009	-.009	-0.27	.099	3.18
Log likelihood at Convergence:		-681.99		-616.29		-735.69
C. With Perceived Prejudice broken down into components:						
Constant	-1.42	-7.74	-0.98	-5.24	-0.97	-5.61
Personal exp.	0.28	2.91	0.21	2.03	0.23	2.44
Prej toward grp	-.001	-.013	-.021	-0.20	0.12	1.24
Fewer opp.	0.12	1.12	0.23	2.00	0.12	1.09
Log likelihood at Convergence:		-680.33		-614.97		-740.45
D. With strength of partisanship and Perceived Prejudice components:						
Constant	-1.41	-7.20	-0.96	-4.78	1.19	6.38
Personal exp.	0.28	2.91	0.21	2.04	0.23	2.40
Prej toward grp	-.001	-.011	-.020	-0.19	0.11	1.13
Fewer opp.	0.12	1.12	0.23	2.02	.095	0.89
Party strength	-.002	-.060	-.009	-0.27	0.10	3.21
Log likelihood at Convergence:		-680.33		-614.94		-735.22
N:		1232		1234		1231

*Probit coefficients
#t-statistics. Critical value of t for p < .05 = 1.96.

for strength of partisanship is reported. The third portion of the table (C) reports estimates for the same model as in part A but with substitution of the three individual measures of discrimination and prejudice for the combined measure, and the fourth portion (D) adds strength of partisanship to these models. Again, as the other coefficients change little, only the coefficients and t-statistics for the constant and the newly introduced variables are reported.

Examination of the log-likelihood ratios at convergence leads to two conclusions about these models. First, strength of partisanship contributes to the explanation of voting and registration, and somewhat less to the explanation of contacting elected officials, but adds little in the estimation of the other variables. The t-statistics for the party strength variable point to the same conclusion. Second, either the combined discrimination scale or the individual measures work equally well as predictors.

Overall, the demographic variables work very much as expected. Persons are more active when they are older (except for the very old). They are also more active if they have more education and wealth or if they speak English. Men are more likely than women to contribute money and to work in groups. (See Uhlaner, Cain, Kiewiet 1989 for a more thorough discussion of these factors and of differences in their effects for different types of activities.) All else equal, members of all three minority groups are less likely to contact elected officials than are non-Hispanic whites. Aside from that, minority participation rates are comparable to those of whites of equivalent characteristics, except that Asian-Americans are less likely to register or to vote, Mexican-Americans are less likely to work in groups, and blacks are less likely to contact news media. Keep in mind that since few whites identified group interests and none, by construction, perceived discrimination, these comparisons really only tell us how the minority group members who do not have interests or perceive discrimination compare with whites.

Against this background, what impact do perceived discrimination and group interests have upon participation? The probability of voting, registering, working in groups, contacting news media, and contacting elected officials is clearly significantly higher for respondents who perceive discrimination than for those who do not. The effect for contributing money is less strong, but in the same direction. Perception of interests has more effect for the nonelectoral activities than for the electoral ones. Persons who identify an ethnic problem are more likely to work in groups or contact the media. Those with a nonethnic identity also are more likely to work in groups and have a higher probability of registering and of contributing money.

Parts C and D of the table indicate that for the electoral activities, all three parts of the discrimination scale are contributing to the effect. That the individual variables are not particularly significant, while the overall scale is, suggests that for purposes of explaining electoral activity, each of the items provides an imperfect measure of underlying "perceived discrimination." While the same point basically holds for the nonelectoral activities, it is nonetheless striking that a personal experience of discrimination seems to provide a substantially more powerful boost to activity than does a generalized perception of the group's position. Persons who report personal discrimination are also those who work in groups, contact news media, and contact elected officials. A perception of the group as having fewer opportunities does also contribute to contacting news media. But those persons who believe Americans are prejudiced toward their group do not try to influence these other Americans through officials, media, or associational activity.

Thus, even after controlling for measures of the respondents' demographic and economic circumstances, those persons who perceive discrimination and those who identify group interests are more likely to be politically active than those who do not. The impact of perceived discrimination extends across both electoral and nonelectoral activities. Notably, those who perceive discrimination are significantly more likely to register and vote. The identification of group problems, however, is primarily of importance in increasing nonelectoral participation such as working in groups and contacting news media. Thus it appears that the overall perception of one's group's position has more impact than a more specifically interest-oriented view.

VARIATIONS BETWEEN RACIAL/ETHNIC GROUPS

Of course, the effect of each independent variable may differ from group to group. In terms of this analysis, if the coefficients for the independent variables are estimated separately for members of different racial/ethnic groups, these coefficients may vary. I thus reanalyzed these data with interactive independent variables, in effect doing a separate estimation for each of the four racial/ethnic groups. In addition, in those estimations I split both the Mexican-American and Asian-American samples into two parts: persons who had immigrated to the United States themselves, and persons who had been born in the United States. The basic conclusions reached above on the effects of the independent variables generally hold. However, a few interesting deviations emerged.

First, the effects of percentage of life spent outside the United States and of not speaking English as a primary language are generally stronger for the Mexican-Americans than for the Asians.

Second, gender matters most for blacks and Asians. Black men are less likely than women to register or vote, but more likely to work in groups. Asian men are more likely than women to register, contribute money (as are white men), work in groups, or contact news media, although they are less likely than women to contact elected officials.

Third, some quirks appear among the income-related variables. Home-ownership is not related to registration or voting for foreign-born Latinos or foreign-born Asians, although it does matter for these Asians for nonelectoral activities. And although living in a household with an unemployed head seems to have no effect overall, it does depress the electoral and contributing activity of whites.

Fourth, even elderly Mexican-Americans—over age 65—are more likely than younger people to work in groups. For voting and registration, the positive slope on age is especially steep for foreign-born Mexican-Americans. Since this is a young population, the net effect of the steep slope is to depress overall amounts of voting and registration.

Fifth, the behavior of the college variable most closely addresses the question of low Asian participation. Despite the ubiquity of the link between education and political activity, participation is not significantly higher among better-educated Asian-Americans than among other Asian-Americans. This result holds whether we use the college dummy, as here, or use years of education. Thus, the high level of education among Asians does not get translated into political activity.

Finally, I examined racial/ethnic group differences on the variables of most theoretical concern. The two measures of interests—identification of a racial/ethnic group-related problem and specification of a nonethnic identity—generally have whatever effects they do upon electoral activities because of their impact for non-Hispanic whites, while their effects for nonelectoral activities are due to their impact for Mexican-Americans and Asian-Americans. Thus, it is mainly those whites who have some nonethnic identity who register with higher probability. There are two interesting exceptions to this generalization. First, native-born Asian-Americans are more likely to contribute money if they have a *non*ethnic identity than if they do not; at the same time, identification of an ethnic problem has no impact for this group on this activity. Second, blacks who identify a group-specific problem are substantially more likely than other blacks to work in groups.

Examination of the prejudice and discrimination items indicates that they have some effect upon participation for members of each of the minority groups, but the effects are more striking for some groups for some activities. Registration and voting rates go up for Mexican-Americans who perceive discrimination and go up particularly steeply for those who perceive other Americans as prejudiced toward their group. Although perceived discrimination only barely affects contributing money in the combined analysis, perception of fewer group opportunities is related to higher donations by immigrant Asian-Americans. Personal experiences of discrimination, especially among Mexican-

Americans and Asians, have particularly strong impact upon working in groups and contacting news media. For blacks, perception of fewer opportunities for the group has more impact, especially in increasing registration and increasing news media contacts. Contacting of elected officials increases with perceived discrimination particularly strongly for native-born Mexican-Americans (responding to personal experience) and for blacks (who perceive bias against the group), but also increases for immigrant Asian-Americans and Mexican-Americans who perceive group disadvantage. Only native-born Asian-Americans are, if anything, less likely to take part in nonelectoral activities if they perceive discrimination.

Thus, analysis of the data separately by racial/ethnic group does not lead overall to any major change in the story that perceptions of both group interests and discrimination lead to increased activity, with the former more important for nonelectoral varieties.

CONCLUSION

Although the majority of Californians perceive opportunities to be available for all, a substantial number, especially among the members of minority groups, do perceive the existence of prejudice or report personal experiences of discrimination. Overall, their perceptions of members of other minority groups suggest that there would be no particular barrier against the formation of a coalition; there is not much sign of intergroup rivalry on this ground.

Analysis of the relationship between these perceptions and participation shows that persons who perceive discrimination or prejudice are also more likely to be politically active. While this agrees with hypotheses in the literature, and, in particular, closely ties into the discussion of group consciousness, it does contradict some reports which would suggest decreased participation by those who perceive discrimination or prejudice. Perceptions of inequity may therefore contribute to the mobilization of political activity. Of course, it is also possible that those who are active are more sensitive to indications of unfair treatment. However, it seems more likely that perceived discrimination and prejudice lead to group consciousness and activity.

The impact of perceptions of discrimination and prejudice seems to be particularly strong for Mexican-Americans and, in some activities, for blacks. The fact that a stronger effect does not appear for blacks in the electoral arena is likely due to their already high rates of participation. Among Asian-Americans, the impact is stronger for immigrants than for those who are native-born. Since few native-born Asian-Americans perceive prejudice or discrimination, the impact for participation by second and third generation Asian-Americans is further lessened. Thus, if ethnic politics were to evolve with a focus upon questions of prejudice and discrimination, any resulting coalition would probably include Mexican-Americans, both immigrant and native born, blacks, and only immigrant generation Asian-Americans. Nonetheless, as shown in other parts of the analysis, the interests and concerns of these groups are not equivalent, so it is unclear what issues such a coalition would address.

Nonetheless, the importance of perceived discrimination and prejudice as factors that enhance the amount of political participation among these groups underscores the importance of group identity as a contributor to activity. "Perceptions"—including those of discrimination and prejudice—can be modified using the resources of education and organization. There are substantial opportunities for a skilled leader to increase the participation of supporters by helping them to perceive their discriminatory experiences and to perceive the prejudice of others toward them. Thus, the analysis of the impact of perceived discrimination and prejudice upon participation illuminates a potent mechanism of political mobilization.

APPENDIX: SAMPLE DESIGN

The major problem we faced in designing the survey was that of efficiently reaching large numbers of adult individuals from the three major racial and ethnic minorities in California—Latinos (primarily Mexican-Americans), blacks, and Asians, who, according to the 1980 census, constituted 19 percent, 8 percent, and 5 percent of the state population respectively. Because of a young age structure, black and Latino percentages of adults are somewhat smaller than their percentages of the total population.

Comparisons between in-person interviews and telephone interviews indicate that the former technique produces a higher response rate. It also avoids bias due to the incomplete saturation of telephone ownership (Thornberry and Massey 1988). We worried, however, that recent immigrants (especially undocumented ones) would be suspicious of interviewers coming to their doors. Telephone interviews seem less obtrusive, and, therefore, arguably preferable. Most importantly, however, telephone interviews cost substantially less; budget constraints ruled out the expense of in-person interviews.

The most common sample selection technique in telephone surveys is random digit dialing. RDD, however, is an extremely inefficient method for contacting members of residentially dispersed groups that make up a small percentage of the population. Since most blacks live in predominantly black neighborhoods, one can draw a sample of telephone exchanges via probability weights that would yield the desired proportion of black respondents. However, among Latinos and Asians, the level of residential concentration (and resultant correlation between telephone exchanges and census units) is too low for this technique to be effective. Asians are an extreme case in this regard. Of the 5,050 census tracts in California in the 1980 census, only 33 (0.6 percent) were 40 percent or more Asian. Even if telephone exchanges could be weighted in a skewed enough fashion to increase significantly the probability of contacting Asian respondents, the resultant sample would be problematic (that is, Asians in heavily Asian neighborhoods are likely to be atypical Asians).

Because of the highly problematic nature of RDD for our purposes, we therefore chose to generate Latino and Asian subsamples from surnames listed in telephone directories. The use of lists of distinctive surnames to find ethnic subpopulations has been shown to produce representative samples (Chang et al. 1988; Himmelfarb, Loar, and Mott 1983), despite some biases introduced by directory sampling relative to RDD (Leuthold and Scheele 1971). Oversampling of blacks, on the other hand, could be done on the basis of residence.

After randomly selecting a list of 300 census tracts in California, we obtained from DialAmerica Corporation of Cleveland, Ohio, the names, current phone numbers, and addresses of 80 to 100 individuals per tract for approximately 90 percent of the tracts, thus yielding a list of 24,523 names. We ran these through Hispanic and Asian surname dictionaries, yielding subsample Ns of 3,306 and 1,170, respectively. We then drew a 20 percent sample of the remaining 20,047 names, doubling the selection probability for census tracts in which 50 percent or more of the residents are black so as to generate another subsample that would contain roughly equal proportions of whites and blacks. Because of this sampling procedure, we use weights on the white and black subsamples when calculating marginal percentages. (The weights give double weight to respondents residing outside the heavily black tracts but are adjusted to keep the total subsample N unchanged.) This procedure produced significantly fewer Hispanic names than their proportions of the total state population in the 1980 census would have predicted (13.5 percent versus 19 percent) and slightly fewer Asian names. While incomplete saturation of telephone ownership probably accounts for some of the discrepancy, the young age structure of the Latino community also contributes. In order to increase our sample of recent Asian immigrants, we drew a supplemental sample of Korean surnames from the 1984 Korean Telephone Directory of Southern California. The creators of this directory believe that it contains the telephone numbers and addresses of over 75 percent of all Koreans in southern California. We ultimately conducted interviews with 80 Korean Americans via this supplemental sample.

The interviewing firm we hired made as many as three attempts to contact each telephone number. Randomization within the household was achieved by asking to speak with whichever adult living at that address would be the next to have a birthday anniversary. The interviewers made no attempt to convert those who did not wish to participate. A completed interview was achieved in 44 percent of the residences with valid telephone numbers (by "valid" we mean that a person with the name identified in our sample resided at that address). The major reasons for failing to obtain an interview included: (1) contacting a minor child, friend, or relative, but not an eligible adult; (2) contacting an eligible respondent, arranging to call back to interview them at a more convenient time, and then failing to reestablish contact; (3) repeatedly reaching an answering machine; (4) refusals to be interviewed; (5) language difficulties. This was primarily a problem with Koreans, and may have cost about a dozen interviews. A Spanish version of the questionnaire and bilingual interviewers were available for all Hispanic surname respondents, and we encountered virtually no language problems with other Asians. Finally, few individuals terminated an interview before completion; we treated any partial interviews as noncompletions.

A response rate of 44 percent is comparable to the rates currently achieved by commercial polling firms (Wiseman and McDonald 1979). It is also close to the 46 percent rate of cooperation estimated by comparing the number of reported telephone contacts to the number of reported telephone interviews in the National Research Council's 1979 survey of the polling experience of the U.S. population. Admittedly, that our response rate is similar to that achieved by others is less reassuring than it might be in light of the increasing nonresponse experienced by telephone (and other) surveys (Steeh 1981). The amount of bias that results from the nonresponse depends critically on how much difference there is between respondents and nonrespondents. Although we cannot directly obtain the characteristics of the nonrespondents to our study, we can partially assess the representatives of our samples by comparing their demographic characteristics with the 1980 census estimates for the corresponding populations.

The figures reported in table 6A.1 indicate that in all four subsamples the reported figures for family income and country of birth (U.S. or not) were quite similar to those reported by the Census Bureau. There are, however, some discrepancies. The percentages of blacks and Latinos in our sample who reported being homeowners were higher than the census figures, and we oversampled Asian men and black women. The largest discrepancies were in reported education. Individuals in all four subsamples were considerably more likely to report having attended college than the 1980 census figures indicate should be the case. This is not surprising. Almost all political surveys show some bias in reported

Table 6A.1
Comparison of Sample and Census Characteristics

	White	Black	Latino	Asian
Percent Male				
Sample 1984	49%	38%	49%	60%
Census 1980	49	49	51	48
Percent Owner Occupiers				
Sample 1984	66	64	52	64
Census 1980	62	45	44	62
Family Income 10K				
Sample 1984	12	25	21	9
Census 1980	16	34	27	14
Family Income 10-25K				
Sample 1984	44	41	47	35
Census 1980	40	40	48	37
Family Income over 25K				
Sample 1984	44	33	32	56
Census 1980	44	26	25	49
Percent Native Born				
Sample 1984	94	98	60	38
Census 1980	90	98	63	42
Percent Some College or Greater				
Sample 1984	60	53	34	77
Census 1980	44	36	20	54

education, and telephone surveys generally fare worse in this regard than do face-to-face surveys. The model estimations in tables 6.13 and 6.14 should be unaffected by the bias in education level, if the models are correctly specified.

NOTES

Data collection for this project was funded by a grant from the Seaver Institute to Bruce E. Cain and D. Roderick Kiewiet. The author thanks Mark Capps for assistance in data analysis.

1. By restricting the analysis to Mexican-Americans, we avoid problems of interpretation that arise from the variety of countries and circumstances that characterize our other Latino respondents, at no real cost in statistical power, as the number of Mexican-Americans is very large. We must also confess, however, that due to an error in programming the survey instrument for the interviewers, non-Mexican Latinos were not asked the prejudice questions. Since they would have to be excluded from that portion of the analysis in any case, they were excluded from the entire analysis.

2. Although the high reported rates of black participation could be an artifact of the high education and income levels of the black sample (see table 6A.1) or of differential overreporting, other evidence suggests that the result is real. Wolfinger, using the Voter Supplement to the 1984 Current Population Survey, found black Californians slightly more likely than whites to register (80 percent versus 78 percent), although less likely to vote once registered (88 percent versus 91 percent); the net effect is virtually equal turnout (Raymond Wolfinger, personal communication). For the 1988 election, the Bureau of the Census reported black voting rates which exceeded white rates in a number of states, including California (*Voting and Registration in the Election of November 1988* (*Advance Report*), 6–9).

3. A number of native-born respondents also claim a language other than English as their primary language and would similarly be limited in political life by this.

REFERENCES

Anderson, Kristi. 1979. *The Creation of a Democratic Majority, 1928–1936*. Chicago: University of Chicago Press.
Bobo, Lawrence. 1983. "Whites' Opposition to Busing: Symbolic Racism or Realistic Group Conflict?" *Journal of Personality and Social Psychology* 45:1196–1210.
Cain, Bruce E., D. Roderick Kiewiet, and Carole J. Uhlaner. 1991. "The Acquisition of Partisanship by Latinos and Asian-Americans." *American Journal of Political Science* 35 (May): 390–422.
Chang, Tsan-kuo, Pamela Shoemaker, Stephen Reese, and Wayne Danielson. 1988. "Sampling Ethnic Media Use: The Case of Hispanics." *Journalism Quarterly* 65:189–191.

Conway, M. Margaret. 1985. *Political Participation in the United States.* Washington, D.C.: CQ Press.

Gurin, Patricia, and E. G. Epps. 1975. *Black Consciousness, Identity, and Achievement.* New York: John Wiley and Sons.

Gurin, Patricia, Shirley Hatchett, and James S. Jackson. 1989. *Hope and Independence: Blacks' Response to Electoral and Party Politics.* New York: Russell Sage Foundation.

Gurin, Patricia, Arthur H. Miller, and Gerald Gurin. 1980. "Stratum Identification and Consciousness." *Social Psychology Quarterly* 43 (1): 30–47.

Henig, Jeffrey R., and Dennis E. Gale. 1987. "The Political Incorporation of Newcomers to Racially Changing Neighborhoods." *Urban Affairs Quarterly* 22 (March): 399–419.

Himmelfarb, Harold, Michael R. Loar, and Susan Mott. 1983. "Sampling by Ethnic Surnames: The Case of American Jews." *Public Opinion Quarterly* 47:247–260.

Keefe, Susan E., and Amado M. Padilla. 1987. *Chicano Ethnicity.* Albuquerque: University of New Mexico Press.

Leuthold, David, and Raymond Scheele. 1971. "Patterns of Bias in Samples Based on Telephone Directories." *Public Opinion Quarterly* 35:249–257.

Miller, Arthur H., Patricia Gurin, Gerald Gurin, and Oksana Malanchuk. 1981. "Group Consciousness and Political Participation." *American Journal of Political Science* 25 (August): 494–511.

National Research Council. 1979. *Privacy and Confidentiality as Factors in Survey Response.* Washington, D.C.: National Academy of Sciences.

Olsen, Marvin E. 1970. "Social and Political Participation of Blacks." *American Sociological Review* 35:682–696.

Portes, Alejandro, and Robert L. Bach. 1985. *Latin Journey: Cuban and Mexican Immigrants in the United States.* Berkeley: University of California Press.

Salamon, Lester M., and Stephen Van Evera. 1973. "Fear, Apathy, and Discrimination: A Test of Three Explanations of Political Participation." *American Political Science Review* 67 (December): 1288–1306.

Sears, David O., and Donald R. Kinder. 1985. "Whites' Opposition to Busing: On Conceptualizing and Operationalizing Group Conflict." *Journal of Personality and Social Psychology* 48 (May): 1141–1147.

Sears, David O., Richard R. Lau, Tom R. Tyler, and Harris M. Allen, Jr. 1980. "Self-Interest vs. Symbolic Politics in Policy Attitudes and Presidential Voting." *American Political Science Review* 74 (September): 670–684.

Sniderman, Paul M., and Philip E. Tetlock. 1986. "Symbolic Racism: Problems of Motive Attribution in Political Analysis." *Journal of Social Issues* 42 (2): 129–150.

Steeh, Charlotte. 1981. "Trends in Nonresponse Rates, 1952–1979." *Public Opinion Quarterly* 45 (Spring): 40–57.

Thornberry, Owen T., Jr., and James T. Massey. 1988. "Trends in United States Telephone Coverage across Time and Subgroups. In *Telephone Survey Methodology,* ed. Robert M. Groves, Paul P. Biemer, Lars E. Lyberg, James T. Massey, William L. Nicholls II, and Joseph Waksberg, 25–49. New York: John Wiley & Sons.

Uhlaner, Carole Jean. 1989a. "Rational Turnout: The Neglected Role of Groups." *American Journal of Political Science* 33 (May): 390–422.

Uhlaner, Carole Jean. 1989b. "'Relational Goods' and Participation: Incorporating Sociability into a Theory of Rational Action." *Public Choice* 62:253–285.

Uhlaner, Carole Jean, Bruce E. Cain, and D. Roderick Kiewiet. 1989. "Political Participation of Ethnic Minorities in the 1980s." *Political Behavior* 11 (September): 195–231.

Verba, Sidney, and Norman Nie. 1972. *Participation in America: Political Democracy and Social Equality*. New York: Harper and Row.

Wiseman, Frederick, and Philip McDonald. 1979. "Noncontact and Refusal Rates in Consumer Telephone Surveys." *Journal of Marketing Research* 16 (November): 478–484.

7 Voting for Judges: Race and Roll-Off in Judicial Elections

Richard L. Engstrom and
Victoria M. Caridas

The typical American ballot presents the voter with multiple decisions. A variety of separate elections are usually contested at any one time. Voters may be asked to choose, on a single ballot, between or among candidates for offices as diverse as president of the United States and county coroner, or governor of a state and traffic court judge. Participation in these various elections is not compulsory, however. Just as eligible voters may stay home on election day, so also may those who sign in to vote decline or neglect to cast votes in some of the elections on the ballot. This type of nonparticipation is not random, of course, but tends to vary with the perceived importance of an office. Most voters are drawn to the polls initially by the high stimulus elections to the more salient offices (contests usually located at or near the top of the ballot). After voting in these contests, however, some "rolloff" (i.e., do not vote) in the elections to offices perceived to be less salient (contests usually located farther down the ballot). Indeed, the "stereotypical voter" has been described as one who

> shows up at the polls intending to vote in one or two salient and well-publicized races or in a controversial referendum. Entering the polling place, the voter is confronted with a bewildering array of contests and choices. After voting on a few salient races, interest is quickly lost as the voter no longer recognizes names of candidates, becomes fatigued, gets careless, and, eventually, goes beyond the point of indifference and stops voting entirely. (Darcy and Schneider 1989, 348)

Students of political participation, like voters, have been most interested in high stimulus elections. Roll-off, as a consequence, has not been studied extensively. This relative inattention to roll-off does not mean that it is a politically unimportant phenomenon, however. To the contrary, due to roll-off, the actual electorate in low stimulus elections can be different in politically significant ways from that in the high stimulus elections. Just as roll-off does not occur randomly across the ballot, neither does its incidence among the voters occur randomly. Certain types of voters therefore can be expected to rolloff more frequently than other types.

One extremely important correlate of roll-off has been the race of the voters. Not only have blacks been found less likely than whites to be among those who sign in on election day, they also have been found more likely to be among the voters who rolloff rather than vote an entire ballot (see Darcy and Schneider 1989; Vanderleeuw and Engstrom 1987; Sheffield and Hadley 1984, 458; Magleby 1984, 103–114; Collins 1980, 333; Clubb and Traugott 1972, 145–146; Walker 1966, 460). The extent to which either form of nonparticipation is attributable to blacks being disproportionately poor and less educated, or to other variables related to race, remains a matter of dispute (see, e.g., Darcy and Schneider 1989, 360–362; Vanderleeuw and Engstrom 1987, 1087–1090; Sheffield and Hadley 1984, 458; Abramson and Claggett 1984, 1986, 1989), but the demographic consequences of the nonparticipation are not disputed. The actual electorate, when compared with the potential electorate, is usually disproportionately white, and becomes increasingly so as it moves down (or across) the ballot from high stimulus to low stimulus contests. This is especially significant given that the candidate preferences of American voters often differ by the voter's race (see, e.g., Bullock 1984, 1985; Collins 1980; Engstrom 1985, 1989; Sheffield and Hadley 1984).

While the elections most affected by roll-off tend to be those for the less salient offices on a ballot, many of those offices are far from unimportant. Salience is a relative matter, of course, and some very important decisions are made by people who occupy these offices. Among these low salience positions, for example, are numerous state and local judgeships. Despite rhetoric about "mechanical jurisprudence" and judges being neutral decisionmakers, judges are widely acknowledged to have considerable discretion when interpreting and applying the law. Different judges, in short, may make different findings and reach different conclusions (see, e.g., Uhlman 1977; Welch, Combs, and Gruhl 1988; Crockett 1976).

JUDICIAL ELECTIONS

Trial and/or appellate court judges are popularly elected in many states (Dubois 1980a; Fund for Modern Courts 1985; Marquardt 1988). Elections to judicial offices are generally low stimulus affairs. Candidates are restricted by ethical canons from certain types of campaign activities, including taking positions on controversial legal and/or political issues (see Alfini and Brooks 1988–89). The media's attention to these more subdued campaigns is usually low, and voters tend to have minimal information about the candidates (Johnson, Shaefer, and McKnight 1978; McKnight, Shaefer, and Johnson 1978; Klots 1973; Landinsky and Silver 1967, 161; Jacob 1966, 818). Not surprisingly, many voters rolloff when they reach the portion of the ballot containing judicial contests. This is especially the case when judicial elections are nonpartisan, or when the ballot format does not facilitate straight-party voting (Dubois 1980a, 1980b, 47–48, 54–57; Berg and Flynn 1980, 168–169; Barber 1971, 772–776, 782–784; Darcy and Schneider 1989, 358; Baum 1987, 72 n.1; Lovrich and Sheldon 1985, 289).

Roll-off in judicial elections may be extremely important politically. Black voters reportedly have a preference for black judges, a preference not generally shared by white voters. Federal courts in Mississippi, Louisiana, and Texas, for example, have found judicial elections involving a choice between or among black and white candidates to be infected with "racially polarized voting."[1] These voting patterns presumably reflect, at least in part, expectations that white and black judges will exercise discretion differently, expectations for which there is some empirical evidence (see Welch, Combs, and Gruhl 1988). When voting is racially divided, the relative levels of participation between blacks and whites in judicial elections may be a critical variable (along with the type of election system employed, see McDuff 1989) affecting black electoral prospects. Indeed, one black jurist has admonished black voters for ignoring judicial elections, stating:

> One judge and one decision can do more to protect your rights than any elected mayor. But we blacks seem to concentrate on electing mayors; we pride ourselves in saying that we have a black mayor who is taking over some bankrupt metropolitan city. When we go to the polls to vote, we don't even look at the judicial ballot. That, I submit, is where the power is. (Crockett 1976, 192)

Empirical research on the extent to which there are racial differences in participation in judicial elections has been very limited, however, and the findings have not been consistent. Support for the assertion that blacks rolloff from judicial elections at rates greater than whites is provided in one study of an election involving a choice between black and white candidates for criminal court judge in New Orleans, Louisiana, in 1982. Based on *reported* participation by the respondents in a postelection survey, Sheffield and Hadley (1984) conclude that while black registered voters turned out at a slightly higher rate than whites in the mayoral election that day (91.9 percent compared to 89.5 percent), black participation was lower than white in the simultaneous judicial election due to roll-off (82.8 percent compared to 86.9 percent). These survey based figures, however, exaggerated significantly the actual participation levels in these elections (1984, 455, 458).

Studies based on actual election returns, rather than surveys, have produced different results. Lovrich, Sheldon, and Wasmann (1988) examined two trial court elections involving a biracial choice of candidates in Multnomah County (Portland), Oregon, in 1984. In predominantly black precincts, 18.8 percent and 24.5 percent of the people signing in to vote that day did not cast a vote in the respective judicial contests. While these figures may be high in an absolute sense, fall-off in these elections in socioeconomically matched white precincts was even higher, 32.1 percent and 30.9 percent (1988, 809). Similar results have been reported by Atkins, DeZee, and Eckert (1984, 1985) for two Florida Supreme Court elections in 1976. In the election involving a choice between two white candidates for the court, turnout in white precincts averaged 28.1 percent of the registered voters, compared to only 13.1 percent in the black precincts. In the other supreme court election on the same ballot, one involving a choice between a black and a white candidate, turnout in the white precincts remained about the same, 27.1 percent, but almost doubled in the black precincts, to 25.6 percent. The resulting racial difference in participation in the black-on-white election was therefore less than two percentage points (1984, 217; 1985, 218). These studies based on actual election returns suggest that the presence of a black candidate for judge may stimulate black voters to participate in judicial elections at rates comparable to, or even higher than, white voters (see more generally Pinderhughes 1985, 534–537; O'Loughlin 1980).

Participation in judicial elections is, unfortunately, a type of political behavior about which very little is known. While we can generalize with confidence that participation in these elections is consistently lower than in high stimulus elections, we know relatively little, for example, about which voters are most likely to rolloff from judicial contests or the conditions affecting the rates at which they do rolloff. The following addresses the racial dimension to both of these issues. Data have been collected for all 52 contested judicial elections held in New Orleans, Louisiana, from 1978 through 1988, of which 32 presented voters with a biracial choice of candidates. Participation levels among black and white registered voters in these, as well as 15 simultaneous elections for major offices, will be estimated and compared, as will the levels of support each group provided particular candidates.[2] The extent to which racial differences in participation may have varied with racial divisions over the candidate choices confronting the voters will be examined to determine whether the racial saliency of a judicial election affects the absolute and/or relative rates of roll-off in these contests.

SETTING AND MEASURES

New Orleans is a city in which a majority of the registered voters is now black. The 1980 census of population reported that blacks comprised 55.3 percent of the city's 557,515 residents (a 1985 Census Bureau estimate placed the black percentage at 58.8). A slight majority of the city's registered voters was black by 1984, a figure that increased to 54.0 percent in 1988. The city has had a black mayor since 1978, a black majority on its council since 1986, and a black majority on its school board since 1988. Blacks remain woefully underrepresented, however, in the local judiciary. In 1988, only six of the 40 elected trial court judgeships in New Orleans were held by blacks, and only one of the eight elected appellate court judgeships apportioned exclusively to New Orleans was held by a black. Judicial seats are increasingly contested by black candidates, however. As noted above, 32 of the 52 (61.2 percent) contested elections between 1978 and 1988 included at least one black candidate. Since 1983, a black has been a candidate in 20 of the 22 (90.9 percent) contested elections.

The large number of contested judicial elections, and the frequency with which blacks have been judicial candidates, make New Orleans a particularly appropriate setting in which to examine the racial dimension to roll-off. Equally important, however, is the fact that voter registration is recorded by race in New Orleans. This greatly facilitates the estimation, through precinct-based registration and election data, of the voting levels and candidate preferences of each racial group. The number of precincts on which these estimates can be based ranged from 428 in 1978 to 465 in 1988. Many of the precincts were racially homogeneous at the time of the elections, meaning 90 percent or more of the registered voters within them were either black or white. In 1978, 81 precincts were homogeneously black, 142 homogeneously white; in 1988, the numbers were 110 and 109, respectively. Problems of ecological inference in this context are probably less serious than either the tendency of respondents in surveys and polls, especially black respondents, to exaggerate their level of electoral participation (Abramson and Claggett 1984, 1986, 1989; Wolfinger and Rosenstone 1980, 115–118), or the tendency among white respondents to misreport their candidate preferences in biracial elections (Pettigrew and Alston 1988, 17–21; Rosenthal 1989).

The candidate choices and participation levels of blacks and whites in these elections have been estimated through ecological regression. The procedure employed is sometimes referred to as "double regression" because the results of two bivariate regressions are combined to produce the estimates (see Grofman, Migalski, and Noviello 1985, 202–205; Engstrom and McDonald 1988, 181; Loewen and Grofman 1989; Engstrom 1989). The independent variable in each regression is the percentage of registered voters in each precinct that was black. The dependent variable is, in one regression, the percentage of registered voters in each precinct that voted for a particular candidate in the election, and in the other, the percentage voting for that candidate's opponent(s). The first regression provides estimates of the percentage of the white and black registered voters voting for that candidate, while the second provides the corresponding figures for the opponent(s). Combining these results provides (1) estimates of the percentages of black and white registered voters casting votes in the election, and (2) among those voting, estimates of the percentages of blacks and whites voting for the candidate and/or the opponent(s).[3]

The methodology is illustrated in figures 7.1 and 7.2. These figures concern a 1982 runoff election for a seat on the criminal district court between a black candidate, Henry Julien, and a white candidate, Shirley Wimberly. Figure 7.1 is a scatterplot of the vote by precinct for Julien. Each precinct has been located in the plot according to the percentage of registered voters within it that was black (the horizontal axis) and the percentage of registered voters within it that cast a vote for Julien (the vertical axis). The line in the figure is a regression line, the straight line that fits most tightly to these points. The association between the racial composition of the precincts and the vote for Julien in this election was very strong, as reflected in the magnitude of the correlation coefficient ($r = .962$).

The regression line begins at the left end of the horizontal axis, the point at which none of the registered voters is black. The value of this intercept, 11.4, provides the estimate of the percentage of white registered voters that cast a vote for Julien. The magnitude of the regression coefficient (b) measures the slope of the regression line, and reflects a tendency for Julien's vote across precincts to increase by .493 of a percentage point for every 1.0 percentage point increase in black registration. The value of the "right intercept," the point at which the regression line ends, where all registered voters are black, is therefore 60.7 [11.4 + .493 (100)]. This provides the estimate of the percentage of black registered voters that voted for Julien.

Figure 7.2 contains the same information as figure 7.1, only the vertical axis now represents the vote for Wimberly, Julien's opponent. Based on the same type of analysis, Wimberly is estimated to have received votes from 58.6 percent of the whites registered to vote, but only 8.2 percent of the blacks. Overall, therefore, the estimated percentage of white registered voters casting a vote in this election is 70.0 (11.4 percent for Julien and 58.6 percent for Wimberly), and among the whites voting, an es-

Figure 7.1
Vote for the Black Candidate

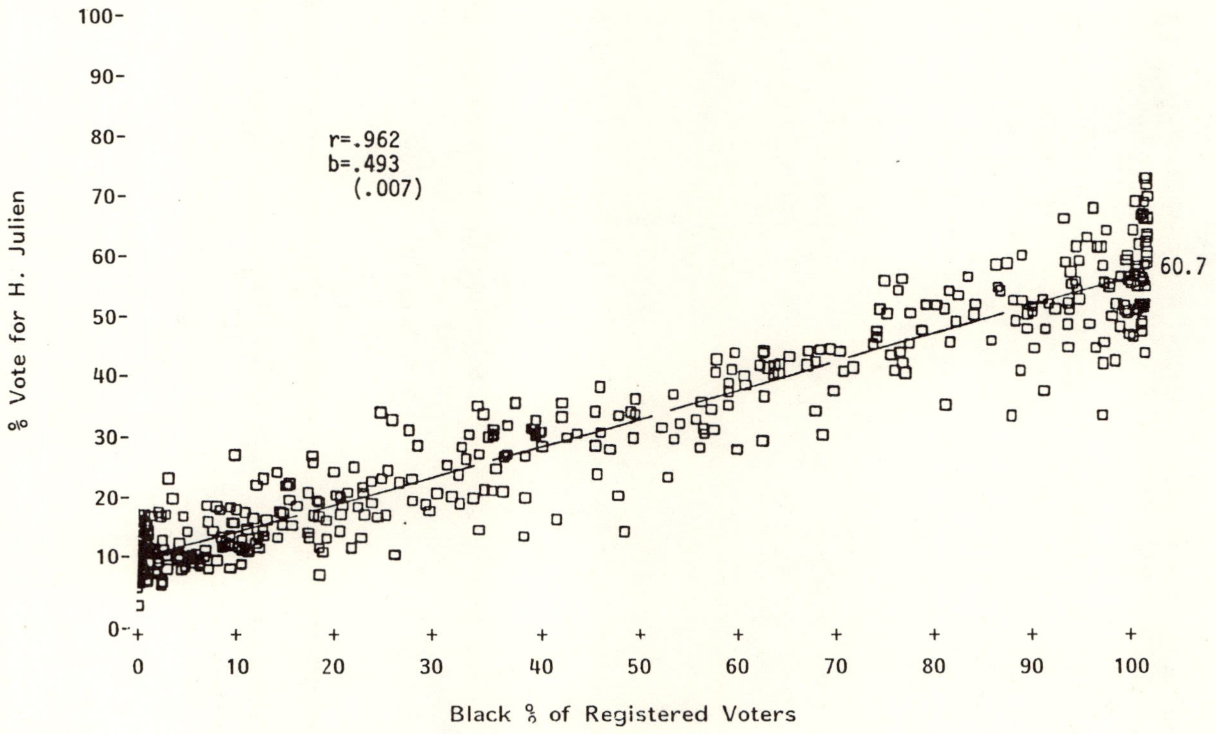

r=.962
b=.493
(.007)

% Vote for H. Julien / Black % of Registered Voters

Figure 7.2
Vote for the White Candidate

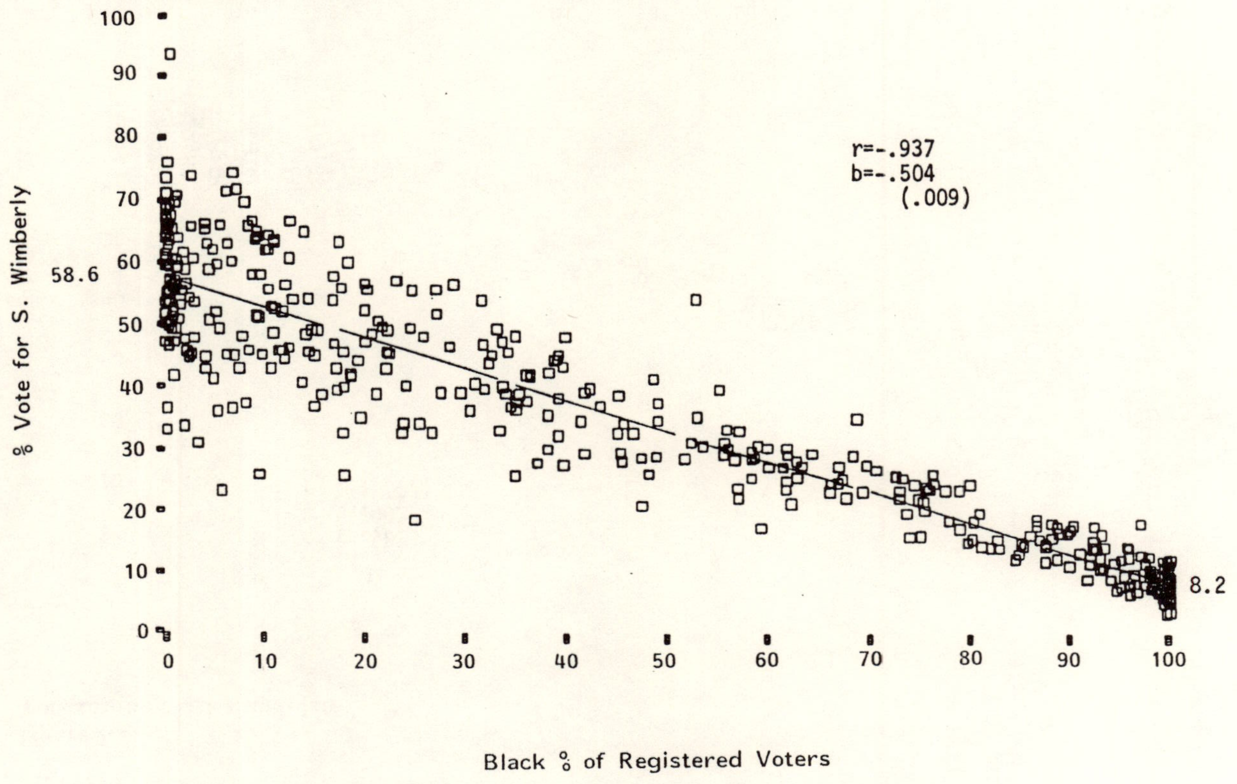

r=-.937
b=-.504
(.009)

% Vote for S. Wimberly

Black % of Registered Voters

timated 16.3 percent (11.4/70.0) voted for Julien. In contrast, an estimated 68.9 percent of the registered blacks cast a vote in this election (60.7 percent for Julien and 8.2 percent for Wimberly), and among the blacks voting, it is estimated that 88.1 percent voted for Julien.

This procedure was used to derive estimates of participation levels and candidate preferences for all 52 judicial elections over the 11 year period and also for the 15 elections for major offices held simultaneously with these judicial elections.

RESULTS

Participation levels across the 52 judicial elections have varied greatly for both blacks and whites. The estimated turnout in these elections among white registered voters, for example, ranged from 20.5 percent to 70.0 percent, with the average being 46.2 percent (st.dev. = 13.8). For blacks, in contrast, the range was even greater, 6.0 percent to 69.0 percent, while the average was lower, 33.9 percent (st.dev. = 14.9). Much of the variation for both groups, of course, is due to large differences in participation levels between the judicial elections held concurrently with elections to major offices and those that were not. Among black registered voters, the average turnout percentage in the 34 judicial elections contested at the same time as a more salient office was 40.7, twice the average for the 17 judicial elections held on a day without a major contest (see table 7.1).[4] For whites, the average turnout in the concurrent judicial elections is about 80 percent higher than that in the others. Not surprisingly, the scheduling of judicial elections along with those for more salient offices has been a major stimulus to voting in judicial contests in New Orleans as elsewhere (see Dubois 1980a, 45; Adamany and Dubois 1976, 743–745; Atkins and McDonald 1977, 31).

While participation is higher in the simultaneous judicial elections than in the others, it is still, for both groups, considerably below that for the major office elections (see table 7.1). This reflects the fact that many voters drawn to the polls by the high stimulus elections do rolloff rather than vote in the judicial contests. These New Orleans elections were conducted through an office-block ballot, so participation in a judicial election did require a voter to locate that election on the ballot and then pull a lever for a specific judicial candidate. This ballot format, not surprisingly, is associated with higher levels of voter roll-off than the party column ballot (Dubois 1980a, 56, Atkins and McDonald 1977, 22; Walker 1966; Scarrow 1986, 243–244). When turnouts in these judicial elections in New Orleans are compared to those in the major elections on the same day, whites on average cast 10.9 percent (st.dev. = 6.9) fewer votes in the judicial elections. However, blacks on average rolloff at almost twice that rate, 20.6 percent (st.dev. = 11.6). The racial gap

Table 7.1
Participation Rates in Judicial and Major Office Elections, by Race

	% of Registered Voters Voting in		
	Judicial Elections		Elections for Major Offices (N=15)
	Without Simultaneous Election to Major Office (N=17)	With Simultaneous Election to Major Office (N=34)	
All Registered Voters			
Mean (St.Dev.)	25.6 (6.0)	47.7 (10.0)	61.5 (11.3)
White Registered Voters			
Mean (St.Dev.)	30.3 (6.9)	54.4 (8.3)	65.6 (9.6)
Black Registered Voters			
Mean (St.Dev.)	20.4 (6.0)	40.7 (13.6)	56.9 (14.0)

in participation therefore is accentuated in the judicial elections. Not only are black registered voters in New Orleans less likely than whites to turnout for the major office elections (table 7.1), they are also more likely to rolloff after voting in the more salient contest. The actual electorate in judicial elections therefore is usually more white than that in the major election on the same day.

The standard deviations reported above indicate, however, that there is considerable within-group variation in roll-off for both blacks and whites. The range in roll-off among blacks is substantial, from only 4.0 percent to 58.8 percent, while that for whites is from 1.3 percent to 34.8 percent. There are even six instances in which black roll-off in judicial elections is lower than that for whites. This raises the question, of course, of what variables or conditions may affect the rate at which voters, black or white, rolloff in these elections. Our data allow us to examine one potentially important condition likely to affect roll-off—the extent to which black and white voters differ in their choice of judicial candidates.

Racial Differences in Candidate Preferences

Black voting may increase dramatically if blacks have a positive incentive to participate (Pinderhughes 1985). Among the major incentives, of course, would be "candidates who are attractive to black voters, which includes, but is not necessarily limited to black candidates" (Pinderhughes 1985, 535; see also O'Loughlin 1980). Limited evidence that black voters may be induced to vote in, rather than rolloff from, judicial elections when presented with the chance to vote for a black candidate has been provided by Atkins, DeZee, and Eckert (1984; 1985) and Lovrich, Sheldon, and Wasmann (1988). As noted above, over 60 percent of the New Orleans judicial elections between 1978 and 1988 presented voters with a biracial choice. These elections provide a particularly good opportunity, therefore, to assess the extent to which racial divisions in candidate choices may affect racial differences in participation.

Louisiana has a unique election system. Voters may specify a party preference when registering to vote, and the partisan registrations of candidates (including judicial candidates) are listed on the ballot. All candidates however, regardless of party registration, compete in a single primary election in which all voters, regardless of their party registration, may vote. If no candidate receives a majority of the votes cast in the primary, the top two, again regardless of party registration, compete in a runoff election. This system, which has been described by one student of Louisiana politics as a "bipartisan" election system, does not necessarily pit Democratic and Republican candidates in head-to-head contests (Parent 1988, 214; see also Hadley 1986; Theodoulou 1985; Kazee 1983). Judicial elections in New Orleans have been, under this arrangement, virtually void of partisan content; indeed, only seven Republicans have been candidates in the 52 elections.

When party cues are not particularly salient, racial cues can be expected to be important (see, e.g., Atkins, DeZee, and Eckert 1984, 1985), and they undoubtedly have been in New Orleans' judicial elections. In the 32 elections involving a choice between or among black and white candidates, black voters preferred a black candidate in all but three. Candidate preference estimates reveal that a majority of blacks voted for a black candidate in 26 (81.2 percent) of the elections, and that a plurality of blacks did in three additional elections (9.4 percent). This preference was never shared by New Orleans' white voters, however. In none of these elections did a plurality, let alone a majority, of the whites voting for judge support a black candidate. The white preference was, in all 32 instances, a white candidate. Racial divisions, while not as dominant, were not uncommon in the 20 white-on-white judicial elections either. In nine of these contests involving a choice between or among whites only, a majority of blacks and a majority of whites voted for different candidates.

While black and white voters were usually divided over their choice of judicial candidates, the degree to which these preferences differed varied greatly. When the estimated percentage of white voters who voted for the candidate most preferred by blacks is subtracted from the estimated black percentage for that candidate, the resulting distribution of differences ranges from 90.4 percentage points to –11.3 percentage points, and has a standard deviation of 28.2 around a mean of 40.7. These differences are most pronounced, not surprisingly, when the black-preferred candidate is a black. In these situations, the average difference is 61.2 percentage points (st.dev. = 17.6), compared to an average of only 14.8 (st.dev. = 13.9) when the black preference is a white candidate.[5]

Candidate Preference Differences and Participation

Variations in racial divisions over candidates may relate to participation in judicial elections. As the divisions increase, and the elections therefore become more racially salient, the stimulus to vote may increase. This could be true for both racial groups, but is most likely to occur among the group that is otherwise less participatory, the blacks (see Pinderhughes 1985; Vanderleeuw and Engstrom 1987). To determine whether there is an empirical linkage between these variables, participation measures have been regressed onto the racial divisions in candidate preferences.

The impact that racial divisions over judicial candidates have on participation appears to depend on whether a major office is also being

Table 7.2
Regression Equations Relating Racially Divided Voting to Black Participation

A: BTURN = 25.8   + .349RDVJ $R^2 = .453$
              (3.4)   (.068)

B: BTURN = 12.8   + .487RDVM $R^2 = .566$
              (4.6)   (.075)

C: BTURN = 8.9   + .378RDVM + .237RDVJ $R^2 = .747$
              (3.6)   (.063)   (.050)

contested at the same time. In the 17 judicial elections held on a day when no major offices were contested, racial divisions in the candidate choices of judicial candidates were *not* related to participation for either group. When the white turnout percentages in these elections (WTURN) are regressed onto the divisions in candidate preferences (RDVJ) the following equation results:

$$WTURN = 32.4 - .057 \, RDVJ$$
$$(2.5) \quad (.052)$$
$$R^2 = .075$$

The magnitude of the regression coefficient (b) in this equation is minimal, only $-.057$, and not reliably different from zero ($S_b = .052$), revealing virtually no relationship between the racial divisions in the vote and white turnout. Similar results are found for black turnout. When black turnout percentages (BTURN) are regressed onto RDVJ, the result is:

$$BTURN = 19.5 + .025 \, RDVJ$$
$$(2.3) \quad (.046)$$
$$R^2 = .019$$

The b is again minimal, .025, and not reliably different from zero ($S_b = .046$), revealing virtually no relationship between racial divisions and black turnout. Participation in these elections is simply not responsive, for either group, to the racial divisions over the judicial candidates. Divisive judicial candidacies apparently are not a sufficient stimulus, absent a major office contest, to bring the more peripheral voters to the polls.

When judicial elections are held simultaneously with an election for a major office, however, the results are in sharp contrast. Racial divisions over judicial candidates are related to voting in these 34 judicial contests by blacks (table 7.2, equation A), and to a much lesser degree, by whites (table 7.3, equation A). Judicial voting among blacks is not as strongly related to these candidate divisions, however, as it is to the racial divisions over the candidates for the major offices (RDVM) (table 7.2,

Table 7.3
Regression Equations Relating Racially Divided Voting to White Participation

A: WTURN = 49.6   + .112RDVJ $R^2 = .123$
              (2.6)   (.053)

B: WTURN = 45.17   + .161RDVM $R^2 = .164$
              (3.9)   (.064)

C: WTURN = 44.0   + .127RDVM + .074RDVJ $R^2 = .212$
              (4.0)   (.068)   (.055)

equation B). This undoubtedly reflects the importance of the major election contest in bringing black voters to the polls. These racial divisions over judicial candidates and over major office candidates are not strongly correlated, however ($r = .369$), and when both are included as independent variables in a multiple regression equation, the racial division over judicial elections does have an independent, although subdued ($b = .237$), impact on black voting (table 7.2, equation C). The standardized regression coefficients in the multiple regression for black turnout are .583 for RBVM and .458 for RBVJ, reflecting the more prounced impact of the candidate choice in the major election. Much weaker relationships are found between participation and candidate divisions among whites (table 7.3).

It is unlikely that divisive judicial choices bring voters to the polls in these simultaneous elections any more than in those held on a day without a major office contest. On the contrary, it is most likely that these divisions related to black participation because black voters, once at the polls, are less likely to rolloff from the most racially salient judicial contests. This expectation is supported when the estimated percentages of blacks rolling off (BROLL) are regressed onto the RDVJ scores for the 34 judicial elections. The resulting equation,

$$\text{BROLL} = 31.4 - .252 \text{ RDVJ}$$
$$(3.2) \quad (.064) \qquad R^2 = .326$$

reveals that black roll-off does decline as the conflict in preferences increases. The magnitude of the relationship is impressive—roll-off tends to drop by a percentage point for every four percentage point increase in the group divisions. A similar relationship does not exist for white voters, however. When the estimates of white roll-off (WROLL) are regressed onto RDVJ, the result is:

$$\text{WROLL} = 9.1 + .043 \text{ RDVJ}$$
$$(2.3) \quad (.046) \qquad R^2 = .163$$

Conflicting preferences have virtually no impact on the participation levels of whites.

The elections in which the two group preferences have contrasted most sharply have been, as noted above, those involving a biracial choice in judicial candidates. It is when black voters prefer a black candidate that the divisions tend to be greatest. It has been in these biracial elections therefore that blacks have tended to rolloff the least, and the racial composition of the actual judicial electorate has been the least distorted. This is illustrated in figure 7.3, in which the racial differences in roll-off (black roll-off percentage minus white roll-off percentage) have been plotted and regressed against the racial divisions over the judicial candidates. Those elections in which the candidate preferred by black voters was black are identified in the plot by a B; those in which the black-preferred candidate was white are identified by a W. The race of the candidate preferred by black voters is obviously an important variable. It was the candidacies of blacks over which the voters were most divided, and it was these candidacies that stimulated black voters to vote in, rather than rolloff from, the simultaneous judicial contests. The more racially salient the election, therefore, the less is the participation gap between blacks and whites (see also Vanderleeuw and Engstrom 1987).

CONCLUSION

No other democracy employs elections to fill the number and variety of offices as does the United States (Lijphart 1985, 19). Students of American electoral politics, however, have focused on participation in the elections to the few major offices such as president, governor, and mayor, while little attention has been devoted to elections to the large number of less salient offices, such as county supervisor or municipal judge. The preoccupation with the "high stimulus" elections is understandable, but unfortunately it does neglect an important type of non-partipation, roll-off. Due to roll-off, the actual electorate may vary from office to office on any particular day, and this variation may be politically important.

One significant dimension on which the electorate may vary is its racial composition. Blacks and whites often have contrasting candidate preferences, so participation differences between these groups are important. Numerous studies have documented the general tendency for blacks to participate in major office elections at a rate below that for whites. Differences in roll-off between the groups can accentuate this participation gap as voters move down or across the ballot to the contests for other offices.

Among the less salient offices filled by election are numerous state and local judgeships. Judicial elections tend to be low stimulus affairs that attract relatively few voters to the polls. When these elections are not held concurrently with those for major offices, participation in them

Figure 7.3
Roll-Off Differences and Racial Voting Divisions

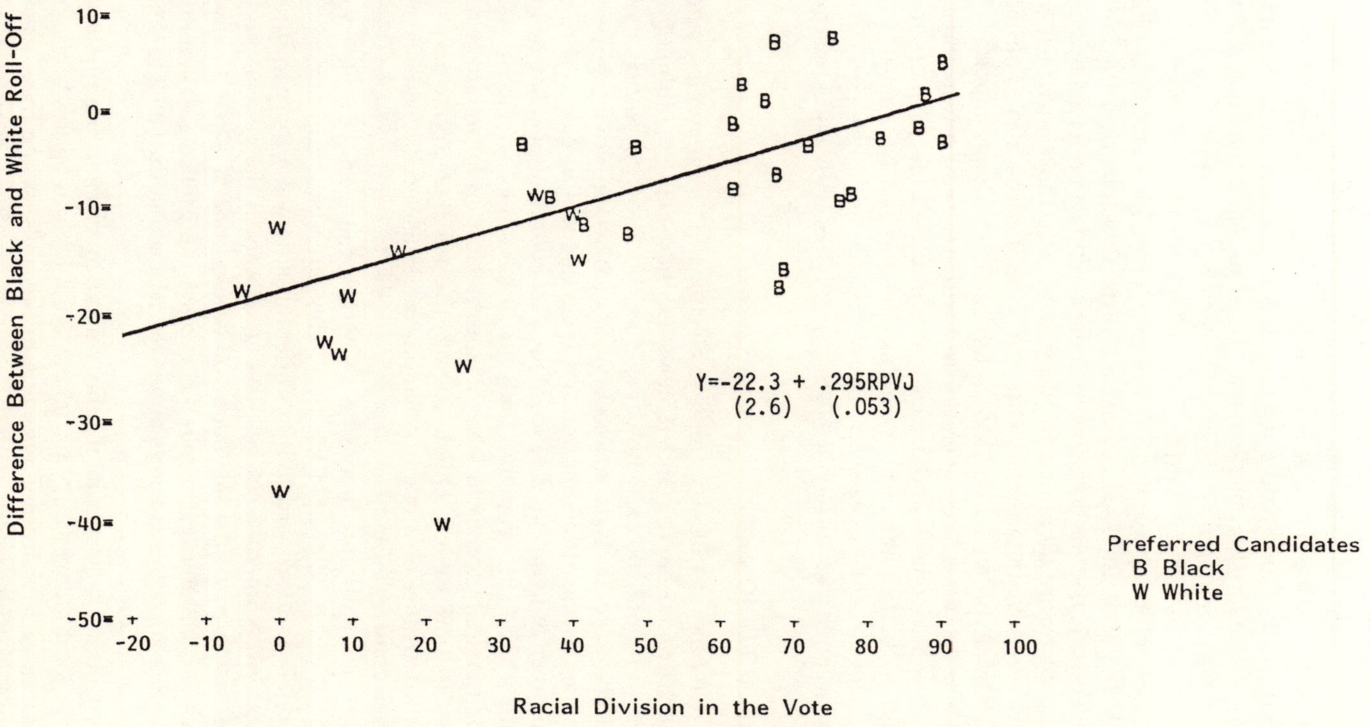

$Y = -22.3 + .295 \text{RPVJ}$
$(2.6) \quad (.053)$

Difference Between Black and White Roll-Off

Racial Division in the Vote

Preferred Candidates
B Black
W White

is usually severely depressed. But even when held simultaneously with a major office contest, participation in judicial elections still tends to be considerably below that in the major office election. Many voters simply rolloff rather than vote for judges.

Roll-off in New Orleans' judicial elections has affected the racial composition of the local judicial electorate. Black voters were found, in over 80 percent of simultaneous judicial elections, to rolloff at greater rates than white voters. The relative rates of roll-off varied, however, depending on the candidate choices presented to the voters. The more racially divided the response to the candidates, the less the difference in participation tended to be. This was primarily attributable to the impact that black candidacies had on the voters, however. It was the black candidates for judicial office over which the voters were most divided, and it was in support of these candidates that black voters tended to "rollon" (Loewen and Grofman 1989, 591) rather than off. Black candidacies undoubtedly provided blacks with an incentive to participate, once at the polls, in these judicial elections. But these black candidacies, it must be remembered, usually only reduced the racial differences in participation, rather than reversed them. Racial differences in roll-off, even when blacks were candidates, generally resulted in a judicial electorate that was, in comparison to the major office electorate, disproportionately white.

NOTES

1. See *Martin* v. *Allain*, 658 F.Supp. 1183 (S.D. Miss. 1987); *Clark* v. *Edwards*, 725 F.Supp. 285 (M.D. La. 1988); *Chisom* v. *Roemer*, Civ. No. 86–4057 (E.D. La. 1989); *Rangel* v. *Mattox*, Civ. No. B–88–053 (S.D. Tx. 1989); and *LULAC* v. *Mattox*, Civ. No. MO–88–CA–154 (W.D. Tx. 1989).

2. These elections were held on a total of 27 separate days from 15 April 1978 through 8 November 1988. The positions at issue in the 52 judicial elections were on the Civil District Court (13), Criminal District Court (11), Juvenile Court (7), Traffic Court (3), Municipal Court (5), First City Court (5), Circuit Court of Appeals (6), and state Supreme Court (2). Voters throughout the City of New Orleans voted in all of these elections except those for First City Court, in which the residents of one ward (comprising the west bank of the Mississippi River) do not participate. The 15 simultaneous major office elections were for President of the United States (3), United States Senator (4), Governor of Louisiana (3), Mayor of New Orleans (4), and District Attorney for the Parish of Orleans (1).

3. For the elections held in 1988, voter sign-in data were available, and these were used in place of the registration data for the purpose of estimating the support for particular candidates among those voting. Registered voters were classified as either white or black until 1986, at which time the category "others" was added. Our comparisons for elections beginning with that of 27 September 1986 therefore are technically between blacks and nonblacks, rather than blacks and whites. The "others" category, however, never execeeded 1.0 percent of

the total of registered voters. All of the double regressions have been weighted to reflect the different number of registered voters (or voters signing in) across the precincts.

4. The one judicial election held concurrently with the 1988 Louisiana presidential primary has not been included in this part of the analysis. Unlike the other major office elections, the presidential primary was a "closed" election in which only those voters registered as Democrats or Republicans could participate, and then only in that party's primary. Only about 15 percent of those not registered with one of the major parties (8.4 percent of the total registered) signed in to vote that day. More importantly, less than 40 percent of the white Democrats (63.3 percent of all white registered voters) signed in to vote, presumably reflecting the widespread disinterest in the Democratic primary within this group.

5. Twenty of the 23 elections in which the candidate preferred by black voters was a white were white-on-white elections. As noted above, black voters preferred a white candidate over a black candidate in only three of the elections.

REFERENCES

Abramson, Paul R., and William Claggett. 1984. "Race-Related Differences in Self-Reported and Validated Turnout." *Journal of Politics* 46:719–738.

Abramson, Paul R., and William Claggett. 1986. "Race-Related Differences in Self-Reported and Validated Turnout in 1984." *Journal of Politics* 48:412–422.

Abramson, Paul R., and William Claggett. 1989. "Race-Related Differences in Self-Reported and Validated Turnout in 1986." *Journal of Politics* 51:397–408.

Adamany, David, and Philip Dubois. 1976. "Electing State Judges." *Wisconsin Law Review*. 731–779.

Alfini, James J., and Terrence J. Brooks. 1988–89. "Ethical Constraints on Judicial Election Campaigns: A Review and Critique of Canon 7." *Kentucky Law Journal* 77:671–722.

Atkins, Burton, and Michael McDonald. 1977. "Electoral Rule Changes and Voter Participation in Judicial Elections: A Longitudinal Analysis of the Florida Supreme Court." Paper presented at the 1977 Meeting of the Florida Political Science Association, Orlando, Florida.

Atkins, Burton, Matthew R. DeZee, and William Eckert. 1984. "State Supreme Court Elections: The Significance of Racial Cues." *American Politics Quarterly* 12:211–224.

Atkins, Burton, Matthew R. DeZee, and William Eckert. 1985. "The Effect of a Black Candidate in Stimulating Voter Participation in Statewide Elections: A Note on a Quiet 'Revolution' in Southern Politics." *Journal of Black Studies* 16:213–225.

Barber, Kathleen L. 1971. "Ohio Judicial Elections—Nonpartisan Premises with Partisan Results." *Ohio State Law Journal* 32:762–789.

Baum, Lawrence. 1987. "Information and Party Voting in 'Semipartisan' Judicial Elections." *Political Behavior* 9:62–74.

Berg, Larry L., and Leo Flynn. 1980. "Voter Participation in Municipal Court Elections in Los Angeles County." *Law and Policy Quarterly* 2:161–180.

Bullock, Charles S., III. 1984. "Racial Crossover Voting and the Election of Black Officials." *Journal of Politics* 46:238–251.

Bullock, Charles S., III. 1985. "Aftermath of the Voting Rights Act: Racial Voting Patterns in Atlanta-Area Elections." In *The Voting Rights Act: Consequences and Implications*, ed. Lorn Foster. New York: Praeger Publishers.

Clubb, Jerome M., and Michael W. Traugott. 1972. "National Patterns of Referenda Voting: The 1968 Election." In *People and Politics in Urban Society*, ed. Harlan Hahn. Beverly Hills, Calif. Sage.

Collins, William. 1980. "Race as a Salient Factor in Nonpartisan Elections." *Western Political Quarterly* 33:330–335.

Crockett, George W. 1976. "The Discretion of Judges." In *Urban Governance and Minorities*, ed. Herrington J. Bryce. New York: Praeger.

Darcy, R., and Anne Schneider. 1989. "Confusing Ballots, Roll-Off, and the Black Vote." *Western Political Quarterly* 42:347–364.

Dubois, Philip L. 1979. "Voter Turnout in State Judicial Elections: An Analysis of the Tail of the Electoral Kite." *Journal of Politics* 41:865–887.

Dubois, Philip L. 1980a. *From Ballot to Bench: Judicial Elections and the Quest for Accountability.* Austin, Tex.: University of Texas Press.

Dubois, Philip L. 1980b. "Public Participation in Trial Court Elections: Possibilities for Accentuating the Positive and Eliminating the Negative." *Law and Policy Quarterly* 2:133–160.

Engstrom, Richard L. 1985. "The Reincarnation of the Intent Standard: Federal Judges and At-Large Election Cases." *Howard Law Journal* 28:495–513.

Engstrom, Richard L. 1989. "When Blacks Run for Judge: Racial Divisions in the Candidate Preferences of Lousiana Voters." *Judicature* 73:87–89

Engstrom, Richard L., and Michael D. McDonald. 1988. "Definitions, Measurements, and Statistics: Weeding Wildgen's Thicket." *Urban Lawyer* 20:175–191.

Fund For Modern Courts. 1985. *The Success of Women and Minorities in Achieving Judicial Office: The Selection Process.* New York: Fund for Modern Courts.

Grofman, Bernard, Michael Migalski, and Nicholas Noviello. 1985. "The 'Totality of Circumstances Test' in Section 2 of the 1982 Extension of the Voting Rights Act: A Social Science Perspective." *Law and Policy* 7:199–223.

Hadley, Charles D. 1986. "The Impact of the Louisiana Open Elections System Reform." *State Government* 58:152–157.

Jacob, Herbert. 1966. "Judicial Insulation—Elections, Direct Participation, and Public Attention to the Courts in Wisconsin." *Wisconsin Law Review*, 801–819.

Johnson, Charles A., Roger C. Shaefer, and R. Neal McKnight. 1978. "The Salience of Judicial Candidates and Elections." *Social Science Quarterly* 59:371–378.

Kazee, Thomas A. 1983. "The Impact of Electoral Reform: 'Open Elections' and the Louisiana Party System." *Publius* 13:132–139.

Klots, Allen T. 1973. "The Selection of Judges and the Short Ballot." In *Judicial Selection and Tenure*, ed. Glenn R. Winters. Chicago: American Judiciature Society.

Landinsky, Jack, and Allan Silver. 1967. "Popular Democracy and Judical Independence: Electorate and Elite Reactions to Two Wisconsin Supreme Court Elections." *Wisconsin Law Review* 1967:128–169.

Lijphart, Arend. 1985. "The Pattern of Electoral Rules in the United States: A Deviant Case Among the Industrialized Democracies." *Government and Opposition* 20:18–28.

Loewen, James W., and Bernard Grofman. 1989. "Recent Developments in Methods Used in Vote Dilution Litigation." *Urban Lawyer* 21:589–604.

Lovrich, Nicholas P., and Charles H. Sheldon. 1985. "Assessing Judicial Elections: Effects Upon the Electorate of High and Low Articulation Systems." *Western Political Quarterly* 38:276–293.

Lovrich, Nicholas P., John C. Pierce, and Charles H. Sheldon. 1989. "Citizen Knowledge and Voting in Judicial Elections." *Judicature* 73:28–33.

Lovrich, Nicholas, P., Charles H. Sheldon, and Erik Wasmann. 1988. "The Racial Factor in Nonpartisan Judicial Elections." *Western Political Quarterly* 41:807–816.

Magleby, David B. 1984. *Direct Legislation: Voting on Ballot Propositions in the United States*. Baltimore: Johns Hopkins University Press.

Marquardt, Ronald G. 1988. "Judicial Politics in the South: Robed Elites and Recruitment." In *Contemporary Southern Politics*, ed. James E. Lea. Baton Rouge: Louisiana State University Press.

McDuff, Robert. 1989. "The Voting Rights Act and Judicial Elections Litigation: The Plaintiffs' Perspective." *Judicature* 73:82–85.

McKnight, R. Neal, Roger Schaefer, and Charles A. Johnson. 1978. "Choosing Judges: Do the Voters Know What They're Doing?" *Judicature* 62:94–99.

O'Loughlin, John. 1980. "The Election of Black Mayors 1977." *Annals of the American Association of Geographers* 70:353–370.

Parent, Wayne. 1988. "The Rise and Stall of Republican Ascendancy in Louisiana Politics." In *The South's New Politics: Realignment and Dealignment*, ed. Robert H. Swansbrough and David M. Brodsky. Columbia, S.C.: University of South Carolina Press.

Pettigrew, Thomas F., and Denise A. Alston. 1988. *Tom Bradley's Campaigns for Governor: The Dilemma of Race and Political Strategies*. Washington, D.C.: Joint Center for Political Studies.

Pinderhughes, Dianne M. 1985. "Legal Strategies for Voting Rights: Political Science and the Law." *Howard Law Journal* 28:515–540.

Pitkin, Hanna Fenichel. 1967. *The Concept of Representation*. Berkeley: University of California Press.

Rosenthal, Andrew. 1989. "Broad Disparities in Polls and Votes Raising Questions." *New York Times* (November 9): 1, 13.

Scarrow, Harold A. 1986. "Ballot Format in Plurality Partisan Elections." In *Electoral Laws and Their Political Consequences*, eds. Bernard Grofman and Arend Lijphart. New York: Agathon Press.

Sheffield, James F., and Charles D. Hadley. 1984. "Racial Voting in a Biracial City: A Reexamination of Some Hypotheses." *American Politics Quarterly* 12:449–464.

Theodoulou, Stella Z. 1985. "The Impact of the Open Elections System and

Runoff Primary: A Case Study of Louisiana Electoral Politics, 1975–1984." *Urban Lawyer* 17:457–471.
Uhlman, Thomas M. 1977. "Race, Recruitment and Representation: Background Differences Between Black and White Trial Court Judges." *Western Political Quarterly* 30:457–470.
Vanderleeuw, James M., and Richard L. Engstrom. 1987. "Race, Referendums, and Roll-Off." *Journal of Politics* 49:1081–1092.
Walker, Jack L. 1966. "Ballot Forms and Voter Fatigue: An Analysis of the Office Block and Party Column Ballots." *Midwest Journal of Political Science* 10:448–463.
Welch, Susan, Michael Combs, and John Gruhl. 1988. "Do Black Judges Make A Difference?" *American Journal of Political Science* 32:126–136.
Wolfinger, Raymond E., and Steven J. Rosenstone. 1980. *Who Votes?* New Haven: Yale University Press.

8 Participation and Political Knowledge
Jane Junn

Since the mid–1830s, when Alexis de Tocqueville penned his famous observations of American democracy, the American polity has been described as exceptional. Political activity in the new world abounded. "No sooner do you set foot on American soil than you find yourself in a sort of tumult; a confused clamor rises on every side, and a thousand voices are heard at once, each expressing some social requirements" (Tocqueville 1966, 242). Unlike European monarchies, American democracy was built on the principle that political participation was not only the privilege of every man, but a necessity in ensuring the efficiency and prosperity of the democratic system. Popular participation constituted a vital component of the theory and practice of American democracy.

Political philosophers, preceding and following the birth of the United States government, declared free expression of political will by individual citizens to be the cornerstone of democracy. The autonomy of the individual and the control of government by the governed were central to democratic government. While there was consensus on the necessity of citizen participation in democracy, there was disagreement over why citizen activity was important. Macrolevel theories of democratic government consider the role of participation important for a variety of reasons: as a stabilizing and legitimizing force, as a process of resource allocation, and as a solvent to social conflict. Microlevel theories, on the other hand, argue that political participation is important because of its effect on individuals. Taking part in political life enhances the level of political efficacy, knowledge, and sense of commitment to the political community that individual citizens have.

Rousseau, Tocqueville, and J. S. Mill were among those theorists interested in the effect of democratic participation on individuals. They supported the notion that political institutions and the citizens that comprise the polity the institutions serve are dependent on one another. In *The Social Contract*, Rousseau argued, among other things, that participation is more than an institutional arrangement in a democratic system, and that the act of engagement in the political community has a psychological effect on the participants. This relationship, then, ensures a continuing interrelationship between political institutions and the individuals interacting within them. Mill considered political participation the means by which self realization could occur. Tocqueville characterized the American democratic system as one with overlapping political and civil spheres; political practices enhanced rather than bound the conduct of private lives. The lessons individuals learned from their political activity influenced the conduct of their civil lives as well, and the act of participating in political life had independent effects on individuals. "A man of the people, when asked to share the task of governing society, acquires a certain self-esteem. . . . He may not be more virtuous or happier than his forebears, but he is more enlightened and active" (Tocqueville 1966, 243).

This chapter presents a model of the individual-level process by which participation in the American democratic system influences citizens' levels of political knowledge. Does the act of taking part in political life influence how much individual citizens know about the system of government that rules them, and those elected officials who lead them? How can the nature of the American democracy be understood *as a result of* its system of government?

The basic principles of individual autonomy and citizen control that form the foundations of the theory of democratic government can be fulfilled only under certain conditions. Individuals can identify and articulate what they want from government only if they can understand and take part in the system that regulates what they get. The link between political knowledge (or political ignorance) and participation becomes clear under these conditions. What and how much individuals know about their government will either enhance or inhibit their ability to get what they want. Knowledge of political facts and an understanding of the political system are prerequisites for the evaluation of political objects, and political knowledge is a necessary condition for political participation. Taking part in political life, in turn, teaches certain cognitive skills: individuals gain a higher level of knowledge and a greater understanding of their political system through their experience.

The feedback between participatory input and output requires a model that accounts for this reciprocal relationship. A nonrecursive simultaneous equation model of the relationship between participation and political knowledge is developed. The model proposes that, while both political activity and political knowledge are fundamentally influenced by individual economic and educational resources, participatory behavior is influenced in particular by knowledge about politics, strong affiliation with a political party, and involvement in labor unions, church and other organized groups. Political knowledge, on the other hand, is influenced by experience in political activity, exposure to political information through the mass media, and the level of individuals' cognitive verbal skills.

POLITICAL PARTICIPATION

Political participation has been studied widely (Verba and Nie 1972; Milbrath and Goel 1977; Nagel 1987; Conway 1985; Bennett and Bennett 1986). Participatory activity is influenced by the amount of economic, educational, and cognitive resources individuals have. In the absence of such resources, group mobilization through political parties or religious groups, for example, can also positively influence how much people participate. The standard socioeconomic model of participation has two basic elements. Higher status individuals have a greater stake in politics, and they act to protect and advance their interests. People with higher socioeconomic status also live and interact with others like them who are active in politics. Through this experience, they develop the civic orientations that lead them to participate (Verba and Nie 1972, chap. 8). Individuals function in an institutional context as well. Organizations can act both as a channel to government access and as a mobilizer for political activity. Individuals who are less likely to participate because of lower levels of socioeconomic resources can become active in politics through involvement in organized groups (Verba and Nie 1972, chap. 11). Through their group membership, individuals broaden their social and political interest by learning from other group members and consequently have a greater inclination to participate.

American democracy and its participatory mechanisms are defined by a multitude of political activities. Participation extends far beyond the act of voting, in both level of difficulty and engagement, as well as in the magnitude of the message sent to government. Political participation is an activity of more than a single dimension, and significantly different modes of participation have been identified (Verba, Nie, and Kim 1971). Consequently, the determinants of the various types of activities may also differ.

Despite the identification of the range of activities political participation characterizes, a significant number of academic investigations in American political science have followed the more limited conceptualization of participation as solely a representative function. By the mid-twentieth century, contemporary American democratic theorists became overwhelmingly preoccupied with the notion of democracy as a political method, and macrolevel concerns dominated investigations of democratic theory. Insofar as democracy is defined as a method, citizen participation was simply a process for electing government officials. The empirical scholarship that has remained loyal to this paradigm focuses on that political activity most closely related to the representative function of democracy: voting. Descriptions of how much voting and by whom, and models of the determinants of vote choice remain popular topics in the field of political behavior studies.

POLITICAL KNOWLEDGE

The conceptualization, the determinants, and the significance of political knowledge, on the other hand, have received far less theoretical and empirical attention. Political information or political knowledge is defined a number of ways: awareness of basic facts about the American democratic system, such as the role of the Supreme Court and the meaning of civil liberties (McCloskey and Zaller 1984); recognition of names of candidates and incumbents and their issue positions (Bennett, 1988; Brady and Ansolabehere 1989; Erikson, Luttbeg, and Tedin 1980; Erskine 1963); or voter "sophistication," often measured as attitude constraint over a series of political issues (Campbell et al. 1960; Converse 1964; Neuman 1986; Luskin 1987; Palfrey and Poole 1987).

Political knowledge defined as political sophistication has received the most attention. Early conceptualizations of political knowledge as attitude consistency were developed by the architects of the American National Election Studies, whose main goal was to explain voting behavior. They found that political attitudes in the American population were only loosely constrained and hence concluded that voters were not terribly sophisticated. The idea of knowledge of political facts, such as the names of political candidates and incumbents and their issue positions, has received a more modest amount of attention. Brady and Ansolabehere emphasize the importance of political information on the structure of individual utility functions and subsequently on vote preference; knowledge is important because it allows voters to decide how to decide (1989, 158).

There are clearly several dimensions of political knowledge; the nature of political information may be understood as attitude consistency, the amount of information individuals have about candidates, or a more varied and complex compilation of facts about the structure and operation of the American democratic system. Regardless of its dimensions, and under various definitions, political knowledge is fundamentally different from political behavior. It is a cognition: an intellectual capacity individuals reach through a process of political learning. Thus, one might

Figure 8.1
Illustration of Political Learning Model

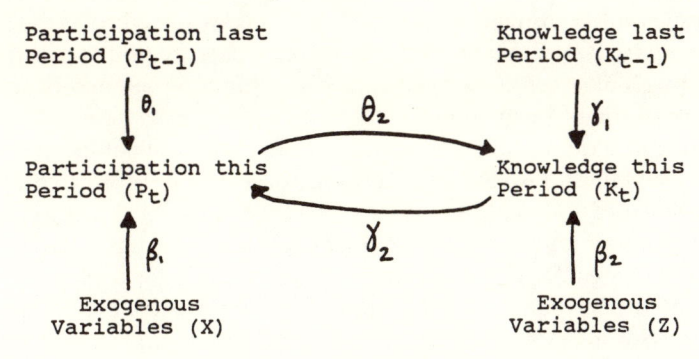

Participation last Period (P_{t-1}) — θ_1 → Participation this Period (P_t)

Knowledge last Period (K_{t-1}) — γ_1 → Knowledge this Period (K_t)

θ_2 (from P_{t-1} toward K_t), γ_2 (from K_t toward P_t)

Exogenous Variables (X) — β_1 → Participation this Period (P_t)

Exogenous Variables (Z) — β_2 → Knowledge this Period (K_t)

expect that parallel processes and a similar set of factors explain how any sort of political knowledge is obtained. The level of political knowledge an individual has is influenced by some of the same resources and conditions that influence participation. However, the ability to learn and retain political facts depends upon the presence of other independent individual factors, including verbal acuity and the exposure to political news and information through various mass media.

A STATISTICAL MODEL OF THE PROCESS OF POLITICAL LEARNING

The first step in determining the importance of participatory behavior to the level of political knowledge is the formulation of an explicit statistical model. The model is illustrated in figure 8.1.

The essence of the model is simple: participation and political knowledge feed on one another. The more a person participates, the more he or she knows about politics; and the more that person knows about politics, the more capable and the more likely he or she is to take part in political life. There are factors which independently influence participation and still others which affect only political knowledge and not political activity. These factors are considered exogenous to the overall learning model.

The equations for this model are specified in equations 1 and 2:

$$P_t = \theta_1 P_{t-1} + \gamma_2 K_t + \beta_1 X + e_1 \tag{1}$$
$$K_t = \gamma_1 K_{t-1} + \theta_2 P_t + \beta_2 Z + e_2 \tag{2}$$

The first equation indicates that participatory behavior at the current time, denoted by (P_t), is related to a set of social and economic variables

(X), the participatory behavior at a previous point in time (P_{t-1}), and the level of political knowledge at the current time (K_t). The set of demographic and organizational variables (X), is expected to be related to how motivated and capable one is to take part in political activities. People in similar social and educational situations are likely to have similar patterns of participation.

The second equation specifies that the level of political knowledge at the current time (K_t) is related to a set of social and economic conditions (Z), the level of political knowledge at a previous point in time (K_{t-1}), and the amount of political participation the individual engages in at the current time (P_t). The demographic variables that are expected to be important in the political knowledge equation are characteristics that make individuals more capable of understanding and retaining political information, and factors which expose individuals to a greater amount of political information.

ESTIMATING THE POLITICAL LEARNING MODEL

In a perfect world where true measurements of distinct concepts were attainable, political participation would be measured as a behavior, something one does. Knowledge of politics, on the other hand, would be measured as a cognitive capacity, something one retains. Different causal mechanisms would affect these two distinct phenomena. Unfortunately, in reality neither the measurements nor the causal relationships are quite so clear. Despite this less than perfect conceptualization of the reciprocal relationship and measurement of the variables, estimating the simultaneous relationship between participation and political knowledge is still possible.

There are two basic problems in testing the structure of the model of political learning set forth in equations 1 and 2. The first is obtaining robust and meaningful measurements of the variables in question, and the second is estimating the coefficients on the determinants of participation and political knowledge in a nonrecursive model. Participation and political knowledge are simultaneously related to each other, and therefore, the error terms, e_1 and e_2, are correlated. Therefore, ordinary least squares estimates of the coefficients will be biased (Hanushek and Jackson 1977). A method of two-stage least squares is used to estimate the system of simultaneous equations in the political learning model.

The model is tested with two unique sets of data with two different survey designs. Panel data from the 1980 National Election Study, conducted by the Center for Political Studies, is used to test the political learning model over the course of a presidential election campaign. The political learning model is also tested with cross-sectional data from the 1987 General Social Survey, conducted by the National Opinion Research

Estimating the Model: Panel Data

The first test of the model is with panel data from the 1980 National Election Study. The data were collected in four waves throughout the year preceding the presidential election of 1980. The interviews for the first wave were conducted before the first national election primaries in January-February; for the second wave after the end of the primary season in June and July; for the third wave in September; and after the election for the fourth wave in November of 1980.[1]

Questions on participatory behavior and political knowledge focused mainly on the electoral behavior of individuals and their knowledge of the issue positions of national candidates. Respondents were asked if they had taken part in a political meeting or rally, if they tried to persuade others to vote for a particular candidate, and how many of the past presidential elections they voted in. Individuals were also asked to place President Jimmy Carter and Ronald Reagan on a scale denoting their respective positions, from liberal to conservative, on general ideology and on the three issues of defense spending, government spending, and the Soviet Union. Political knowledge was measured as the number of times an individual correctly named Jimmy Carter as more liberal than Ronald Reagan.

Equations 3 and 4 detail the structure of the model of political learning in the panel data.

$$P_t = \theta_1 P_{t-2} + \gamma_2 K_t + \beta_1 V + e_1 \qquad (3)$$
$$K_t = \gamma_1 K_{t-2} + \theta_2 P_t + \beta_2 W + e_2 \qquad (4)$$

Before the model can be estimated, the equations must be explicitly specified. First, some theory must guide the exclusion and inclusion of variables that belong in each equation. Within the set of variables (V) in the participation equation, there are four variables which are assumed to affect participation independently of the other factors in the system of equations. In the knowledge equation, there are three variables within the set of factors (W), which affect political knowledge independently of the other variables. Table 8.1 details the variables used to test the learning model with the panel data.

Equations 3 and 4 are estimated using the third data collection, roughly a month before election day, and the first data collection, taken in the winter of 1980 before the start of the primary season. In equation 3, P_t is a measure of the participatory activity of the individual in the third wave, and P_{t-2} is a measure of activity at the first wave. K_t is the measure

Table 8.1
Included Exogenous Variables: 1980 Panel

Variable	Included in equation Participation	Knowledge
participation at first wave	P_{t-2}	
church attendance	V_1	
strong party affiliation	V_2	
union membership	V_3	
years of education	V_4	W_1
gender	V_5	W_2
race	V_6	W_3
have children	V_7	W_4
employed	V_8	W_5
watch television news		W_6
attention to political news		W_7
knowledge at first wave		K_{t-2}

of political knowledge of the relative positions of the two presidential candidates. The set of variables (V) denotes other factors which affect participation. These include education, gender, race, whether the individual has children, and his or her employment status. In addition to political activity earlier in the campaign, three additional variables are expected to influence participation independently of political knowledge. Participation in three types of organizations will directly influence participation, since organizational affiliation mobilizes people to action above and beyond activity that might be expected based upon the individual's socioeconomic level. Membership in a labor union and being a strong partisan affiliator are expected to positively influence participatory activity. Affiliation with religious groups was measured by the frequency the individual reported attending religious services.

In equation 4, political knowledge (K_t) is the level of political knowledge an individual has at the third wave of the panel, and K_{t-2} is the level of information at the first wave. The set of variables (W) designates other factors that affect political knowledge. In addition to the demographic factors common to the participation equation, political knowledge is influenced independently by the level of political knowledge at the first wave (K_{t-2}) and two additional variables. Exposure to political news, measured by how often the individual watches television news, and how much attention the person pays to news on politics and government, independently influence the level of political knowledge.

Estimating the Model: Cross-Sectional Data

The political learning model was also tested with cross-sectional data from the 1987 General Social Survey (GSS). The GSS replicated the participation module of the 1967 Verba-Nie study of political participation. The measurements for both participation and political knowledge in these data are of greater depth and breadth than those of the 1980 National Election Study. The 1967 study, which remains the benchmark of participation studies, queried the respondent on participatory activity for eleven different acts of participation: voting in national elections, voting in local elections, persuading others how to vote, being a member of a political club, working for a political candidate or party, attending political meetings or rallies, contributing money to a party or candidate, forming a group to solve local problems, working with others in the community to solve a problem, contacting local officials, and contacting state or national officials. The act of contacting officials was split into contacting on particularized problems and on problems of a broader social referent. Overall participatory activity was measured on a scale of 1 to 13 by the number of political acts the respondent reported engaging in.[2] The 1987 study also asked people to give the names of the head of the local school board, the U.S. representative from the district, and the governor of the state. Political knowledge is measured by the number of correct names the individual gave to the three questions. No questions on candidate recognition or issue position were asked on the GSS study, but individuals were tested for their level of verbal acuity with a 10-word vocabulary test.

Equations 5 and 6 specify the structure of the model of political learning in the cross-sectional data. The major difference in the structure of the political learning model for the cross-sectional data from the model for the panel data is the absence of a lagged variable for participation and knowledge. In the cross-section, no such measurements for prior behavior and level of knowledge are available. Table 8.2 details the specification of the system of equations for the test of the learning model with the cross-sectional data.

$$P = \gamma K + \beta_1 A + e_1 \tag{5}$$
$$K = \theta P + \beta_2 D + e_2 \tag{6}$$

Equation 5 indicates that participation, (P) is influenced by knowledge (K) and a set of social and demographic variables (A). The set of variables (A) includes factors that affect participation, including education, gender, race, whether the individual has children, and his or her employ-

Table 8.2
Included Exogenous Variables: 1987 Cross-Section

Variable	Included in equation Participation	Knowledge
church attendance	A_1	
strong party affiliation	A_2	
organizational affiliation	A_3	
years of education	A_4	D_1
gender	A_5	D_2
race	A_6	D_3
have children	A_7	D_4
out of labor force	A_8	D_5
employed full time	A_9	D_6
news media exposure		D_7
verbal acuity		D_8

ment status. In addition, three variables are expected to influence participation independently of political knowledge. As in the model using the 1980 panel data, participation is assumed to be influenced by organizational activity independently of other variables in the system of equations. Involvement with religious groups was measured by the frequency of church service attendance. Affiliation with a political party was measured by whether or not the individual has a strong attachment to a political party. Overall organizational affiliation was measured by the number of times the individual reported being an active member of fifteen different types of organizations active in community problems.[3]

Equation 6 indicates that political knowledge (K) is a function of participation (P) and a set of social and demographic variables, (D). In addition to the social and demographic factors such as education and gender, political knowledge in the participation equation is expected to be influenced independently by two additional variables measuring cognitive verbal skills and how intensely the individual is exposed to political news and information. These two variable represent the number of correct answers the respondent received on 10-word vocabulary test and how frequently the individual reported reading a newspaper.

EMPIRICAL ESTIMATES OF THE POLITICAL LEARNING MODEL

1980 Panel Study

The results from the two-stage least squares estimation of the political learning model with the panel data are presented in tables 8.3 and 8.4. The unstandardized regression coefficients for the factors affecting participation (P_t) in equation 3 are shown in table 8.3. The coefficient representing the influence of participation at the first wave to activity in the third wave (Θ_1) is the strongest coefficient in the equation. For each additional act of participation an individual reported taking part in during the first wave, participation in the third wave (P_t) increases by .507. The coefficient γ_2, representing the influence of political knowledge in the third wave (K_t) to participation, is the second strongest coefficient in the equation. For every additional issue the individual correctly placed Carter as more liberal than Reagan, participation increases by .210 acts. Having children and being active in church organizations also increase political activity. Higher levels of education and strong political party affiliation also positively influence participation, though the coefficients are not statistically significant.

Table 8.4 details the results of the estimation of the learning model for the political knowledge equation with the panel data. Political knowledge is strongly influenced by participation (P_t), level of political knowledge in the first wave (K_{t-2}), level of education, and gender. The coefficient Θ_2 shows that every additional participatory activity the individual engages in increases level of political knowledge by .555. Knowing where the presidential candidates stood relative to each other early in the campaign also influenced individuals in getting correct answers on the same set of questions at the third wave of the panel. The coefficient γ_1 on knowledge at the first wave was .329. Having a higher level of education and paying attention to political news also positively influence the likelihood that an individual will know where the candidates stand. Being male and being white are also favorable to individuals' levels of political knowledge.

1987 Cross-Section Study

The results of the two-stage least squares estimation of the political learning model for the cross-sectional data are provided in tables 8.5 and 8.6.[4] The unstandardized regression coefficients for the factors affecting participation are shown in table 8.5. The coefficient representing

Table 8.3
Two-Stage Least Squares Coefficients of Participation Equation: 1980 Panel

Variable	unstandardized coefficient
political knowledge (K_t)	.210 *** (.050)
participation (P_{t-2})	.507 *** (.042)
education	.019 (.012)
gender	.000 (.052)
race	-.030 (.082)
employed	-.076 (.051)
have children	.164 *** (.052)
strong party affiliator	.025 (.049)
frequent church attendance	.045 *** (.016)
union member	-.040 (.056)
constant	-.295 (.140)

Adjusted R^2 = .42

Valid N = 694

*** significant at .01
** significant at .05
* significant at .10

Table 8.4
Two-Stage Least Squares Coefficients of Political Knowledge Equation: 1980 Panel

Variable	unstandardized coefficient
participation (P_t)	.555 *** (.114)
political knowledge (K_{t-2})	.329 *** (.037)
education	.082 *** (.018)
gender	.239 *** (.089)
race	.337 ** (.144)
employed	.070 (.094)
have children	-.177 * (.097)
watch television news	-.056 (.038)
attention to political news	.223 ** (.100)
constant	-.327 (.280)

Adjusted R^2 = .365

Valid N = 693

*** significant at .01
** significant at .05
* significant at .10

Table 8.5
Two-Stage Least Squares Coefficients of Participation Equation: 1987 Cross-Section

Variable	unstandardized coefficient	
political knowledge	2.204 (.254)	***
education	.101 (.027)	***
gender	-.000 (.142)	
race	-.129 (.222)	
out of labor force	.056 (.211)	
employed full time	-.173 (.196)	
have children	.038 (.162)	
strong party affiliator	.368 (.141)	***
church attendance	-.018 (.029)	
affiliated with organization	.621 (.068)	***
constant	-1.462 (.433)	

Adjusted R^2 = .262

Valid N = 1516

*** significant at .01

** significant at .05

* significant at .10

Table 8.6
Two-Stage Least Squares Coefficients of Political Knowledge Equation: 1987 Cross-Section

Variable	unstandardized coefficient	
participation	.149 (.022)	***
education	-.009 (.010)	
gender	.020 (.049)	
race	.160 (.072)	**
out of labor force	.002 (.073)	
employed full time	.047 (.067)	
have children	.152 (.054)	***
news media exposure	.146 (.023)	***
verbal acuity	.026 (.013)	**
constant	.044 (.158)	

Adjusted R^2 = .165

Valid N = 1516

*** significant at .01
** significant at .05
* significant at .10

the importance of political knowledge in predicting participation (γ) is 2.204. One more correct answer in naming local and elected officials increases participation 2.204 acts on a scale from 0 to 13. Level of education also has a strong positive effect on participation (.101). Being a strong political party affiliator and being involved in organizations that work in the community also strongly influence participation.

Table 8.6 presents the results of the two-stage least squares estimation for the political knowledge equation in the cross-sectional data. The coefficient representing the effect of participation on political knowledge (Θ) indicates that for every additional act of political activity individuals engage in, their level of political knowledge increases .149. Exposure to political news through reading the newspaper also increases levels of political knowledge by roughly the same magnitude. Level of cognitive verbal skills is also important to political knowledge; and every additional correct answer increases the score on the political knowledge scale by .026. Having children and being white are also positively related to political knowledge.

CONCLUSION

The results of the empirical tests of the political learning model support the theory that a reciprocal relationship exists between participation and political knowledge. Participation plays multiple roles in a polity: it is a forum under which the political preferences of individuals are expressed; it is a system by which public policy decisions are made and resources are allocated. But participation is also an activity that has significant microlevel effects. Individuals gain cognitive skills or knowledge from their experience participating in the political system, and taking part in political activity enhances the level of knowledge individuals have of their government.

What is most striking in the results of the statistical tests of the political learning model is the strength and the magnitude of the effect of participation on political knowledge and knowledge on political activity in both of the two sets of data. The estimates of the relationships in the panel data, with limited measures of both participation and political knowledge, yielded strong positive results. In the cross-sectional data, where far superior measures of a broader range of participatory activities were available, the relationship between participation and knowledge is even more pronounced.

The contemporary focus in the study of American democratic theory has revolved around macrolevel concerns, and little attention has been directed toward questions of the consequences of the democratic system on the individual. The questions we pose about American democracy have been limited by this emphasis on macrolevel processes and by the notion that the sole function of popular participation is to elect government officials. In order to understand the macrolevel importance and consequences of participation for democracy, however, it is equally important to understand what effect the democratic system has on its citizens.

NOTES

The data in this paper were originally collected by the National Opinion Research Center, University of Chicago, and the Center for Political Studies, University of Michigan, and made available by the Inter-University Consortium for Political and Social Research. I express my appreciation to Norman Nie, Henry Brady, Chris Achen, Patricia Conley, Fay Booker, Steve Shulman, and Margaret Trevor for their many helpful ideas and comments.

1. See Markus (1982) for a full description of the 1980 sample and data collection.

2. The measurement of participation as an additive scale of activities was used for two reasons. The measurement is a valid measure of overall activity, and there is a reasonably close fit between the overall measure of participation and the individual items used in this scale. The modes of activity—vote, campaign, communal, and contacting—are correlated to the overall scale at .64 or above, with the exception of contacting, which is correlated at .43. Distinction between the modes of participation is sacrificed in order to present an easily interpretable scale of activity.

3. The fifteen types of organizations are: fraternal groups; service clubs; veterans' groups; political clubs; labor unions; sports groups; youth groups; school service groups; hobby or garden clubs; school fraternities or sororities; nationality groups; farm organizations; literary, art, discussion, or study groups; professional or academic societies; and any other groups.

4. Separate analyses for the political learning model were run for participation divided into the modes of voting, campaign activity, communal participation, and contacting. The reciprocal relationship between participation and political knowledge is strong and positive for all four types of political activity.

REFERENCES

Achen, Christopher H. 1975. "Mass Political Attitudes and the Survey Response." *American Political Science Review* 69 (December): 1218–1231.

Aristotle. 1984. *The Politics*, trans. Carnes Lord. Chicago: University of Chicago Press.

Bachrach, Peter. 1980. *The Theory of Democratic Elitism: A Critique*. Washington, D.C.: University Press of America.

Barber, Benjamin R. 1984. *Strong Democracy: Participatory Politics for a New Age*. Berkeley, Calif.: University of California Press.

Barnes, Samuel H., and Max Kaase. 1979. *Political Action: Mass Participation in Five Western Democracies*. Beverly Hills, Calif.: Sage Publications.

Bartels, Larry M. 1985. "Expectations and Preferences in Presidential Nominating Campaigns." *American Political Science Review* 79 (September): 804–815.

Bennett, Stephen E. 1988. " 'Know-Nothing' Revisited: The Meaning of Political Ignorance Today," *Social Science Quarterly* 69: 476–490.

Bennett, Stephen E., and Linda L.M. Bennett. 1986. "Political Participation." In *Annual Review of Political Science*, ed. Samuel Long. Norwood, N.J.: Ablex Publishing.

Berelson, Bernard R., Paul F. Lazarsfeld, and William N. McPhee. 1954. *Voting: A Study of Opinion Formation*. Chicago: University of Chicago Press.

Brady, Henry E., and Stephen Ansolabehere. 1989. "The Nature of Utility Functions in Mass Publics." *American Political Review* 83 (March): 143–163.

Campbell, Angus, Philip E. Converse, Warren E. Miller, and Donald E. Stokes. 1960. *The American Voter*. New York: John Wiley and Sons, Inc.

Carmines, Edward G., and John P. McIver. 1983. "An Introduction to the Analysis of Models with Unobserved Variables." *Political Methodology* 9:51–102.

Converse, Philip E. 1964. "The Nature of Belief Systems in Mass Publics." In *Ideology and Discontent*, ed. David E. Apter. New York: The Free Press.

Conway, Margaret. 1985. *Political Participation in the United States*. Washington, D.C.: Congressional Quarterly Press.

Dahl, Robert A. 1956. *Preface to Democratic Theory*. Chicago: University of Chicago Press.

Davis, James Allan, and Tom W. Smith. 1987. *General Social Surveys, 1972–1987*. (Machine-readable data file.) Principal Investigator, James A. Davis; Senior Study Director, Tom W. Smith. NORC ed. Chicago: NORC, producer; Storrs, CT: The Roper Center for Public Opinion Research, University of Connecticut, distributor. 1 data file (21,875 logical records) and 1 codebook (682 pp.).

Downs, Anthony. 1957. *An Economic Theory of Democracy*. New York: Harper and Row.

Eckstein, Harry. 1961. *A Theory of Stable Democracy*. Princeton, N.J.: Center of International Studies.

Erikson, Robert S., Norman R. Luttbeg, and Kent L. Tedin. 1980. *American Public Opinion: Its Origins, Content, and Impact*, 2nd ed. New York: John Wiley and Sons, Inc.

Erskine, Hazel Gaudet. 1963. "Textbook Knowledge." *Public Opinion Quarterly* 27:491–500.

Ferber, Robert. 1956. "The Effects of Respondent Ignorance on Survey Results." *Journal of the American Statistical Association*. 51 (December): 576–587.

Finkel, Steven E. 1985. "Reciprocal Effects of Participation and Political Efficacy: A Panel Analysis." *American Journal of Political Science* 29 (November): 891–913.

Fiske, S. T., and S. T. Taylog. 1984. *Social Cognition*. Reading, Mass.: Addison-Wesley.

Franklin, Charles, and John E. Jackson. 1983. "The Dynamics of Party Identification." *American Political Science Review* 77 (December): 957–974.

Graber, Doris. 1984. *Processing the News: How People Tame the Information Tide*. New York: Longman.

Gutmann, Amy. 1987. *Democratic Education*. Princeton, N.J.: Princeton University Press.
Hanushek, Eric, and John E. Jackson. 1977. *Statistical Methods for Social Scientists*. New York: Academic Press.
Jackson, John E. 1975. "Issues, Party Choices and Presidential Votes." *American Journal of Political Science* 19 (May): 161–185.
Key, V. O. 1961. *Public Opinion in American Democracy*. New York: Alfred A. Knopf.
Lane, Robert. 1959. *Political Life and Why People Get Involved in Politics*. Glencoe, Ill.: Free Press.
Luskin, Robert C. 1987. "Measuring Political Sophistication." *American Journal of Political Science* 31 (November): 856–899.
Markus, Gregory B. 1982. "Political Attitudes During an Election Year: A Report on the 1980 NES Panel Study." *American Political Science Review* 76 (September): 538–560.
McCloskey, Herbert, and John Zaller. 1984. *The American Ethos: Public Attitudes Toward Capitalism and Democracy*. Cambridge, Mass.: Harvard University Press.
Milbrath, Lester W., and M. L. Goel. 1977. *Political Participation*, 2nd ed. Chicago: Rand McNally.
Mill, John Stuart. 1873. *Representative Government*. New York: Holt.
Nagel, Jack. 1987. *Participation*. Englewood Cliffs, N.J.: Prentice-Hall.
Neuman, W. Russell. 1986. *The Paradox of Mass Politics: Knowledge and Opinion in the American Electorate*. Cambridge, Mass.: Harvard University Press.
Nie, Norman H., and Jane Junn. 1988. "Participation and Democratic Values." Paper presented at the Second Symposium of the Joint U.S.-U.S.S.R. Commission on Political Participation.
Nie, Norman H., Sidney Verba, Henry E. Brady, Kay Lehman Schlozman, and Jane Junn. 1988. "Participation in America: Continuity and Change." Paper presented at the annual meeting of the Midwest Political Science Association.
Norpoth, Helmut, and Milton Lodge. 1985. "The Difference Between Attitudes and Non-Attitudes in the Public: Just Measurement?" *American Journal of Political Science* 29 (May): 291–307.
Palfrey, Thomas R., and Keith T. Poole. 1987. "The Relationship Between Information, Ideology, and Voting Behavior." *American Journal of Political Science* 31 (August): 511–530.
Pateman, Carole. 1970. *Participation and Democratic Theory*. New York: Cambridge University Press.
Rousseau, Jean Jacques. 1966. *The Social Contract*, M. Cranston, ed. New York: Penguin Books.
Schumpeter, Joseph A. 1943. *Capitalism, Socialism, and Democracy*. London: George Allen and Unwin Press, Inc..
Shklar, Judith N. 1969. *Men and Citizens: Rousseau's Social Theory*. London: Cambridge University Press.
Tocqueville, Alexis de. 1966. *Democracy in America*, edited by J. P. Mayer, translated by George Lawrence. New York: Harper and Row Publishers.

Verba, Sidney, and Norman H. Nie. 1972. *Participation in America: Political Democracy and Social Equality*. New York: Harper and Row, Inc.

Verba, Sidney, Norman H. Nie, and Jae-On Kim. 1971. *The Modes of Democratic Participation: A Cross-National Comparison*. Beverly Hills, Calif.: Sage Publications.

Verba, Sidney, Norman H. Nie, and Jae-On Kim. 1978. *Participation and Political Equality: A Seven Nation Comparison*. New York: Cambridge University Press.

Bibliography

Abramson, Paul R. 1983. *Political Attitudes in America*. San Francisco: W. H. Freeman.

Abramson, Paul R., and John H. Aldrich. 1982. "The Decline of Electoral Participation in America." *American Political Science Review* 76:502–521.

Achen, Christopher H. 1975. "Mass Political Attitudes and the Survey Response." *American Political Science Review* 69:1218–1231.

Adamany, David, and Philip Dubois. 1976. "Electing State Judges." *Wisconsin Law Review*, 731–779.

Alfini, James J., and Terrence J. Brooks. 1989. "Ethical Constraints on Judicial Election Campaigns: A Review and Critique of Canon 7." *Kentucky Law Journal* 77:671–722.

Andersen, Kristi J. 1979. *The Creation of the Democratic Majority, 1928–1936*. Chicago: University of Chicago Press.

Aristotle. 1984. *The Politics*, trans. Carnes Lord. Chicago: University of Chicago Press.

Ashenfelter, Orley, and Stanley Kelley, Jr. 1975. "Determinants of Participation in Presidential Elections." *Journal of Law and Economics* 18:695–731.

Atkins, Burton, and Michael McDonald. 1977. "Electoral Rule Changes and Voter Participation in Judicial Elections: A Longitudinal Analysis of the Florida Supreme Court." Paper presented at the 1977 Meeting of the Florida Political Science Association, Orlando, Florida.

Atkins, Burton, Matthew R. DeZee, and William Eckert. 1984. "State Supreme Court Elections: The Significance of Racial Cues." *American Politics Quarterly* 12:211–224.

Atkins, Burton, Matthew R. DeZee, and William Eckert. 1985. "The Effect of a Black Candidate in Stimulating Voter Participation in Statewide Elections: A Note on a Quiet 'Revolution' in Southern Politics." *Journal of Black Studies* 16:213–225.

Bachrach, Peter. 1980. *The Theory of Democratic Elitism: A Critique*. Washington, D.C.: University Press of America.

Barber, Benjamin R. 1984. *Strong Democracy: Participatory Politics for a New Age*. Berkeley, Calif.: University of California Press.

Barber, Kathleen L. 1971. "Ohio Judicial Elections—Nonpartisan Premises with Partisan Results." *Ohio State Law Journal* 32:762–789.

Barnes, Samuel H., and Max Kaase. 1979. *Political Action: Mass Participation in Five Western Democracies*. Beverly Hills, Calif.: Sage Publications.

Bartels, Larry M. 1985. "Expectations and Preferences in Presidential Nominating Campaigns." *American Political Science Review* 79:804–815.

Baum, Lawrence. 1987. "Information and Party Voting in 'Semipartisan' Judicial Elections." *Political Behavior* 9:62–74.

Baxter, Sandra, and Marjorie Lansing. 1983. *Women and Politics: The Visible Majority*. Ann Arbor: University of Michigan Press.

Bennett, Stephen E., and Linda L.M. Bennett. 1986. "Political Participation." In *Annual Review of Political Science*, ed. Samuel Long. Norwood, N.J.: Ablex Publishing.

Berelson, Bernard R., Paul F. Lazarsfeld, and William N. McPhee. 1954. *Voting: A Study of Opinion Formation*. Chicago: University of Chicago Press.

Berg, Larry L., and Leo Flynn. 1980. "Voter Participation in Municipal Court Elections in Los Angeles County." *Law and Policy Quarterly* 2:161–180.

Bobo, Lawrence. 1983. "Whites' Opposition to Busing: Symbolic Racism or Realistic Group Conflict?" *Journal of Personality and Social Psychology* 45:1196–1210.

Brady, Henry E., and Stephen Ansolabehere. 1989. "The Nature of Utility Functions in Mass Publics." *American Political Review* 83:143–163.

Brady, Henry E., and Paul M. Sniderman. 1985. "Attitude Attribution: A Group Basis for Political Reasoning." *American Political Science Review* 79:1061–1078.

Brody, Richard A. 1977. "Stability and Change in Party Identification: Presidential to Off-Years." Paper delivered at the annual meeting of the American Political Science Association, Washington, D.C., September 1–4.

Brody, Richard A. 1978. "The Puzzle of Political Participation in America." In *The New American Political System*, ed. Anthony King. Washington, D.C.: American Enterprise Institute.

Brody, Richard A., and Benjamin I. Page. 1973. "Indifference, Alienation and Rational Decision: The Effects of Candidate Evaluations on Turnout and the Vote." *Public Choice* 15:1–17.

Brown, Courtney. 1987. "Mobilization and Party Competition Within a Volatile Electorate." *American Sociological Review* 52:59–72.

Buder, Leonard. 1989. "Local Boards Often Fail to Reflect Schools." *New York Times*. February 16.

Buder, Leonard. 1989. "School Boards: More Women, Fewer Incumbents." *New York Times*. June 11.

Bullock, Charles S., III. 1984. "Racial Crossover Voting and the Election of Black Officials." *Journal of Politics* 46:238–251.

Bullock, Charles S., III. 1985. "Aftermath of the Voting Rights Act: Racial Voting

Patterns in Atlanta-Area Elections." In *The Voting Rights Act: Consequences and Implications*, ed. Lorn Foster. New York: Praeger Publishers.

Burnham, Walter Dean. 1965. "The Changing Shape of the American Political Universe." *American Political Science Review* 59:7–28.

Burnham, Walter Dean. 1970. *Critical Elections and the Mainsprings of American Politics*. New York: Norton.

Burnham, Walter Dean. 1974. "Theory and Voting Research: Some Reflections on Converse's 'Change in the American Electorate' ". *American Political Science Review* 68:1002–1023.

Burnham, Walter Dean. 1974. "The United States: The Politics of Heterogeneity." In *Electoral Behavior*, ed. Richard Rose. New York: Free Press.

Burnham, Walter Dean. 1982. *The Current Crisis in American Politics*. New York: Oxford University Press.

Cain, Bruce, and Ken McCue. 1985. "The Efficacy of Registration Drives." *Journal of Politics* 47:1221–1230.

Cain, Bruce E., D. Roderick Kiewiet, and Carole J. Uhlaner. 1989. "The Acquisition of Partisanship by Latinos and Asian-Americans: Immigrants and Native-Born Citizens." Mimeo.

Campbell, Angus, Gerald Gurin, and Warren E. Miller. 1954. *The Voter Decides*. Evanston, Ill.: Row, Peterson.

Campbell, Angus, Philip E. Converse, Warren E. Miller, and Donald E. Stokes. 1960. *The American Voter*. New York: John Wiley and Sons.

Campbell, Donald T. 1969. "Reforms as Experiments." *American Psychologist* 24:409–429.

Campbell, Donald T., and Donald W. Fiske. 1959. "Convergent and Discriminant Validation by Multitrait-Multimethod Matrix." *Psychological Bulletin* 56:81–105.

Campbell, Donald T., and Julian C. Stanley. 1966. *Experimental and Quasi-Experimental Designs for Research*. Chicago: Rand McNally.

Campbell, James E. 1985. "Sources of the New Deal Realignment: The Contributions of Conversion and Mobilization to Partisan Change." *Western Political Quarterly* 38:357–376.

Carmines, Edward G., and John P. McIver. 1983. "An Introduction to the Analysis of Models with Unobserved Variables." *Political Methodology* 9:51–102.

Carroll, Susan J. 1985. *Women and Candidates in American Politics*. Bloomington: Indiana University Press.

Cassel, Carol A., and David B. Hill. 1981. "Explanations of Turnout Decline: A Multivariate Test." *American Politics Quarterly* 9:181–195.

Cassel, Carol A., and Robert C. Luskin. 1988. "Simple Explanations of Turnout Decline." *American Political Science Review* 82:1321–1330.

Cavanagh, Thomas E. 1981. "Changes in American Voter Turnout, 1964–1976." *Political Science Quarterly* 96:53–66.

Cavanagh, Thomas E. 1985. *Inside Black America*. Washington, D.C.: Joint Center for Political Studies.

Cavanagh, Thomas E., ed. 1987. *Strategies for Mobilizing Black Voters*. Washington, D.C.: Joint Center for Political Studies.

Citrin, Jack. 1974. "Comment: The Political Relevance of Trust in Government." *American Political Science Review* 68:973–988.

Clubb, Jerome M., and Michael W. Traugott. 1972. "National Patterns of Referenda Voting: The 1968 Election." In *People and Politics in Urban Society*, ed. Harlan Hahn. Beverly Hills, Calif.: Sage.

Collins, William. 1980. "Race as a Salient Factor in Nonpartisan Elections." *Western Political Quarterly* 33:330–335.

Conover, Pamela Johnson. 1984. "The Influence of Group Identifications on Political Perception and Evaluation." *Journal of Politics* 46:760–785.

Converse, Philip E. 1964. "The Nature of Belief Systems in Mass Publics." In *Ideology and Discontent*, ed. David E. Apter. New York: Free Press.

Converse, Philip E. 1969. "Survey Research and the Decoding of Patterns in Ecological Data." In *Quantitative Ecological Analysis in the Social Sciences*, ed. M. Dogan and S. Rokkan. Cambridge, Mass.: MIT Press.

Converse, Philip E. 1972. "Change in the American Electorate." In *The Human Meaning of Social Change*, ed. A. Campbell and P. E. Converse. New York: Russell Sage.

Conway, M. Margaret. 1985. *Political Participation in the United States*. Washington, D.C.: Congressional Quarterly Press.

Cox, Gary W., and Michael C. Munger. 1989. "Closeness, Expenditures, and Turnout in the 1982 U.S. House Elections." *American Political Science Review* 83:217–231.

Crockett, George W. 1976. "The Discretion of Judges." In *Urban Governance and Minorities*, ed. Herrington J. Bryce. New York: Praeger.

Dahl, Robert A. 1956. *Preface to Democratic Theory*. Chicago: University of Chicago Press.

Darcy, R., and Anne Schneider. 1989. "Confusing Ballots, Roll-Off, and the Black Vote." *Western Political Quarterly* 42:347–364.

Davis, James Allan, and Tom W. Smith. 1987. *General Social Surveys 1972–1987*. (Machine-readable data file.) Principal Investigator, James A. Davis; Senior Study Director, Tom W. Smith. NORC ed. Chicago: NORC, producer; Storrs, CT: The Roper Center for Public Opinion Research, University of Connecticut, distributor. 1 data file (21,875 logical records) and 1 codebook (682 pp.).

Degler, Carl N. 1964. "American Political Parties and the Rise of the City: An Interpretation." *The Journal of American History* (June): 41–59.

DeNardo, James. 1980. "Turnout and the Vote: The Joke's on the Democrats." *American Political Science Review* 74:406–420.

Downs, Anthony. 1957. *An Economic Theory of Democracy*. New York: Harper and Row.

Dubois, Philip L. 1979. "Voter Turnout in State Judicial Elections: An Analysis of the Tail of the Electoral Kite." *Journal of Politics* 41:865–887.

Dubois, Philip L. 1980. *From Ballot to Bench: Judicial Elections and the Quest for Accountability*. Austin, Tex.: University of Texas Press.

Dubois, Philip L. 1980. "Public Participation in Trial Court Elections: Possibilities for Accentuating the Positive and Eliminating the Negative." *Law and Policy Quarterly* 2:133–160.

Easton, David, and Jack Dennis. 1967. "The Child's Acquisition of Regime Norms: Political Efficacy." *American Political Science Review* 61:25–38.

Easton, David, and Jack Dennis. 1969. *Children in the Political System*. New York: McGraw-Hill.

Eckstein, Harry. 1961. *A Theory of Stable Democracy*. Princeton, N.J.: Center of International Studies.

Eldersveld, Samuel J. 1949. "The Influence of Metropolitan Party Pluralities in Presidential Elections Since 1920." *American Political Science Review* 43:1189–1205.

Engstrom, Richard L. 1985. "The Reincarnation of the Intent Standard: Federal Judges and At-Large Election Cases." *Howard Law Journal* 28:495–513.

Engstrom, Richard L. 1989. "When Blacks Run for Judge: Racial Divisions in the Candidate Preferences of Louisiana Voters." *Judicature* 73:87–89.

Engstrom, Richard L., and Michael D. McDonald. 1988. "Definitions, Measurements, and Statistics: Weeding Wildgen's Thicket." *Urban Lawyer* 20:175–191.

Erikson, Robert S., Norman R. Luttbeg, and Kent L. Tedin. 1980. *American Public Opinion: Its Origins, Content, and Impact*, 2nd ed. New York: John Wiley and Sons.

Erskine, Hazel Gaudet. 1963. "Textbook Knowledge." *Public Opinion Quarterly* 27:491–500.

Ferber, Robert. 1956. "The Effects of Respondent Ignorance on Survey Results." *Journal of the American Statistical Association* 51:576–587.

Ferejorn, John, and Morris Fiorina. 1974. "The Paradox of Not Voting: A Decision Theoretic Analysis." *American Political Science Review* 67:525–536.

Finifter, Ada. 1970. "Dimensions of Alienation." *American Political Science Review* 64:389–410.

Finkel, Steven E. 1985. "Reciprocal Effects of Participation and Political Efficacy: A Panel Analysis." *American Journal of Political Science* 29:891–913.

Fiske, S. T., and S. T. Taylog. 1984. *Social Cognition*. Reading, Mass.: Addison-Wesley.

Franklin, Charles, and John E. Jackson. 1983. "The Dynamics of Party Identification." *American Political Science Review* 77:957–974.

Fund for Modern Courts. 1985. *The Success of Women and Minorities in Achieving Judicial Office: The Selection Process*. New York: Fund for Modern Courts.

Gamson, William A. 1968. *Power and Discontent*. Homewood, Ill.: Dorsey.

Gosnell, Harold F. 1930. *Why Europe Votes*. Chicago: University of Chicago Press.

Graber, Doris. 1984. *Processing the News: How People Tame the Information Tide*. New York: Longman.

Grofman, Bernard, Michael Migalski, and Nicholas Noviello. 1985. "The 'Totality of Circumstances Test' in Section 2 of the 1982 Extension of the Voting Rights Act: A Social Science Perspective." *Law and Policy* 7:199–223.

Gurin, Patricia, and E. G. Epps. 1975. *Black Consciousness, Identity, and Achievement*. New York: John Wiley and Sons.

Gurin, Patricia, Shirley Hatchett, and James S. Jackson. 1989. *Hope and Independence: Black's Response to Electoral and Party Politics*. New York: Russell Sage Foundation.

Gurin, Patricia, Arthur H. Miller, and Gerald Gurin. 1980. "Stratum Identification and Consciousness." *Social Psychology Quarterly* 43:30–47.
Gutmann, Amy. 1987. *Democratic Education*. Princeton, N.J.: Princeton University Press.
Hadley, Charles D. 1986. "The Impact of the Louisiana Open Elections System Reform." *State Government* 58:152–157.
Hanushek, Eric, and John E. Jackson. 1977. *Statistical Methods for Social Scientists*. New York: Academic Press.
Hardin, Russell, and Brian Barry, eds. 1982. *Rational Man and Irrational Society? An Introduction and Source Book*. Beverly Hills, Calif.: Sage.
Henig, Jeffrey R., and Dennis E. Gale. 1987. "The Political Incorporation of Newcomers to Racially Changing Neighborhoods." *Urban Affairs Quarterly* 22:399–419.
Hyman, Herbert H. 1960. "Reflections on Reference Groups." *Public Opinion Quarterly* 24:383–396.
Hyman, Herbert H., and Eleanor Singer, eds. 1968. *Readings in Reference Group Theory and Research*. New York: Free Press.
Jackson, John E. 1975. "Issues, Party Choices and Presidential Votes." *American Journal of Political Science* 19:161–185.
Jacob, Herbert. 1966. "Judicial Insulation—Elections, Direct Participation, and Public Attention to the Courts in Wisconsin." *Wisconsin Law Review*:801–819.
Jennings, M. Kent, and Richard C. Niemi. 1974. *The Political Character of Adolescence*. Princeton, N.J.: Princeton University Press.
Jensen, Richard J. 1971. *The Winning of the Midwest*. Chicago: University of Chicago Press.
Johnson, Charles A., Roger C. Shaefer, and R. Neal McKnight. 1978. "The Salience of Judicial Candidates and Elections." *Social Science Quarterly* 59:371–378.
Kagay, Michael R. 1979. "What's Happening to Voter Turnout in American Presidential Elections." *Vital Issues* 29, no.4.
Karnig, Albert K., and B. Oliver Walter. 1986. "Municipal Voter Turnout: A Longitudinal View." Presented at the annual meeting of the American Political Science Association, Washington, D.C.
Kazee, Thomas A. 1983. "The Impact of Electoral Reform: 'Open Elections' and the Louisiana Party System." *Publius* 13:132–139.
Keefe, Susan E., and Amado M. Padilla. 1987. *Chicano Ethnicity*. Albuquerque: University of New Mexico Press.
Kelley, Stanley, Jr., et al. 1967. "Registration and Voting: Putting First Things First." *American Political Science Review* 61:359–379.
Key, V. O., Jr. 1949. *Southern Politics*. New York: Alfred A. Knopf.
Key, V. O., Jr. 1955. "A Theory of Critical Elections." *Journal of Politics* 17:3–18.
Key, V. O., Jr. 1961. *Public Opinion in American Democracy*. New York: Alfred A. Knopf.
Key, V. O., Jr. 1966. *The Responsible Electorate*. Cambridge, Mass.: Belknap Press.
Kim, Jae-On, John R. Petrocik, and Stephen N. Enokson. 1975. "Voter Turnout Among the American States: Systemic and Individual Components." *American Political Science Review* 69:107–131.

Kimball, Penn. 1972. *The Disconnected*. New York: Columbia University Press.
Kleppner, Paul. 1979. *The Third Electoral System: 1853–1892*. Chapel Hill, N.C.: University of North Carolina Press.
Kleppner, Paul. 1982. *Who Voted?* New York: Praeger.
Kleppner, Paul. 1985. *Chicago Divided*. DeKalb, Ill.: Northern Illinois University Press.
Klots, Allen T. 1973. "The Selection of Judges and the Short Ballot." In *Judicial Selection and Tenure*, ed. Glenn R. Winters. Chicago: American Judiciature Society.
Kousser, J. Morgan. 1974. *The Shaping of Southern Politics*. New Haven, Conn.: Yale University Press.
Lane, Robert. 1959. *Political Life and Why People Get Involved In Politics*. Glencoe, Ill.: Free Press.
Lasswell, Harold D. 1930. *Psychopathology and Politics*. Chicago: University of Chicago Press.
Lasswell, Harold D. 1936. *Politics: Who Gets What, When, and How*. New York: Whittleysey House.
Lasswell, Harold D. 1948. *Power and Personality*. New York: Norton.
Lijphart, Arend. 1985. "The Pattern of Electoral Rules in the United States: A Deviant Case Among the Industrialized Democracies." *Government and Opposition* 20:18–28.
Lindinsky, Jack, and Allan Silver. 1967. "Popular Democracy and Judicial Independence: Electorate and Elite Reactions to Two Wisconsin Supreme Court Elections." *Wisconsin Law Review*:128–169.
Loewen, James W., and Bernard Grofman. 1989. "Recent Developments in Methods Used to Vote Dilution Litigation." *Urban Lawyer* 21:589–604.
Long, J. Scott. 1983. *Covariance Structure Models: An Introduction to LISREL*. Beverly Hills, Calif.: Sage.
Lovrich, Nicholas P., and Charles H. Sheldon. 1985. "Assessing Judicial Elections: Effects Upon the Electorate of High and Low Articulation Systems." *Western Political Quarterly* 38:276–293.
Lovrich, Nicholas P., John C. Pierce, and Charles H. Sheldon. 1989. "Citizen Knowledge and Voting in Judicial Elections." *Judicature* 73:28–33.
Lubell, Samuel. 1952. *The Future of American Politics*. New York: Harper and Row.
Luskin, Robert C. 1987. "Measuring Political Sophistication." *American Journal of Political Science* 31:856–899.
Magleby, David B. 1984. *Direct Legislation: Voting on Ballot Propositions in the United States*. Baltimore: Johns Hopkins University Press.
Markus, Gregory B. 1982. "Political Attitudes During an Election Year: A Report on the 1980 NES Panel Study." *American Political Science Review* 76:538–560.
Marquardt, Ronald G. 1988. "Judicial Politics in the South: Robed Elites and Recruitment." In *Contemporary Southern Politics*, ed. James E. Lea. Baton Rouge: Louisiana State University Press.
Marquette, Jesse F., and Katherine A. Hinckley. 1988. "Voter Turnout and Candidate Choice: A Merged Theory." *Political Behavior* 10:52–76.
Matthews, Donald, and James Prothro. 1966. *Negroes and the New Southern Politics*. New York: Harcourt Brace and World.

McCloskey, Herbert, and John Zaller. 1984. *The American Ethos: Public Attitudes Toward Capitalism and Democracy*. Cambridge, Mass.: Harvard University Press.

McDuff, Robert. 1989. "The Voting Rights Act and Judicial Elections Litigation: The Plaintiffs' Perspective." *Judicature* 73:82–85.

McKnight, R. Neal, Roger Schaefer, and Charles A. Johnson. 1978. "Choosing Judges: Do the Voters Know What They're Doing?" *Judicature* 62:94–99.

McPhee, William A., and R. A. Smith. 1962. "A Model for Analyzing Voting Systems." In *Public Opinion and Congressional Elections*, ed. W. McPhee and William Glaser. New York: Free Press.

Merriam, Charles E., and Harold F. Gosnell. 1924. *Non-Voting*. Chicago: University of Chicago Press.

Milbrath, Lester W., and M. L. Goel. 1977. *Political Participation*, 2nd ed. Chicago: Rand McNally.

Mill, John Stuart. 1873. *Representative Government*. New York: Holt.

Miller, Arthur H. 1974. "Rejoiner to 'Comment' by Jack Citrin: Political Discontent or Ritualism?" *American Political Science Review* 68:989–1001.

Miller, Arthur H., Patricia Gurin, Gerald Gurin, and Oksana Malanchuk. 1981. "Group Consciousness and Political Participation." *American Journal of Political Science* 25:494–511.

Nagel, Jack. 1987. *Participation*. Englewood Cliffs, N.J.: Prentice-Hall.

Nelson, William E., Jr. 1982. "Cleveland: The Rise and Fall of the New Black Politics." In *The New Black Politics*, ed. Michael B. Preston, Lenneal J. Henderson, Jr., and Paul Puryear. New York: Longman.

Nelson, William E., Jr., and Philip J. Meranto. 1977. *Electing Black Mayors*. Columbus: Ohio State University Press.

Neuman, W. Russell. 1986. *The Paradox of Mass Politics: Knowledge and Opinion in the American Electorate*. Cambridge, Mass.: Harvard University Press.

Nie, Norman H., and Jane Junn. 1988. "Participation and Democratic Values." Paper presented at the Second Symposium of the Joint U.S.-U.S.S.R. Commission on Political Participation.

Nie, Norman H., Sidney Verba, Henry E. Brady, Kay Lehman Schlozman, and Jane Junn. 1988. "Participation in America: Continuity and Change." Paper presented at the annual meeting of the Midwest Political Science Association.

Norpoth, Helmut, and Milton Lodge. 1985. "The Difference Between Attitudes and Non-Attitudes in the Public: Just Measurement?" *American Journal of Political Science* 29:291–307.

O'Loughlin, John. 1980. "The Election of Black Mayors 1977." *Annals of the American Association of Geographers* 70:353–370.

Olsen, Marvin E. 1970. "Social and Political Participation of Blacks." *American Sociological Review* 35:682–696.

Palfrey, Thomas R., and Keith T. Poole. 1987. "The Relationship Between Information, Ideology, and Voting Behavior." *American Journal of Political Science* 31:511–530.

Parent, Wayne. 1988. "The Rise and Stall of Republican Ascendancy in Louisiana Politics." In *The South's New Politics: Realignment and Dealignment*, ed.

Robert H. Swansbrough and David M. Brodsky. Columbia, S.C.: University of South Carolina Press.
Pateman, Carole. 1970. *Participation and Democratic Theory*. New York: Cambridge University Press.
Patterson, Samuel C., and Gregory A. Caldeira. 1983. "Getting Out the Vote: Participation in Gubernatorial Elections." *American Political Science Review* 77:675–689.
Petrocik, John R. 1981. *Party Coalitions: Realignments and the Decline of the New Deal Party System*. Chicago: University of Chicago Press.
Petrocik, John R. 1981. "Voter Turnout and Electoral Oscillation." *American Politics Quarterly* 9:161–180.
Petrocik, John R. 1987. "Voter Turnout and Electoral Preference: The Anomalous Reagan Elections." In *Elections in America*, ed. Kay Lehman Schlozman. Boston: Allen and Unwin.
Petrocik, John R. 1988. "Party System Structure and Electoral Change." Unpublished paper.
Pettigrew, Thomas F., and Denise A. Alston. 1988. *Tom Bradley's Campaigns for Governor: The Dilemma of Race and Political Strategies*. Washington, D.C.: Joint Center for Political Studies.
Pinderhughes, Dianne M. 1985. "Legal Strategies for Voting Rights: Political Science and the Law." *Howard Law Journal* 28:515–540.
Pitkin, Hanna Fenichel. 1967. *The Concept of Representation*. Berkeley: University of California Press.
Piven, Frances Fox, and Richard A. Cloward. 1985. "Prospects for Voter Registration Reform: A Report on the Experiences of the Human SERVE Campaign." *PS* 18:582–593.
Piven, Frances Fox, and Richard A. Cloward. 1988. *Why Americans Don't Vote*. New York: Pantheon Books.
Portes, Alejandro, and Robert L. Bach. 1985. *Latin Journey: Cuban and Mexican Immigrants in the United States*. Berkeley: University of California Press.
Powell, G. Bingham. 1980. "Voting Turnout in Thirty Democracies: Partisan, Legal, and Socio-Economic Influences." In *Electoral Participation*, ed. Richard Rose. Beverly Hills, Calif.: Sage.
Powell, G. Bingham. 1986. "American Voter Turnout in Comparative Perspective." *American Political Science Review* 79:17–43.
Preston, Michael B. 1984. "The Resurgence of Black Voting in Chicago: 1955–1983." In *The Making of the Mayor: Chicago, 1983*, ed. Melvin G. Holli and Paul M. Green. Grand Rapids, Mich.: William B. Eerdmans.
Przeworski, Adam, and John Sprague. 1971. "Concepts in Search of Explicit Formulation: A Study in Measurement." *Midwest Journal of Political Science* 15:183–218.
Rae, Douglas W. 1967. *The Political Consequences of Electoral Laws*. New Haven: Yale University Press.
Ranney, Austin. 1972. "Turnout and Representation in Presidential Primary Elections." *American Political Science Review* 66:21–37.
Reiter, Howard L. 1979. "Why is Turnout Down?" *Public Opinion Quarterly* 43:297–311.

Riker, William H., and Peter C. Ordeshook. 1973. *An Introduction to Positive Political Theory*. Englewood Cliffs, N.J.: Prentice-Hall.

Rose, Richard. 1974. "Comparability in Electoral Studies." In *Electoral Behavior*, ed. Richard Rose. New York: Free Press.

Rosenstone, Steven J., and Raymond E. Wolfinger. 1978. "The Effect of Registration Laws on Voter Turnout." *American Political Science Review* 72:22–45.

Rosenthal, Andrew. 1989. "Broad Disparities in Polls and Votes Raising Questions." *New York Times* (November 9):1, 13.

Rousseau, Jean Jacques. 1966. *The Social Contract*, M. Cranston, ed. New York: Penguin Books.

Rusk, Jerrold G. 1970. "The Effects of the Australian Ballot Reform on Split Ticket Voting: 1876–1908." *American Political Science Review* 64:1220–1238.

Rusk, Jerrold G. 1974. "The American Electoral Universe: Speculation and Evidence." *American Political Science Review* 68:1028–1049.

Rusk, Jerrold G., and John J. Stucker. 1972. "Legal-Institutional Factors in American Voting." Ann Arbor, Mich. Unpublished manuscript.

Rusk, Jerrold G., and John J. Stucker. 1978. "The Effect of the Southern System of Election Laws on Voting Participation: A Reply to V. O. Key." In *The History of American Electoral Behavior*, ed. Joel Sibley, et al. Princeton: Princeton University Press.

Sait, Edward M. 1938. *Political Institutions: A Preface*. New York: Appleton, Century and Croft.

Salamon, Lester M., and Steven Van Evera. 1973. "Fear, Apathy, and Discrimination: A Test of Three Explanations of Political Participation." *American Political Science Review* 67:1288–1306.

Salmore, Stephen A., and Barbara G. Salmore. 1985. *Candidates, Parties and Campaigns*. Washington, D.C.: CQ Press.

Sapiro, Virginia. 1983. *The Political Integration of Women*. Urbana: University of Illinois Press.

Scarrow, Harold A. 1986. "Ballot Format in Plurality Partisan Elections." In *Electoral Laws and Their Political Consequences*, ed. Bernard Grofman and Arend Lijphart. New York: Agathon Press.

Schattschneider, E. E. 1960. *The Semi-Sovereign People*. New York: Holt, Rinehart and Winston.

Schlesinger, Arthur M., and Erik M. Erikson. 1924. "The Vanishing Voter." *The New Republic* 40:162–167.

Schumpeter, Joseph A. 1943. *Capitalism, Socialism, and Democracy*. London: George Allen and Unwin Press.

Sears, David O., and Donald R. Kinder. 1985. "Whites' Opposition to Busing: On Conceptualizing and Operationalizing Group Conflict." *Journal of Personality and Social Psychology* 48:1141–1147.

Sears, David O., Richard R. Lau, Tom R. Tyler, and Harris M. Allen, Jr. 1980. "Self-Interest vs. Symbolic Politics in Policy Attitudes and Presidential Voting." *American Political Science Review* 74:670–684.

Sheffield, James F., and Charles D. Hadley. 1984. "Racial Voting in a Biracial City: A Reexamination of Some Hypotheses." *American Politics Quarterly* 12:449–464.

Shklar, Judith N. 1969. *Men and Citizens: Rousseau's Social Theory.* London: Cambridge University Press.
Sibley, Joel, Allan Bogue, and William Flanigan, eds. 1978. *The History of American Electoral Behavior.* Princeton: Princeton University Press.
Sigelman, Lee, Philip W. Roeder, Malcolm E. Jewell, and Michael A. Baer. 1985. "Voting and Nonvoting: A Multi-Election Perspective." *American Journal of Political Science* 29:749–765.
Simon, Herbert A. 1985. "Human Nature in Politics: The Dialogue of Psychology with Political Science." *American Political Science Review* 79:293–304.
Smolka, Richard G. 1977. *Election Day Registration.* Washington, D.C.: American Enterprise Institute.
Sniderman, Paul M., and Philip E. Tetlock. 1986. "Symbolic Racism: Problems of Motive Attribution in Political Analysis." *Journal of Social Issues* 42:129–150.
Southwell, Priscilla L. 1985. "Alienation and Nonvoting in the United States: A Refined Operationalization." *Western Political Quarterly* 38:663–674.
Stokes, Donald E. 1965. "A Variance Components Model of Political Effects." In *Mathematical Applications in Political Science*, ed. Joseph L. Bernd. Dallas: Southern Methodist University. Pp. 120–147.
Theodoulou, Stella Z. 1985. "The Impact of the Open Elections System and Runoff Primary: A Case Study of Louisiana Electoral Politics, 1975–1984." *Urban Lawyer* 17:457–471.
Tocqueville, Alexis de. 1966. *Democracy in America*, ed. J. P. Mayer, trans. George Lawrence. New York: Harper and Row Publishers.
Tuchman, Barbara W. 1962. *The Guns of August.* New York: Macmillan.
Uhlaner, Carole Jean. 1989. "Rational Turnout: The Neglected Role of Groups." *American Journal of Political Science* 33: 390–422.
Uhlaner, Carole Jean. 1989. " 'Relational Goods' and Participation: Incorporating Sociability into a Theory of Rational Action." *Public Choice* 62:253–285.
Uhlaner, Carole Jean, Bruce E. Cain, and D. Roderick Kiewiet. 1989. "Political Participation of Ethnic Minorities in the 1980s." *Political Behavior* 11:195–231.
Uhlman, Thomas M. 1977. "Race, Recruitment and Representation: Background Differences Between Black and White Trial Court Judges." *Western Political Quarterly* 30:457–470.
U.S. Bureau of the Census. 1987. Voting and Registration in the Election of November 1986. *Current Population Reports.* Ser. P–20, no. 414. Washington, D.C.: U.S. Government Printing Office.
U.S. Bureau of the Census. 1989. Voting and Registration in the Election of November 1988 (Advance Report). *Current Population Reports.* Ser. P–20, no. 435. Washington, D.C.: U.S. Government Printing Office.
Vanderleeuw, James M., and Richard L. Engstrom. 1987. "Race, Referendums, and Run-Off." *Journal of Politics* 49:1081–1092.
Verba, Sidney. 1961. *Small Groups and Political Behavior.* Princeton, N.J.: Princeton University Press.
Verba, Sidney, and Norman H. Nie. 1972. *Participation in America: Political Democracy and Social Equality.* New York: Harper and Row, Inc.
Verba, Sidney, Norman H. Nie, and Jae-On Kim. 1971. *The Modes of Democratic*

Participation: A Cross-National Comparison. Beverly Hills, Calif.: Sage Publications.

Verba, Sidney, Norman H. Nie, and Jae-On Kim. 1978. *Participation and Political Equality: A Seven-Nation Comparison.* New York: Cambridge University Press.

Walker, Jack L. 1966. "Ballot Forms and Voter Fatigue: An Analysis of the Office Bloc and Party Column Ballots." *Midwest Journal of Political Science* 10:448–463.

Walton, Hanes. 1985. *Invisible Politics: Black Political Behavior.* Albany: State University of New York Press.

Wanat, John. 1979. "The Application of a Non-Analytic Most Possible Estimation Technique: The Relative Impact of Mobilization and Conversion of Votes in the New Deal." *Political Methodology* 6:357–374.

Wanat, John, and Karen Burke. 1982. "Estimating the Degree of Mobilization and Conversion in the 1890s: An Inquiry into the Nature of Electoral Change." *American Political Science Review* 76:360–370.

Welch, Susan, Michael Combs, and John Gruhl. 1988. "Do Black Judges Make A Difference?" *American Journal of Political Science* 32:126–136.

White, Theodore H. 1961. *The Making of the President, 1960.* New York: Atheneum.

Williamson, Chilton. 1960. *American Suffrage: From Property to Democracy, 1760–1860.* Princeton: Princeton University Press.

Wolfinger, Raymond E., and Steven J. Rosenstone. 1980. *Who Votes?* New Haven, Conn.: Yale University Press.

Index

Abortion, 10
Abramson, Paul R., 32, 94
Absentee balloting, 80
Abstention, 104
Age, and voter turnout, 30–32, 55, 57, 71
AIDS, 10
Aldrich, John H., 94
Alienation, 42–43, 49, 57. See also Alienationist theory
Alienationist theory, 39–40, 50, 52–57, 60–61; comparison with other theories, 36–39; the demographic approach, 30–32; as different rationalist theory, 34; of turnout, 27–28, 29, 30
American Voter, The, 24–29, 52, 60. See also Turnout
Ansolabehere, Stephen, 196
Apathy, and nonvoting, 15–18
Asian-Americans, 140, 142, 144–155, 161–163
Asians, 139. See also Asian-Americans
Atkins, Burton, 174, 181
Attitude consistency, 196
Attitude constraint, 196
Attitudinal analysis of voting, 79
Automatic registration system, 80, 92

Bach, Robert L., 149
Baer, Michael A., 52
Belgium, 84
Bennett, Stephen Earl, 20
Blacks, 20, 107; in Chicago, 98; in Cleveland, 97–98; in New Orleans, 175; in New York City, 98; and prejudice, 144–155, 161–163; and roll-off, 172; and structural barriers, 91; and voter turnout, 71
Bobo, Lawrence, 20
Brady, Henry E., 196
Brody, Richard H., 28, 93
Burnham, Walter Dean, 91, 117, 127
Bush, George, 16, 18, 101

Cain, Bruce E., 155
California, 142
Campbell, Angus, 60
Campbell, Donald, 17, 121, 125, 127, 131, 134
Candidate differences, index, 47–48
Candidate preference, 75, 77
Carter, Jimmy, 75, 77, 84, 199, 203
Catholics. See Religion
Challengers, 100, 105
Chicago, 98, 107
Chicanos, 140

Citizenship, and duty to vote, 40, 41, 57, 76
City elections. *See* Local election turnout
Civic duty. *See* Citizenship, and duty to vote
Class bias. *See* Social class, and participation
Cleveland, 97–98
Cloward, Richard, 79, 91, 106
Coalitions, 11–15, 79; of minorities, 139, 144, 163–164; and nonvoters, 11
Colorado, 107
Community organizations, 109
Competition, 8, 106
Conservative turnout, 73
Conversion of voters, 101, 104
Cuban immigrants, 149

Dahl, Robert A., 19
Death penalty, 10
Defense spending, 73
Democratic Party, 6, 11, 73, 84–85, 104, 106, 107, 108
Democratic theory, 196, 208–209
Democratic thought, and levels of participation, 4
Demographic variables, 30–32, 55, 69–72, 160–161, 202
DeNardo, James, 108
DeZee, Matthew R., 174, 181
Disadvantaged, 91, 96, 109. *See also* Education; Income; and voter turnout
Discrimination, 140, 141, 147–155; and electoral participation, 155–168
Domestic policy, 9
Downs, Anthony, 33, 77; "opportunity cost" model, 117. *See also* Rationalism
Downsian positive theory, 33–36, 38, 39, 40–41, 48–50, 77. *See also* Downs, Anthony
Drugs, 10
Dukakis, Michael, 16, 18, 101

Eckert, William, 174, 181
Education: and political knowledge, 200; and voter turnout, 30–32, 55, 57, 69–70, 90–91, 92, 93, 94, 152
Eighteen-year-old voters, 94
Eisenhower, Dwight D., 84–85
Election day registration, 80, 92, 109
Election laws, 114, 131
Elections: closeness of, 47, 81; competitiveness of, 81, 106; high stimulus, 172, 185; low stimulus, 172, 185. *See also* Judicial elections
Elections, off-year, 121, 128
Electoral index, 130
Employment status, and political knowledge, 200
Empowerment, and political participation, 20
Environmental factors. *See* Political environment
Ethnicity. *See* Race

Fair Deal, 97
Ferejohn, John, 35
Fiorina, Morris, 35
Foreign policy, issue differences and participation, 9

Gale, Dennis E., 141
Gays, 10
Gender. *See* Sex
Gillian, Franklin D., Jr., 20
Gosnell, Harold F., 24
Government performance, 49
Group consciousness, 140
Group identification, 140–141
Group interests, 160–161
Gurin, Patricia, 140

Hadley, Charles D., 173
Henig, Jeffrey R., 141
Hispanics, in New York City, 98

Ideology, and nonvoting, 6–9, 49–50, 73
Immigrants, 149
Income, and voter turnout, 55, 57, 69, 91
Incumbent party, 105–106
Incumbents, 100, 105

Index of turnout behavior, 40, 50
Institutional factors, and nonparticipation, 5
Interest groups, role in politics, 43
Interparty competition, 81
Issue differences: and choice, 77; and nonvoting, 6-10, 78

Jackman, Robert W., 2
Jackson, Jesse, 106
Jewell, Malcolm E., 52
Jews. *See* Religion
Johnson, Lyndon B., 84
Judicial elections, 172-175; in New Orleans, 174; racial divisions in, 182-185

Kagay, Michael R., 60
Karnig, Albert K., 92
Keefe, Susan E., 140
Kelley, Stanley, 117
Kennedy, John F., 84
Kentucky, 82
Key, V. O., 96
Kiewiet, Roderick, 155
Kleppner, Paul, 90, 91

Labor union membership, 200
Lasswell, Harold D., 26
Latinos, 139, 142, 144-145. *See also* Hispanics
Lazarsfeld, Paul F., 27
Learning model. *See* Political learning
Learning theory, 115
Left, 91
Legal systems, 79, 84, 113
Legitimacy of government, 67
Liberal turnout, 73
Literacy tests, 91
Local election turnout: research designs, 109; turnout, 92, 105, 109
Louisiana, 181. *See also* New Orleans
Lourich, Nicholas P., 174, 181

Mail-in registration, 109
Majoritarianism, 43-44
Marital status, and voter turnout, 71
McPhee, William, 115, 118

Merriam, Charles E., 24
Mexican-Americans, 139, 142, 144-155, 161-163. *See also* Hispanics; Latinos
Mill, J. S., 193, 194
Minimax-regret theory, 33, 38, 46-47, 51. *See also* Rationalism
Minnesota, 80, 92
Mississippi, 141
Mobilization, 99, 100-108, 164; of blacks, 106-107; index of, 117, 119-120, 125; organizations' role in, 195
Mondale, Walter, 75, 77

National Election Studies (NES), 27, 196
Netherlands, 82
New Deal, 97
New Orleans, 174-181
New York City, 93, 98
Nie, Norman, 140, 195
Nineteenth Amendment, 123
Nixon, Richard M., 84-85
Nonparticipation: and ideology, 6-9; and institutional factors, 5-6; and political attitudes, 5; profile of nonparticipants, 4-21; and registration, 5-6. *See also* Political participation; Voter participation
Nonpolicy attitudes, 75-76
"Nonvoter candidate," 67
Nonvoters, 6-9, 82-83, 84; assessment of problem, 69; chronic nonvoters, 83; and coalitions, 11-15; demographics related to, 72, 73; and education, 90; and policy preferences, 73-75, 78-79; and political apathy, 15-18; and social status, 91, 97. *See also* Nonparticipation; Political participation
North, 91

Office-block ballot, 179
Opportunity cost model, 117
Opportunity structure, 144-146
Ordeshook, Peter C., 35
Orren, Gray, 19

Padilla, Amado M., 140
"Paradox of not voting," 40
Participation, varieties of, 201. *See also* Nonvoters; Turnout; Voting
Participation index, 117, 125. *See also* Political participation; Voter participation
Partisanship, 42, 157–161, 200
Party column ballot, 179
Party competition, 91, 92
Party differences, 75, 77
Party identification, 94
Party pluralism, 43
Party preference, and social status, 89
Party realignment, 68
Party system, 84
Pateman, Carol, 19, 20
"Peripheral" political population, 109
Piven, Frances Fox, 79, 91, 106
Policy demands voting, 44–45. *See also* Rationalism
Policy issues, and voting, 73–75
Political alienation, 40. *See also* Alienationist theory
Political attitudes, and voting, 5
Political culture, 82–83
Political efficacy, 41, 42, 76, 94–96
Political elites, 90
Political environment, 96, 109
Political information, 196. *See also* Political knowledge
Political information processing, motivation, 48–49. *See also* Downsian theory
Political knowledge, 193–195; defined, 196–197; model, 199–208
Political learning, a statistical model, 197–202, 203–208
Political news, exposure to, 200, 202
Political norms, 84
Political participation: and empowerment, 20; and group identity, 27; and institutional factors, 5; patterns of, 1–2; and political attitudes, 5; and presidential elections, 11–15, 18–19; and social class, 2; and the United States, 1–2. *See also* Nonparticipation; Turnout; Voter participation
Political parties: class-based, 97; and social groups, 2; and voter participation, 10–11
Poll taxes, 91
Portes, Alejandro, 149
Powell, G. Bingham, Jr., 2, 5, 6, 79
Prejudice, 140–141; and electoral participation, 155–168; perceptions of, 142–155
Presidential elections: of 1988, 4–5; and turnout, 68
Primaries, 105
Protestants. *See* Religion
Przeworski, Adam, 117, 126

Quasi-experimental research designs, 121–122

Race: and attitudes, 150–155; and candidate preference, 181–185; and identity, 41; and political knowledge, 200; and voter turnout, 71, 73, 97. *See also* Discrimination; Prejudice
Racially polarized voting, 173, 182–185
Racism, 141
Rational abstentionism, 45, 46, 50, 57. *See also* Rationalism
Rationalism, 39–40, 47–48, 52–57, 60–61; comparison with other theories, 36–39; indexes, 44–48; theory of turnout, 33–36
Reagan, Ronald, 75, 77, 199, 203
Registration: as a barrier, 91–92; drives, 80, 105–106; and turnout, 8, 96; and voting, 5
Religion, 200; fundamentalists, 97; and voter turnout, 71–72, 97
Republican National Committee, 107
Republican Party, 6, 10, 11, 73, 84–85, 104, 106, 108
Research designs: quasi-experimen-

tal, 121; state and city level, 109
Resnick, David, 20
Retention, 104
Riker, William H., 35
Roeder, Philip W., 52
Roll-off, 171–172, 181, 184–185. *See also* Judicial elections
Roll-on, 187
Rosenstone, Steven J., 90, 107
Rousseau, Jean Jacques, 193–194

Salamon, Lester M., 141
Same-day registration. *See* Election day registration
Schattschneider, E. E., 20
School board elections, 93, 98
School prayer, 10
Self-interest motivation, 45. *See also* Rationalism
Sex: and political knowledge, 200; and turnout, 118–120
Sheffield, James F., 173
Sheldon, Charles H., 174, 181
Sigelman, Lee, 52, 82
Social class, and participation, 2, 69, 97
Social Contract, The, 194
Social Democratic Party, 91, 97
Social status, 89, 90–91
Social variables, 202
Social welfare, and voting, 73, 75
Socioeconomic model of participation, 195
South, 1, 91, 132
South Africa, 1
South Dakota, 80
Southwell, Priscilla L., 52
Soviet Union, 73, 199
Sprague, John, 117, 126
State elections: research designs, 109; turnout, 92, 105
Structural factors: barriers, 91, 97; and turnout, 89–90
Suffrage law, 122
"Surge and decline," 92, 128
Switzerland, 1
Systemic variables, 79, 83, 84
System of 1896, 132

Television: and political knowledge, 200, 202; as a source of information, 15–16
Theories of democratic government, 193–195, 196
Tocqueville, Alexis de, 193, 194
Trade unions, 97
Turnout, 79–83, 119; comparison of theories, 36–39; by ethnic groups, 155–168; index of, 120–121; political bias of, 85; rate, fluctuation in, 68; in state and local elections, 92–93; theories of, 23–29; and women's suffrage, 129–135. *See also American Voter, The*; Nonvoting; *Voter Decides, The*
Turnout behavior index, 40, 50
Two-party competition, 81

Uhlaner, Carole Jean, 155
United States: comparison of participation with other nations, 2; fluctuation in election turnout, 68–69; and political participation, 1, 2
Universal registration, 109
Utility calculation, 44. *See also* Rationalism
Utility maximization, 33

Van Evera, Stephen, 141
Verba, Sidney, 140, 195
Voter Decides, The, 24–26. *See also* Turnout
Voter participation: differences between voters and nonvoters, 4–6; and political knowledge, 197–208; and social status, 89; and union membership, 200. *See also* Nonparticipation; Political participation
Voter qualifications, 114–115
Voters, 9; habitual, 100–101, 102, 104–105; mobilized 100–101, 102; and racial divisions, 182–185. *See*

also Nonvoters; Political participation; Voter participation
Voting, 3; and education, 90; and racial polarization, 173. *See also* Nonparticipation

Walter, B. Oliver, 92
Washington, D.C., 141
Washington, Harold, 97
Wasmann, Erik, 174, 181
Western Europe, 96
White primary, 91
Wisconsin, turnout studies, 38–44, 92
Withdrawal, 104
Wolfinger, Raymond E., 90, 107
Women: suffrage, 123–136; and voting, 10, 73
Women's suffrage, 115, 126, 129; regional differences, 131–134

About the Contributors

VICTORIA M. CARIDAS is a Program Officer with the Southern Regional Council's Voting Rights Project in Atlanta, Georgia. She holds a M.A. degree in political science from the University of New Orleans.

THOMAS E. CAVANAGH is director of the Johns Hopkins University Center for the Study of American Government. He has previously been a senior research associate at the Joint Center for Political Studies and a member of the senior staff which produced the National Academy of Sciences report, *A Common Destiny: Blacks and American Society* (1989). He is the author of numerous monographs and articles on black politics, voter turnout, congressional organization, and the American party system.

WILLIAM CROTTY is Professor of Political Science at Northwestern University. He is a former president of the Policy Studies Organization and chair of its committee on electoral policy. He specializes in the study of electoral processes and policy and political parties. Among his publications are *Party Game* (1985), *Primaries and Presidential Nominations* (coauthored, 1985), and *Paths to Political Reform* (1980), edited for the Policy Studies Organization.

JACK DENNIS is Professor of Political Science at the University of Wisconsin at Madison. He is a former Rhodes Scholar, Ford Foundation Fellow, and Fellow for the Center for Advanced Study in the Behavioral Sciences. Dennis has published extensively in the area of elections, political behavior, public opinion, and political attitudes. His works include

Children in the Political System (1969) and *Socialization to Politics* (coauthor, 1973), and his articles on mass support for the political system have been recognized by the Political Organizations and Parties section of the American Political Science Association for the excellence of their contributions to political science.

RICHARD L. ENGSTROM is Research Professor of Political Science at the University of New Orleans. He has done extensive research on the political participation of African-Americans. Among his recent publications are "Race, Referendums, and Rolloff," *Journal of Politics* (1987) (with James Vanderleeuw) and "When Blacks Run for Judge," *Judicature* (1989). He was Senior Research Fellow at the Institute of Irish Studies, Queen's University of Belfast, in 1990.

JANE JUNN is a Ph.D. candidate in political science at the University of Chicago. Her dissertation, "Learning about Politics: Sources and Consequences of Political Knowledge in America" (1991), answers the questions: How much do Americans know about politics? What factors influence what and how much they know about politics? What are the consequences for American democracy of a politically knowledgeable—or politically ignorant—citizenry? Her research and teaching interests include political participation, public opinion, minority politics, and democratic theory.

JOHN R. PETROCIK is Professor of Political Science at the University of California, Los Angeles. His research concentrates on elections and political parties. Along with Sidney Verba and Norman Nie, he received the Woodrow Wilson Award for *The Changing American Voter*. He has also published *Party Coalitions* (1981), a book describing the realignment of the groups which constituted the support base for the Democratic and Republican parties since the New Deal. His current work focuses on issue ownership in elections and its relationship to the realignment of the parties.

JERROLD G. RUSK is Professor of Political Science at the University of Arizona. Professor Rusk has been a Senior Fulbright Scholar to Denmark (1973–74), Fellow to the Netherlands Institute for Advanced Study in the Humanities and Social Sciences (1977–78), Member of the Editorial Board of the *American Political Science Review* (1982–85), and Chairman of the Political Science Department at the University of Arizona (1983–88). Professor Rusk's publications include *Measures of Political Attitudes* and several articles on historical and contemporary electoral behavior in such journals as the *American Political Science Review* and the *American Journal of Political Science*.

DARON SHAW is a Ph.D. candidate in Political Science at the University of California, Los Angeles. His research interests include political parties, public opinion and voting behavior, and ethnic policies. His awards include the Charles F. Scott Fellowship, the Spence Reese Political Science Scholarship, and the Center for American Politics and Public Policy Fellowship.

JOHN J. STUCKER is on the staff of Carger Goble Associates of Columbia, S.C., and Washington, D.C., specializing in criminal justice systems analysis and policy evaluation. An Adjunct Professor of Political Science at the University of South Carolina, Dr. Stucker teaches courses in American government and American political institutions.

CAROLE JEAN UHLANER is Associate Professor of Political Science at the University of California, Irvine. Her research has involved the study of political participation, including ethnic politics and public choice. She has also done work on women and politics, and received the Breckenridge Prize from the Midwest Political Science Association in 1985. She was a visiting fellow at the Russell Sage Foundation (1986–87). Her publications include "Rational Turnout: The Neglected Role of Groups," *American Journal of Political Science* (1989); " 'Relational Goods' and Participation: Incorporating Sociability into a Theory of Rational Action," *Public Choice* (1989); and "Candidate Gender and Campaign Finance," *Journal of Politics* (1986).